Reclaiming Our Democracy

Twentieth Anniversary Edition

Reclaiming Our Democracy

Healing the Break Between People and Government

Sam Daley-Harris
Founder of RESULTS

CAMINO BOOKS, INC.
Philadelphia

To the volunteers of RESULTS and Citizens Climate Lobby,
who inspire me every day,
and to Valerie Harper,
who brought her light to my work
and to the first edition of this book

Manufactured in the United States of America

1 2 3 4 16 15 14 13

Library of Congress Cataloging-in-Publication Data

Daley-Harris, Sam, 1946–
Reclaiming our democracy : healing the break between people and government / Sam Daley-Harris, founder of RESULTS. — Twentieth anniversary edition.
pages cm
ISBN 978-1-933822-84-6 (alk. paper)
1. Lobbying—United States. 2. Political participation—United States. 3. RESULTS (Group) I. Title.
JK1118.H35 2013
324'.40973—dc22

2013024942

ISBN 978-1-933822-84-6 (paper)
ISBN 978-1-933822-85-3 (e-book)

Cover design: Jerilyn Bockorick
Cover photo: Shutterstock, Inc./Oledjio

This book is available at a special discount on bulk purchases for promotional, business, and educational use.

Publisher
Camino Books, Inc.
P.O. Box 59026
Philadelphia, PA 19102
www.caminobooks.com

CONTENTS

Twentieth Anniversary Edition

Foreword by Muhammad Yunus

It must have been remarkable to many when leading climate scientist James Hansen wrote, "If you want to join the fight to save the planet, to save creation for your grandchildren, there is no more effective step you could take than becoming an active member of Citizens Climate Lobby." He could have named any of a number of much larger and more established environmental organizations, but instead he named what was then a four-year-old group with 46 chapters and a staff of five headquartered in San Diego, California.

Hansen's remarks may have been remarkable to many, but not to me. What Hansen saw was a young organization unbelievably effective for its size and effective on the right things.

That is what I saw when I first met Sam Daley-Harris and RESULTS. It was the summer of 1987 and I was rushed into a small second-floor office on Capitol Hill. I was a few minutes late for the first of two conference calls—each with 14 editorial writers from around the United States. I had never been on a conference call before but as I walked in Sam was giving instructions to the group and before I knew it I was making my opening remarks and taking questions from the editorial writers.

During a short break at the end of the first call, one of the participants, Kristin Helmore of the *Christian Science Monitor*, asked if she could join the second call too. Sam said she could stay on but asked her to let the next group of callers ask their questions first. The second call began and 14 more editorial writers from 14 new cities were on the line. After these calls Helmore wrote a four-part series that caught the eye of CBS *60 Minutes* and prompted them to come to Bangladesh in 1989 and do a story on Grameen Bank.

How do you get editorial writers from 28 U.S. cities on a one-hour conference call in 1987 with a little-known Bangladeshi who makes tiny loans in some of the poorest villages in that country—and do it without celebrities? Your most expensive public relations firms couldn't do it in 1987 and they couldn't do something similar today.

Those 28 editorial writers agreed to join the call because each had a relationship that was initiated by a RESULTS volunteer in their community. None of the volunteers was an expert on microcredit or on working with the media before they joined RESULTS and none of the editorial writers was enlisted by a member of RESULTS' tiny staff. But that staff, led by Sam, coached and empowered the volunteers to these breakthroughs and to many more.

I understand how it is a major gift for someone like Hansen to finally see his proposal for a fee on carbon with the fee returned to the public championed in newspapers and Congressional offices across the country thanks to the efforts of Citizens Climate Lobby volunteers, because that is what RESULTS did with microcredit in 1987 and continues to do to this day. I am also sure that the late Jim Grant, Executive Director of UNICEF, experienced the same feeling of hope in 1986 after RESULTS generated 90 editorials supporting a successful effort to triple the child survival fund when he wrote, "I thank you in my mind at least weekly for what you and your colleagues are accomplishing. . . ."

What runs through Hansen and Grant's experience and mine too is the brilliance of Sam Daley-Harris, the brilliance of a methodology that he and others began developing at RESULTS in 1980 and shared with Citizens Climate Lobby in 2007, and the brilliance of every volunteer who has ever seriously embraced that methodology.

Make no mistake, this book is not about advocacy by mouse click, phone messages left at Congressional switchboards, handwritten letters drafted during coffee hour and then forgotten, or lighting up Facebook and Twitter. It is about uncovering and then lighting up the unquenchable desire in each of us to make a difference in the world. It is about providing a powerful structure of support so that our courage is what drives us, not our fear. That is why this 20th anniversary edition of *Reclaiming Our Democracy* is so critically important. The courage this book shows us how to unleash is our only hope to save creation for our grandchildren and for theirs.

Tenth Anniversary Edition

Foreword by Marian Wright Edelman

This tenth anniversary edition of *Reclaiming Our Democracy: Healing the Break between People and Government* demonstrates the commitment of RESULTS, its volunteers, and its founder Sam Daley-Harris over the past quarter-century to the long, hard work that is required for world-transforming change. And so I hope that Sam and the RESULTS activists will take it as a compliment when I herald them as a mighty group of fleas.

One of my heroines, Sojourner Truth, a slave woman who could neither read nor write, told of being heckled, while she was speaking out against slavery, by a white man who said: "I don't care any more for your anti-slavery talk than I do for the bite of a flea." Sojourner replied, "Perhaps not, but the Lord willing, I'll keep you scratching!" Indeed, she and others did until slavery was abolished.

In many ways, RESULTS and its volunteer activists are like Sojourner Truth's fleas. They aren't big or flashy, but they are persistent, and they have made some powerful political forces very uncomfortable.

RESULTS activists kept them scratching until they dramatically expanded the Child Survival Fund and UNICEF from $42.5 million in 1984 to more than $470 million a year in 2004, which is helping to save the lives of more than 11,000 children each day.

RESULTS activists kept them scratching until they took seriously the potential of microcredit to transform the lives of the world's poorest people, especially women. In 1986, barely 1 million families around the world were being reached with microcredit. By the end of 2002, more than 40 million of the world's poorest families received these tiny loans to work their way out of poverty.

And RESULTS activists kept them scratching as they worked with the Children's Defense Fund and others to defend the successful Head Start program.

I am grateful for the tireless work RESULTS has done to make the world a better place for children and the poorest families. In the pages that follow, I hope you will hear the call to be a tenacious activist and be reassured that you don't have to be rich or well connected to make a difference in the lives of children. You just have to be persistent enough to make our leaders scratch!

Marian Wright Edelman is founder and president of the Children's Defense Fund and author of a number of books, which include Lanterns *and* The Measure of Our Success.

Tenth Anniversary Edition

Foreword by Marianne Williamson

Several years ago, a quote was circulated that was attributed to Nelson Mandela's 1994 Inaugural Address. The quote actually came from a book I had written, titled, *A Return to Love*. As honored as I would have been had President Mandela quoted my words, indeed, he did not.

Part of what I said was "... our deepest fear is not that we are inadequate. Our deepest fear is that we are powerful beyond measure.... We ask ourselves, who am I to be brilliant, gorgeous, talented, fabulous? Actually, who are you not to be? ... Your playing small doesn't serve the world. We are all meant to shine, as children do.... And as we let our own light shine, we unconsciously give other people permission to do the same. As we're liberated from our own fear, our presence automatically liberates others."

This tenth anniversary edition of *Reclaiming Our Democracy* is filled with examples of people liberating themselves from their own fears in a way that truly does serve the world. In the voices of dozens of RESULTS volunteers, you will hear people confronting the pernicious myth that has hold of so many of us, an entrenched belief that we don't make a difference. The transformations that are so exquisitely told in the stories in this book outline the changes people make when they move from a life rooted in "I don't make a difference" to a life rooted in the truth that each of us can and does make a difference.

Beneath the images of fingers nervously dialing the phone number of an editorial writer, voices quivering in a public presentation, and knees knocking together during a meeting with a Member of Congress are the actions needed to change the world—and change the world they have. RESULTS volunteers have played a critical role in having U.S. funding for Child Survival and UNICEF grow from $42.5 million a year in 1984 to more than $470 million a year in 2004, which has contributed to saving the lives of more than 11,000 children per day.

As you bask in the light shining from these brave souls, give yourself permission to let your own light shine as well.

Marianne Williamson is an author and lecturer. She has published eight books, including A Return to Love *and* Healing the Soul of America.

First Edition

Foreword by Valerie Harper

Reclaiming Our Democracy chronicles the process of creating political will—in this case to end hunger and poverty—but it serves as a powerful tool for anyone concerned about the health of our planet. Political will is not imposed from the top down by politicians, but comes from the bottom up, from concerned citizens. This is a story of ordinary people finding their voice, their power, to effect change.

I've been asked to write this foreword partly because I am a celebrity, but also because I am a citizen and I have my own story to contribute.

My mother, Iva McConnell, was a nurse. She entered her chosen field of endeavor, medicine, over her parents' objections. The family thought it unseemly that a young woman become a doctor, so Mom went to teachers' college. After a few years, she was able to save up money from the salary she received from teaching in one-room schoolhouses on the Canadian prairie and pay her own way through nurse's training. She worked as a nurse on and off until she was past 70, not out of need, but because she loved the work and the satisfaction it brought her.

I speak of this because my mother's commitment to service has had a major impact on me throughout my life. During all the years I pursued my passion—the performing arts—a little voice deep inside asked, "But is this of *real* value? Should I be doing something of more service—like Mom, who is a teacher and a nurse?

As things turned out, I have achieved a degree of fame, and that has helped me have an impact on issues I care about. My "celebrity" has been a tool I've used to contribute to my community and to my world. But I must make the choice to do so and find the means. I feel this is true for each one of us—whatever our "tools"—because we all have ourselves to share.

After several years of participating in benefits, actions, projects, and campaigns on children's issues, women's rights, homelessness, the environment, and on ending hunger, I began to feel that although these were valuable endeavors, there must be more that I could do—there must be a stronger, more productive course of action I could take. But what should it be and what organizations should I get behind?

Enter RESULTS, in the form of a soft-spoken, powerful, yet immensely practical visionary, Sam Harris. I had worked peripherally with Sam and RESULTS for several years, but only after a lunch meeting during one of Sam's trips to Los Angeles did the power and beauty of the work of RESULTS hit home. We sat across from each other at a Mexican restaurant on Wilshire Boulevard and engaged in a real examination of what RESULTS actually does. My ignorance of the workings of my government and the basic American political process was a barrier, but Sam persisted: "Val, you *know* we have the resources to end world hunger. You *know* we can save the lives of the 40,000 children under the age of 5 who die each day of preventable causes. But it's one thing to *know* it, and it's another to *deliver* it—to be able to speak about it powerfully and inspire others to get involved."

So I joined with my partners in RESULTS, began to master the facts about what is possible in ending hunger and poverty, moved into action, and watched our work unfold. I listened in to a telephone conference call as 30 editorial writers discussed protecting the world's children with the director of the UN Children's Fund (UNICEF). I moderated a conference call connecting news conferences in 28 cities, focused on the state of the world's children. I watched funding priorities change and mortality rates drop. I listened as 30 editorial writers discussed unleashing the power of the world's poorest women by providing tiny loans that allow the women to start little businesses and transform their lives. And the editorial writers on these calls and the journalists at these news conferences were all brought together by my favorite "celebrities," RESULTS volunteers—ordinary citizens who moved from knowing important information to taking action.

The importance of this book is that it shatters the notion "I don't make a difference," and de-mystifies the question "What can I do?" *Reclaiming Our Democracy* shows, by example, what we can and must do. It chronicles the birth, the growing pains, the struggles, and the triumphs of a wish made manifest—that our lives can contribute to building a saner, safer world where human dignity is the birthright of each person.

My mother's commitment to service is alive and vital in my life and in my work in RESULTS. And like her, I love the satisfaction it brings me.

Twentieth Anniversary Edition

Introduction

The premise of this book is that citizens, working within a powerful structure of support, can make a real difference in creating the political will to solve national and global problems including a dramatic reduction in child mortality and hunger around the world. But for most people that premise is doubtful at best and absurd at worst. We are haunted by this secretly held, and for many, unconscious belief: while we know we can love and nurture those close to us and can make a difference in our communities, most of us mistakenly believe that we don't really make a difference in the larger world. The idea that we can be anything more than mere spectators to change at the national or international level, especially with our voices as citizens, seems ludicrous to most people.

This book aims to lay to rest that mistaken belief. You will learn how the grassroots advocacy organization RESULTS empowered citizens, beginning in 1980, to make a quantum leap in changing government policy to save children's lives and promote microfinance around the world. You will see that this was accomplished using techniques that are every bit as effective today.

This 20th anniversary edition has a new chapter on the groundbreaking work of Citizens Climate Lobby, an increasingly powerful new advocacy group following the RESULTS model, and another new chapter on the Center for Citizen Empowerment and Transformation, a new initiative focused on spreading the original concepts developed by RESULTS.

When examined more closely, the approaches laid out in this book help dispel the myth that you and I are powerless to make a difference in the world. Let's start by looking at what deep citizen engagement has helped accomplish.

Launching a Child Survival Revolution

RESULTS started working with UNICEF Executive Director James P. Grant in the mid-1980s to make the survival of children a global priority. At the time 15 million children were dying each year from largely preventable malnutrition and disease. One little-known child survival intervention, oral rehydration therapy, allowed families to prepare a sugar, salt, and water solution that could save the lives of some 5 million children who died each year from dehydration coupled with malnutrition. Another child survival intervention, vaccination against six child-killers like measles and tetanus, could save an additional 3.5 million young lives a year.

After RESULTS volunteers generated 90 editorials in 1986 in a successful lobbying campaign to triple the child survival fund from $25 million to $75 million, Jim Grant penned the following in a hand-written note:

> I want to convey my heartfelt thanks for the unflagging and satisfyingly successful efforts of RESULTS on behalf of vulnerable children and mothers everywhere. I thank you in my mind weekly, if not more often, for what you and your colleagues are accomplishing—but I thought I should do it at least once this year in writing.

Four years later RESULTS Educational Fund organized candlelight vigils around the world seven days before the 1990 World Summit for Children. In his opening remarks to 71 heads of state and government at the Summit, Grant said:

> One week ago over a million candles were lit by ordinary people around the world for the success of this Summit. Each of those candles represented the inextinguishable hope in the hearts of people everywhere that, amid all the problems and dangers of the years ahead, the world can still be made a better place.

RESULTS' advocacy on child survival, begun in 1984, has continued to this day. Over the last 29 years child death rates have dropped from 41,000 a day in the early 1980s to 19,000 a day in 2012. Now there are credible calls to reduce preventable child deaths to zero by 2035. The work continues as does the need for more and more empowered citizens. (See Chapters 4, 7, 8, 22, and 28.)

Microfinance: A Hand Up, Not a Hand Out

From the mid-1980s through today RESULTS and RESULTS Educational Fund's Microcredit Summit Campaign have worked with Grameen Bank founder and Nobel Peace Prize Laureate Muhammad Yunus and others to launch the microfinance revolution. This work has taken a little known phenomenon and helped make it a world-wide intervention that, when applied correctly, can powerfully address poverty. In 1987 RESULTS volunteers persuaded editorial writers from 28 U.S. cities to join a conference call with Professor Yunus, 19 years before he received the Nobel Peace Prize.

When RESULTS first lobbied for microfinance at the end of 1986 fewer than one million of the poor around the world had access to a microloan. By the 1997 Microcredit Summit there were 7.6 million with a microloan, and by 2011 the count had risen to more than 124 million very poor families affecting more than 621 million family members. The 124 million families was actually the first decline in 15 years of counting and was primarily caused by institutions that had lost their way and were focusing more on the well-being of their investors than on the well-being of their clients.

After receiving the Nobel Peace Prize in 2006 Muhammad Yunus said:

> No other organization has been as critical a partner in seeing to it that microcredit is used as a tool to eradicate poverty and empower women than RESULTS and RESULTS Educational Fund's Microcredit Summit Campaign.
>
> [See Chapters 15, 21, and 28.]

But this book is not only about progress begun 30 years ago nor, with this edition, is it about the work of just one group on just one issue. In fact, a new generation of advocates is using these time tested approaches to address new global issues like climate change.

Citizens Climate Lobby

In 2007 businessman and RESULTS volunteer Marshall Saunders came to me for assistance in applying RESULTS' methodology to the issue of climate change. Years earlier Saunders had been inspired by Grameen Bank and started a microcredit program in Mexico, Grameen del la Frontera. Later he saw the Al Gore documentary *An Inconvenient Truth* three times over a 10-day period. When he learned that much of the work of microcredit programs in Bangladesh could be wiped out if millions of people had to escape rising sea levels because of climate change, he joined more than one thousand people who traveled to Nashville, Tennessee, to be trained to lead the slide show.

Saunders returned to San Diego, California, and led the presentation 43 times. He soon realized that the material was almost exclusively focused on the problem of climate change and included very little on what people could do about it. He also knew that participants could not change enough light bulbs or buy enough hybrid cars to make up for what the government was or wasn't doing. Just as RESULTS worked to create the political will to end poverty, he knew that there had to be a major grassroots effort to create the political will for a stable climate.

Saunders asked several large environmental organizations if they would train a small portion of their members to go far beyond mouse-click advocacy and become deep advocates on the issue. They all said no.

That was when Saunders asked me to coach him on starting Citizens Climate Lobby (CCL). When he called he had no volunteers, no groups—not even a serious mailing list. What he did have was his experience with RESULTS, his commitment to doing something significant about climate policy, and a radical honesty about what he saw was needed in the world.

Futurist and inventor R. Buckminster Fuller once said: "The things to do are the things that need doing, that you see need to be done and that no one else seems to see needs to be done." Saunders saw something that needed to be done and either very few others saw it or, if they did, few had any hope in finding an effective way to address it.

What is critical to the premise of this book is not just the first purpose of RESULTS and CCL, creating the political will to end poverty or creating the political will for a stable climate. Perhaps even more important is the second purpose which is to empower individuals to have breakthroughs in expressing their personal and political power. This will be discussed more in depth in Chapter 30 when I outline the 13 commitments needed for citizen empowerment and transformation to succeed.

CCL's first chapters were started in October 2007. By February 2013, they had grown to more than 80 chapters in the U.S. and Canada. While an organization can boast 50, 100, or 500 chapters, the question always comes down to this: "What are the chapters accomplishing?"

CCL has seen exponential growth not only in the number of chapters but also in their members' effectiveness as advocates. Between 2010 and 2012, just a three year period, the number of letters to the editor their volunteers have had published has grown more than 14-fold from 36 in 2010 to 537 in 2012. The number of op-ed pieces their volunteers have had published has grown more than four-fold from 20 in 2010 to 87 in 2012. The number of meetings with members of Congress or their staff has grown more than five-fold from 105 meetings in 2010 to 534 meetings in 2012. These are tremendous accomplishments for a group that didn't even exist before October 2007. These accomplishments have helped CCL play a key role in helping move climate change back onto the national policy agenda. (See Chapter 29.)

The Center for Citizen Empowerment and Transformation

Since the publication of the 10th anniversary edition of this book there has been an avalanche of on-line advocacy. But as *Soul of a Citizen* author Paul Rogat Loeb has said, those e-mail petitions are counted in Congressional offices, but they are also discounted. Yes, mouse-click advocacy can and does make a difference, but if you are truly passionate about an issue, once the mouse had been clicked, the Facebook friends alerted, and the action tweeted, there is often a feeling of some emptiness, a yearning for something deeper. The real question is "What can be done to provide that 'something deeper'?"

When the first edition of *Reclaiming Our Democracy* was published some 20 years ago I was near the end of my 15-year tenure as founder and Executive Director of RESULTS and about to launch the Microcredit Summit Campaign.

When the 10th anniversary edition was published I was past the mid-point in my time as Director of the Campaign. In the years leading up to this 20th anniversary edition I was approaching my sixties and began to think about what my next, and perhaps last, focus would be. I began asking myself this question: "What in my work life has lit me up the most, but is least implemented in the world?" The answer was clear. It is the *grassroots empowerment* that led to the RESULTS victories begun some 30 years ago and the breakthroughs of Citizens Climate Lobby in recent years that inspires me the most and is still, even today, so desperately missing in the world.

In Chapter 29, one of the two new chapters in this edition, I quote Cheryl McNamara, a Citizens Climate Lobby volunteer in Canada, who after participating in a protest *outside* Parliament asked this question: "What was preventing us from going inside and actually talking to policy and law makers about this pressing problem? Why weren't we doing that?" This is how I addressed McNamara's epiphany.

> Her question reverberates through our mostly hollow lives as citizens. It is the question for all mouse-click advocates who are serious about systemic change and who want to do more than just lift a finger for the next mouse-click. The sad answer as to why we aren't going inside and actually talking to the law makers is that most people who want big change cannot find an organization capable of empowering them at a level equal to their desire for change. Most organizations ask us for nothing more than a click and a check. They see us as little children who are too busy with play, too distracted, too naïve, and too incapable of doing the homework necessary to go really deep with our democracy.

In 2012, I set out to change that when I left the Microcredit Summit Campaign and launched the Center for Citizen Empowerment and Transformation (CCET). CCET works to help non-governmental organizations (NGOs) find and train that small portion of their members who want to go far beyond mouse-click advocacy and create champions in Congress and the media for their cause.

The breakthroughs of RESULTS are discussed in Chapters 1–28, those of Citizens Climate Lobby are discussed in more detail in Chapter 29 and the vision of the Center for Citizen Empowerment and Transformation, including 13 commitments needed to succeed at empowerment and transformation, are discussed in Chapter 30. This book provides an answer to these two questions: "Why aren't we going inside and talking to the policy makers and what can be done about it?" It also reminds us that some people already are going inside and that we can follow their lead.

First Edition

Introduction

Voter discontent boiled over during the 1992 presidential elections with George Bush losing 30 percent of the vote in early Republican primaries and third-party candidate Ross Perot garnering 19 million votes in the general election. But this was just a symptom of a deeper civic dysfunction in this country. One member of Congress expressed his own frustration by doing what elected officials almost never do in public—he pointed the finger back at the electorate.

"All you hear from the people is that *none* of the presidential candidates is any good," he said in the months leading up to the election. "And they don't just stop with the presidential candidates," the congressman continued. "They complain that the House of Representatives is no good, and they feel the same way about the Senate. Well let me tell you," he concluded, "the American public is no great bargain either."

Our nation faces a crisis of democracy. People feel cynical and impotent. Where does our cynicism come from? Is it from Vietnam or Watergate? Is it from the assassinations of the Kennedys and King? Is it from the deluge of negative campaigning or the Clarence Thomas hearings? Or is it from the gnawing sense that money talks, and if you don't have it, you don't have a voice? Whatever its origins, this crisis of democracy has left most of us frustrated—unsure of what to do or whether doing anything is even a good idea.

We've heard all the reasons: "You can't fight city hall!" "Voting is a waste of time!" "They're all a bunch of crooks!" "I'm not political." "Good government is an oxymoron."

What do we get from all of our complaining? We get hopelessness and a sense of alienation; and in the process, we lose our sense of vision. "Why dream about how the world could be," we might ask, "when we don't have the ability to change it?"

Reclaiming Our Democracy is a book that challenges this civic despair and offers a new model of citizen empowerment and leadership. It's the story of

RESULTS, an organization that is committed to healing the break between people and government—committed to helping people take back their democracy. RESULTS is an international citizens' lobby dedicated to creating the political will to end hunger. While RESULTS' focus is ending world hunger, its methods could be used to address any issue, such as protecting our fragile environment or improving our educational system.

At its heart, however, this book is not about hungry children or the deterioration of our environment. It is about our own hunger to make a difference and our hunger to halt the deterioration of our democracy. But it's not about taking direct action, such as working in soup kitchens or changing showerheads to conserve water, important as those actions are. It's about working in the political arena and changing the way we view our role in establishing government priorities.

When I spoke about RESULTS to a class of graduate students in public health at the University of California at Berkeley, I told stories of RESULTS volunteers' successes and discussed the healing that was taking place between people and government. But as I spoke, I felt a growing uneasiness in the room.

"Is there something I've said that has put you off?" I asked.

After what seemed to be a long silence, a student raised her hand. "When it all seemed hopeless, we were off the hook," she said. "But if you're right, if individuals *can* make a difference with their government, that means we might have to *do* something. *That's* what is making us uncomfortable."

Reclaiming Our Democracy is a call to action. The book will not leave the reader altogether comfortable, because it's meant to intrude on the false notion that someone else will come to our rescue. But it's also meant to offer inspiration and show that we are our only hope. There are many with whom responsibility can be shared, and I intend to point out how each of us has helped create the mess we are in through our cynicism and apathy and how we are central to resolving it.

Some might ask, aren't our elected officials the ones to take responsibility for the state of our planet and its people—the deterioration of our environment and the poverty of over a billion humans? I think Apollo astronaut Rusty Schweickart answered the question best when he said, "We aren't passengers on spaceship earth. We're the crew...."

But most of us see ourselves as passengers in the mission of stewarding the health of this planet and its people, *not* as crew. During the 1980s, a number of us began to get up out of our passenger seats, walk to the cockpit, and realize—there was nobody up there.

Those cockpit seats are *our* seats. This book is about the migration to the cockpit by ordinary citizens. It shows that some of us have started, and how the rest of us can follow.

In the early days of RESULTS, I assumed that our elected leaders were taking care of the essential business of the planet. But my view changed in 1982 when I called Rep. Mervyn Dymally (D-CA), a member of the House Foreign Affairs Committee, to see if he would participate as a panelist in the World Food Day Forum on Ending Hunger that we were organizing in Los Angeles.

"Yes, I'll come to the Forum," the congressman said to me over the phone, "but I'll sit in the audience."

I was perplexed and said, "But you're supposed to be on the panel."

"Well, you see, hunger's not one of my issues," he responded.

"But Congressman," I said, "we've already sent your office all the questions we'll be asking."

"The questions aren't my problem," the congressman replied. "It's the answers I'm concerned about."

"Well, we've asked nine experts to answer the questions, and we've sent you their responses along with a three-page summary of their answers," I informed him.

"OK," the congressman said, "I'll be there and I'll be part of the panel."

I'd learned two years earlier why members of Congress could say "hunger is not one of my issues." It was at RESULTS' first meeting with a U.S. congressman, Rep. Dan Lungren (R-CA). We were a fledgling, grassroots, anti-hunger lobby with just six groups in the Los Angeles area. We showed Rep. Lungren *I Want to Live,* a film narrated by John Denver that portrayed the tragedy of world hunger. The congressman was visibly shaken by the unnecessary suffering that he was seldom asked to address by his constituents. He spoke in halting phrases.

When he finished, one of the group asked, "Do you get many letters on hunger?"

The congressman stared at the ceiling, thought for awhile, and then looked at us and replied, "There's this Methodist minister in Long Beach."

It's lonely out there for that Methodist minister in Long Beach. He needs our help, and so do our members of Congress. Whether your primary concern is the environment, the quality of our educational system, homelessness, or some other issue—your voice is not being heard.

We often forget that members of Congress are usually lawyers or businesspersons who ran for office and they know everything about these issues any successful businessperson or lawyer would know—which isn't very much. Some of us believe our elected officials should be mind readers. They aren't! We believe they should know what we want. They don't! You could say that members of Congress know everything we ever asked them to know—which, again, isn't very much.

If active citizen involvement is so important to solving the problems we face, then why are most of us so alienated, so politically naive? Is it that we don't care? "Americans do care about politics," says *Citizens and Politics: A*

View from Main Street America, prepared for the Kettering Foundation by the Harwood Group, "but they no longer believe they can have an effect. They feel politically impotent."

The purpose of this book is to show how we can take back our democracy. No more waiting for elected officials to lead. No more waiting for non-elected community leaders. No more waiting for the big shots to handle it. That's a lesson I learned long ago.

In 1979, I spoke with Dr. Henry King Stanford, the President of the University of Miami, who also was chairman of the local Human Relations Commission. His ramrod posture and his extended chest seemed filled with the pride that comes from years of building institutions of higher learning. With his shiny bald head, he looked every bit a pillar of the South Florida community. It was a simple interaction with an unexpected result. I asked if he'd heard about The Hunger Project, a group with which I'd been volunteering.

"No," he answered, "but I have a feeling I'm about to."

I started talking, and after a few moments he stopped me in mid-sentence and said, "You know, somewhere along the line I kind of gave up on our ability to ever end hunger in the world."

My esteem for the man skyrocketed; his honesty was liberating. But at the same time, it shook one of my precious assumptions. I thought I was going to speak to students and ordinary folks about world hunger. I thought that while I worked with grassroots people, the big shots would handle the details of ending hunger—big shots like him. But the big shots *aren't* handling it. The change that is needed will have to come from the bottom. We must stop waiting for our leaders to save us. We have to save ourselves.

The British departure from India was not an initiative from the top. The expansion of civil rights in the United States was not an initiative from the top. The fall of the Berlin Wall was not an initiative from the top. In each case, the people led the government.

"Each of the great social achievements of recent decades has come about *not* because of government proclamations," said James Grant, Executive Director of the United Nations Children's Fund (UNICEF), "but because people organized, made demands, and made it good politics for governments to respond. It is the political will of the people that makes and sustains the political will of governments."

That's both the good news and the bad news, because if the political will of the people is asleep at the wheel, then the political will of the government will be asleep at the wheel. So we must wake up, we must organize, make demands and make it good politics for governments to respond. But, so far, most of us haven't. Why?

The late Bartlett Giamatti, former President of Yale University and Commissioner of Major League Baseball, said it's our disdain for politics and politicians. "What concerns me most today," Giamatti commented at a Yale graduation in the mid-1980s, "is the way we have disconnected ideas from power in America and created for ourselves thoughtful citizens who disdain politics and politicians when more than ever we need to value politics and what politicians do."

But do elected officials deserve the disdain most of us heap on them? I say they don't.

I tried to convey the extent to which we are the missing link in comments at a 1988 conference in Colorado. I was one of four people to lead small-group workshops at the Windstar Foundation in Aspen. There were 1,000 people in the audience, and the four workshop leaders had three minutes each to describe the sessions we were about the lead. John Denver was the moderator. I completed my three minutes and started to sit down.

"I have one more question," John said, calling me back. "Do you know members of Congress?"

"Yes," I responded, "I know some members of Congress."

"What are they like?" he asked.

At that moment I felt a thousand pairs of ears lean forward as if to hear something mysterious or titillating. From my more than ten years of talking with people about hunger and politics, I knew that at best, most people were oblivious to members of Congress, and at worst, they disdained them. And now Denver had asked me, "What are they like?" I prayed for something useful to say.

"By and large," I replied, "members of Congress are dedicated, committed people who got caught without *us*. We sent them to Washington and then we abandoned them there. It's time for *us* to get back into action."

But we won't get back into action until we discard the armor of hopelessness and denial we wear and then educate ourselves for action. I've been told that people don't get involved in issues like world hunger because it doesn't seem to affect them directly. But I say we always wear a cloak of apathy, even around issues that have a direct and obvious effect on us.

In 1980, my first summer in Los Angeles, the smog was oppressive. The problem was right in our faces, in our eyes—we breathed it in. But I heard no clamor for an extensive system of light rail. I saw no mass rallies demanding stricter pollution controls on automobiles. All I heard was the daily weather and smog report on the local news which from time to time let us know that "Today's air quality is unhealthful for everyone."

It's time for us to breathe the fresh air of democracy and reclaim what's rightfully ours. It's time for us to realize that democracy is not a spectator sport.

Preface

How RESULTS Works

Woven through the personal stories of the RESULTS volunteers reclaiming their democracy is the story of how RESULTS works. The final chapters of the book focus on specific how-to's. What follows, in brief, are the basics on the organization.

The purpose of RESULTS is to create the political will to end hunger and to break through the thought that "I don't make a difference." There are more than 100 RESULTS chapters in the United States and an additional 40 chapters in eight other countries. Each group has a minimum of four key volunteers we call partners. The RESULTS partners agree to participate in three meetings per month: (1) a nationwide telephone conference call linking 200 to 300 volunteers to each other and to a guest speaker; (2) a delivery meeting at which the partners learn to speak about issues; and (3) an education and action meeting where the partners invite their friends to join in educating themselves and in writing letters to elected officials and the media. There are 25 volunteer regional coordinators who link each week with a member of the RESULTS staff. The 25 regional coordinators then call the 100-plus RESULTS group leaders, sharing information and coaching the group leaders on specific projects which include meetings with members of Congress, meetings with editorial writers, and hosting news conferences. RESULTS is an acronym for Responsibility Ending Starvation Using Legislation, Trimtabbing,[1] and Support.

RESULTS is funded primarily by individuals who contribute a set amount each month. Contributions to RESULTS are not tax-deductible because we are a non-partisan citizens' lobby. *Entry Point* is our quarterly newsletter. Each

[1]A trimtab is the small rudder found on the back of a larger rudder on an ocean liner. The trimtab is easier to turn. Buckminster Fuller coined our usage of the term when he said that if you wanted to turn the ship of state, you shouldn't try to push the ship around from the front or even try turning the rudder, but find the trimtab and turn that, and then the rudder and ship will turn more easily.

issue includes a domestic action sheet and a global action sheet. RESULTS Educational Fund is the sister organization of RESULTS and is tax-deductible. Its primary project is the World Summit for Children Keeping the Promise campaign.

CHAPTER 1

Getting Started

From Hopelessness to Action

Visionaries are possessed creatures, men and women in the thrall of belief so powerful that they ignore all else—even reason—to ensure that reality catches up with their dreams...for always behind the action is an idea; a passionate sense of what is eternal in human nature and also of what is coming, but as yet unseen, just over the horizon.

Time *magazine, 1992*

The story of RESULTS begins with my own hopelessness about ending hunger, something I carried throughout my first 31 years. Actually it was hopelessness about any major issue—cleaning up the environment, stopping the nuclear threat, and so forth.

In 1976 I was in Manhattan reading a poster advertising a concert by Harry Chapin to raise money for the fight against world hunger. "I'm glad there are people in the world like *him,*" I thought to myself, "people who would do something about a hopeless problem." Several months later, comedian-turned-activist Dick Gregory ran across the United States—50 miles a day for some 70 days—to bring to the public's attention the problem of world hunger and poverty. I was touched that there were people in the world like *him*—people who would take such action for something that was hopeless.

If we want to move into action or move others into action, we must face the hopelessness that's in most of us. Without facing it, it's impossible to move past it to effective action. My own initial involvement in world hunger came through a presentation I attended almost by accident.

"There'll be no class October 5," announced my yoga teacher. "There's a presentation on ending world hunger that evening."

It was 1977 and I was intrigued by his announcement. First of all, he never canceled yoga class. Secondly, hunger was inevitable. I asked how I could get a ticket. The presentation was one of the 11 launching events for The Hunger Project, an international organization committed to letting large numbers of people know that the end of hunger is possible. A large banquet room at the Carillon Hotel in Miami Beach was set with hundreds of chairs, lecture-style. The concepts were simple and earth-shattering. Everything you do or have is an idea first. The pen I used to write my first draft was an idea first. The book you're holding was an idea before it was a book. So, too, with world hunger, or more particularly with ending world hunger. The ideas feed the final outcome. You might say predict the final outcome. If the predominant ideas are "it can't be done," or "hunger is inevitable," or "there are no solutions," then the final outcome will be congruent with these ideas.

It was a remarkable evening. As layers of hopelessness and misinformation were stripped away, I realized that *my* basic assumption was that hunger was inevitable—something that would always be with us. But as I looked deeper, I realized that there was nothing particularly mysterious about growing food. There was nothing particularly mysterious about access to basic health care, clean water, basic education, and the like. It turned out that I wasn't hopeless about the technical feasibility of ending hunger, I was hopeless about human nature. I feared *people* would never get it together. That night, however, I realized there was a particular part of human nature I had some influence over—my own. Up to that point, for me, commitment had a certain "I will if you will" quality to it. "I'll recycle if you will," I might have thought. "Oh, you won't? Then I won't either." In that darkened hotel banquet hall, I experienced commitment in a new way, a kind of "I will whether you will or not."

But more than anything, the evening tore the veil of despair that covered my view of the world. That was what was most exciting and most liberating.

The evening also provided another way of looking at what needed to be done. "Nothing is so powerful as an idea whose time has come," said Victor Hugo. No matter how powerful the resistance is to something happening, once it becomes an idea whose time has come, nothing can stop it. The fall of the Berlin Wall and the democracy movement in Eastern Europe were powerful examples of the fact that when an idea's time comes, nothing can stop it. Of course, the $64,000 question is: "How do you make an idea's time come?" I don't know a simple answer to that. If I did, I'd be in greater demand than I am. But at the time I did think that making an idea's time come might have something to do with talking with people. So I did that—mostly with young people, and it took me to the next step of my journey.

In 1978, I was a high school music teacher and a percussionist with the Miami Philharmonic. The symphony became a full-time job that year, and I took a leave from teaching, which actually gave me time to speak to hundreds of high school classes about world hunger. I was preparing to speak to my first three classes and had been reading quotes from experts and panels calling for the "political will" to end hunger. "If there is the political will in this country and abroad," said the National Academy of Sciences World Food and Nutrition Study, "...it should be possible to overcome the worst aspects of widespread hunger and malnutrition within one generation." I didn't have any real sense of what "political will" was, but I knew it might start with a basic awareness of who represented us in government. So, at the beginning of the first class, I asked the 25 students a simple question. The responses changed my life.

The question was: "Who knows the name of your member of Congress?" I added: "I don't want to know if you've written them or met them, just their names."

Five hands went up.

"Only five hands?" I thought.

But it got worse. I called on the first student. He named the governor.

"No," I said, "I'm looking for the name of the person who serves you in the U.S. House of Representatives."

He didn't know. Four out of 25 did. In the next classroom *none* of the 28 students knew. I was hooked. Over the next two years, 1978 and 1979, I asked 7,000 high school students to name their member of Congress—200 knew the answer, 6,800 didn't. Later, when RESULTS started and things got difficult, this experience served as a part of my foundation, a part of my grounding. It gave me a very direct sense of what needed to be done. We had to find a way to generate the political will—we had to teach the skills of democracy and acquaint people with their government, starting at the most basic level. The seed had been planted.

During this time, I volunteered with the local Hunger Project group which met weekly. It was a tax-deductible group doing educational work. Because of this, we couldn't do much citizen lobbying, such as writing members of Congress on specific legislation, because it would put the organization's tax-deductible status in jeopardy. So, once a month we'd end our meeting early and pass out a newsletter from Bread for the World, a Christian anti-hunger lobby, and write letters to our members of Congress.

In October 1979, I moved from Miami to Los Angeles. I extended my leave from teaching and took a leave from the symphony. I was off to get rich as a songwriter so I could have more time to speak to high school students about world hunger. It didn't work out that way—but it did work out.

I spent my first six months in Los Angeles writing songs, substitute teaching, and working on The Los Angeles World Hunger Event, which was intended to inspire celebrities and other community leaders to commit themselves to ending hunger.

At the event I met a couple, actress Wendy Schaal and songwriter Stephen

Michael Schwartz. They told me they were inspired by the gathering, but frustrated. They didn't know what to do. I told them about my group of friends in Miami who used to write letters to Congress once a month. We agreed to invite friends to Wendy and Stephen's home to do the same. Five days later there were 12 people in their living room. We hadn't planned on starting an organization. We hadn't planned to write letters at any other locations. But it was from that evening that the organization RESULTS grew.

Wendy was an actress on the ABC-TV sitcom *It's a Living*, as was Gail Edwards, a former girlfriend of mine from Miami. We invited Gail to the first meeting. She couldn't make it and urged us to have another meeting at her house the following week. We did, and now we had two letter-writing groups in Southern California, one in Van Nuys and one in Santa Monica. Within two months I was driving to six different locations each month to lead meetings. I would show the film *I Want to Live*, pass out Bread for the World newsletters, and lead the letter-writing sessions. From time to time I would go to the Southern California Interfaith Hunger Coalition to rent a film of the *60 Minutes* segment, "Into the Mouths of Babes," documenting the death and illness that came with inappropriate promotion and use of infant formula in the Third World. We'd write letters to Nestlé, the infant formula manufacturer. It was the summer of 1980. Our experiment had begun.

As I look back on that time, I say something now that I wouldn't have said then: "We were fortunate that no one came up to us and said, 'Creating the political will to end hunger—that's vitally important. Here's $50,000. Let's get this organization up and running in the next six months.'" If someone had said that, I probably would have gotten on a plane, flown to Washington, D.C., and tried to find out how everyone else did it. But luckily, no one offered the $50,000 in start-up money. So all we had was time, our commitment, and the question, How can we be effective on Capitol Hill *from* Los Angeles? I remained a substitute teacher for the next 4 1/2 years as we trial-and-errored our experiment in citizen empowerment. It turned out to be an exciting exercise in getting our democracy back.

CHAPTER 2

Getting to the Media

Finding a Public Voice

Be outrageous. It's the only place that isn't crowded.
Anonymous

The first 18 months (May 1980 to October 1981) were simple times. The leaders of the six groups would meet once a month to write letters and then go out and lead letter-writing sessions in their own living rooms. As we grew, and our members dispersed, they'd join monthly gatherings of group leaders by conference call. We were rather content writing letters to and getting responses from our members of Congress. And we were rather harmless because we hadn't yet learned to work with the media.

But in October 1981, we began to focus on the line-up of candidates running for the U.S. Senate seat in California, a number of whom had direct links to the presidency or to presidential aspirations. Candidate Maureen Reagan's father was president. Rep. Barry Goldwater, Jr.'s father had run for president. Rep. Pete McCloskey and Gov. Jerry Brown had both run for president. Other candidates included Rep. Bob Dornan, author Gore Vidal, and the eventual winner, San Diego mayor Pete Wilson. We decided we would invite the candidates to speak and call it the U.S. Senate Candidate Forum on Ending Hunger. This sleepy little all-volunteer, anti-hunger lobby was about to get a wake-up call and, along with it, a crash course in working with the local media.

Inviting Senate candidates to speak on hunger was one thing, but getting them to come was quite another. First we had to develop some credibility for the Forum. We had to arrange for organizational cosponsors and an advisory committee. I stood at a pay phone in the asphalt yard behind Le Conte Junior

High in Hollywood, California. Over the next several years, junior high pay phones would be my daytime office with "office hours" being moments snatched during planning periods and lunch. I had just spoken with Rev. Stephen Commins, head of the Food and Agriculture Project of the African Studies Center at UCLA. Steve agreed to have his group serve, along with our non-lobbying education arm, RESULTS Educational Fund, as one of the co-sponsors of the Senate Candidate Forum. I talked next with Pat Rief, head of the Southern California Interfaith Hunger Coalition. She didn't think co-sponsorship would be a problem and invited me to speak at the next coalition meeting where they would vote on it. We were off and running.

We sent invitations on our new candidate forum letterhead. We organized letter-writing parties from San Diego to San Francisco and generated 700 personally written letters of invitation to each of the 11 candidates.

"Where can I get volunteers like yours?" asked Maureen Reagan's husband as the deluge of letters started to arrive at her campaign headquarters.

But one invitation on fancy letterhead wasn't going to get the candidates there and neither were 700 letters from future constituents in a state whose population topped 26 million. We had to get the Forum covered in the media. Most of the candidates wanted to be seen, and we needed to demonstrate that this forum was a place where that would happen.

It was during the Senate Candidate Forum in Los Angeles that we began to learn how to work with the media. We continued our training with World Food Day Forums in Los Angeles and New York City six months later. These three events formed the foundation of our prowess with the local media. What we learned, we learned as volunteers. We spent the next decade sharing our knowledge with volunteers across the country and around the world.

I coordinated the two Los Angeles Forums, and Cameron Duncan, assistant to the window designer at Bendel's department store and a new RESULTS leader, coordinated the New York City event. Over the phone we held each other's hand and kept creating answers to the question: "Who are we to coordinate candidate forums in the two largest cities in the country?"

We dedicated the entire year to the candidate forums, and we tried everything. In Los Angeles, our only advantage was our relationship with several celebrities I'd met at the Los Angeles World Hunger Event during my first six months in town. In every other way, we were rank beginners with the media. On most days I was a substitute teacher in junior high schools throughout East Los Angeles. On a few other days, I took off from subbing and appeared on *A.M. Los Angeles* with actor Jeff Bridges or actress Didi Conn or accompanied Harvey Corman to an appearance on *Good Morning L.A.* Our forum moderator, Alicia Sandoval, hosted a mid-day television show and had me and other forum organizers on her program. Alicia would call the campaign headquarters of frontrunners Jerry Brown and Barry Goldwater, Jr. on-air and ask why they hadn't yet committed to coming to the Senate Forum. On most days, Cameron was at Bendel's department store. On a few others, he was doing a citizen editorial on WNBC-TV or a one-hour TV interview along with actor Raul Julia.

During the three candidate forums that year, we had specific events to promote and, of course, the celebrities. First we decided which radio and television interview programs we wanted to get on. Then we found out the names of the producers. We became expert at the 7:00 a.m. Sunday morning radio interview and the 8:00 a.m. Sunday morning religious television programs. We called and we called and we called. We generated 13 television interviews, 23 radio interviews, 4 television editorials, 7 feature articles, more than 12,000 personally written letters urging the candidates to attend, and 14 members of Congress participating at the three candidate forums. All of this was accomplished by volunteers for a grand total of $11,500, which was spent on printing, photocopying, postage, telephone calls, and room rentals.

The one area we hadn't cracked was generating a newspaper editorial. I'd spent my first 33 years in Miami, Florida, and felt that editorial writers at the *Miami Herald* and now the *Los Angeles Times* sat in an ivory tower to which I had no key. This was all to change as a result of an interview with Kathy Hendrix, a writer for the *Los Angeles Times*. Kathy was interviewing me for an article on the World Food Day Forum in Los Angeles. I told her about our request to television and newspaper editorial writers for editorials urging candidates to speak out on hunger. She was shocked when I told her most of the television editorial writers declined because they didn't see hunger as a state or local issue. I heard some concern in her voice when she asked if we'd called the *Los Angeles Times* about an editorial. "Yes, we did," I told her, "but the *Times* wouldn't even return our calls."

She advised me to call Kay Mills and tell her Kathy Hendrix said to call. Kay Mills was the only woman on the *Los Angeles Times* editorial board at the time.

My first call to Kay Mills was from a phone booth in the main office of a junior high school in East Los Angeles. I walked in, closed the door behind me, and put my diary and grade book on a built-in ledge. "We don't usually do editorials on days—World Food Day or Labor Day," Kay said after a brief conversation. "Let's pick an issue and do one."

I promised to mail materials on key anti-hunger legislation Bread for the World had been pushing and follow up by phone. The fourth period bell rang. I said good-bye and hurried back to my classroom. That telephone call and the editorial that followed altered my sense of myself and of what was possible. It was normal for me to distribute 100 photocopies of an action sheet or important article. But when that first editorial appeared, I remember thinking, "not only has the *Los Angeles Times* written this editorial, but they've made one million copies of it and they've delivered it for us, too. How marvelous."

My early morning dash to the front yard to pick up the *Los Angeles Times* was my run to democracy. I realized that I had the right job to make a difference: substitute teacher. I realized that I had the right training to make a difference: music. I realized that I had the right bank account to make a difference: nearly zero. I realized that making a difference wasn't a function of any of these. It was a function of commitment and persistence.

"Editorials flogging RESULTS' pet issues," the *Miami Herald* would write eight years later, "a hefty stack of 90 piled up during a fierce lobbying effort [in 1986] for the Child Survival Fund—are photocopied and distributed [to members of Congress] by the pound."

This first editorial weighed a fraction of an ounce, but it was a hefty beginning.

CHAPTER 3

Expanding Nationwide

Learning the Importance of Speaking Powerfully

Never doubt that a small group of thoughtful, committed citizens can change the world; indeed, it's the only thing that ever has.

Margaret Mead

"I remember the first time Sam Harris called and asked if I'd be interested in starting a RESULTS group," said Scott Swearingen, a member of the communications faculty at Tulsa University. "I said it sounded like a good idea, but my wife and I were trying to get the house in shape (nine years later we still are, incidentally), so all I could do was to say that I would write my member of Congress using the Bread for the World newsletter I received each month. That seemed fine by Sam.

"Then he called back six months later," Scott continued. " 'So, how are the letters going?' Sam asked. That was when I had one of the primary revelations of being a RESULTS volunteer: without other people to work with and encourage me, I wasn't ever going to do anything significant on the issue I felt deeply about. It wasn't a lack of information that kept me from acting, but a lack of connection, of affiliation with other people—a lack of support."

I often look back to those early years to try to figure out what allowed RESULTS to blossom and grow. Common Cause had John Gardner, the respected Secretary of Health, Education, and Welfare. It was able to place full-page ads in the *New York Times* 10 years earlier—ads to which I responded as an early member. Bread for the World had its links to the Christian community and helped fulfill the biblical commands to work on behalf of the poor. But as I looked around, most of the people I talked to were more likely to ask, "Why are you doing this?" than "What can I do?" There was one group, however, that asked what they could do. It was the volunteers from The Hunger Project. As we entered our period of greatest expansion, I turned there again and again in my search for people to host RESULTS presentations.

At the beginning of 1983, there were only 12 RESULTS groups in three states, and our entire budget was $15,000. I first talked to Abby Press, our treasurer, about a 21-city trip I wanted to take in the summer of 1983. She knew we didn't have the $649 for air fare, $60 a day for the 15 weekdays I'd be on the road and not substitute teaching, and the extra cost of phone calls to set up the presentations. Three weeks of travel would cost $2,000, nearly 15 percent of our annual budget. But we decided to take the risk.

It paid off so well that within two years we grew to 50 groups in 33 states. Eastern and Delta airlines offered 21 flights for $649 if flown within a 21-day period. I made five 21-city trips and led a total of 105 presentations between October 1983 and March 1985.

My substitute teaching job was perfect for planning the trip and for the travel portion itself. Each day I was a sub I would take roll, have a brief conversation with the class, give them their assignment and, when it was appropriate, sit at my desk and pore over the Eastern Airlines flight schedule, figuring how to get myself from city to city.

When I got home from school, I would hit the phones, looking for hosts in each of the cities I planned to visit. Besides finding a room for the meeting and inviting their friends, my hosts would pick me up at the airport, put me up in their home, and take me back to the airport the next day. On my first trip, 89 people became monthly sponsors, contributing an average of $10 per month. The trip in 1983 and three more in 1984 more than tripled RESULTS' 1983 budget of $15,000 to $53,000 in 1984. More than anything, the expansion allowed RESULTS to become a growing voice on Capitol Hill for the Third World poor. We were now able to play more of a leadership role in legislative campaigns.

At the end of 1983, we went from two meetings a month—the national telephone conference call[2] and the education and action meeting[3]—to three meetings a month. The newest meeting was the delivery meeting, where the

---

[2]The telephone conference call connects the RESULTS partners each month and includes a guest speaker. As RESULTS grew, so would the call. Now, between 200 and 300 people are on the call. The telephone conference call is described in detail in Chapter 25.

[3]The education and action meeting is held at the end of each month. RESULTS partners invite their friends to learn about an issue and write letters to elected officials and the media.

"Bones Exercise"[4] allowed the groups to write a two-minute talk we called the "Laser Talk."[5]

The decision to move to three meetings a month was cemented in October 1983, during my first 21-city trip. Among the cities I visited were Pittsburgh, Cleveland, and Detroit, three places I'd been to several months earlier on a short speaking tour. On this second visit, I made the two-hour drive from Pittsburgh to Cleveland with RESULTS' Pittsburgh leader, Linda Braun. It was cold and rainy that night, and when we arrived in Cleveland there were only two people in the living room where the meeting was held—four including Linda and me. It was a transformative evening. The need for the third monthly meeting to learn to speak powerfully quivered through my body. I gave everything I had that night, and each word reinforced my resolve to take RESULTS volunteers to the next level as spokespersons. Near empty rooms like this one were the result of uninspired speaking—an inability to convey the vision of RESULTS and the power of its mission.

After the meeting, Linda returned to Pittsburgh, and I was given the pull-out couch in the living room, but I couldn't fall asleep. I wrote a letter to all the RESULTS groups about the need for powerful speaking and a third meeting each month to develop that skill, but I still couldn't fall asleep.

There was a stereo and headphones in the living room. I put on a Bob Seeger album and played the same song over and over: "I know it's late. I know you're weary. I know your plans don't include me...." It was as if I had reverted to my high school guitar teacher days. I started writing down the lyrics, "both of us lonely. Longing for shelter..." and figuring out the chords. It was difficult on the road, pushing through a shyness that had been with me throughout my life, but that night I realized the missing link in my RESULTS lesson plan. Up until then I had asked the question most would ask, "What's the least I can ask of people?" Now I saw I had to ask even more of people; I had to ask them to learn to speak powerfully. It was something I was willing, even eager, to do.

What in my background had led me to this living room in Cleveland on the first leg of a 21-city trip whose mission was to heal the break between people and government? My father was a quiet man, uncomfortable with displays of affection. The grandson of a Lithuanian rabbi, my father went to synagogue twice a day, every day. His religious fervor, commitment, and

[4]The Bones Exercise enables a group to take a powerful article and action sheet and create a brief talk which includes a statement of the problem, the possible solutions, and the opportunities for action. The refinement of this talk is the Laser Talk. The Bones Exercise is described in detail in Chapter 25.

[5]The Laser Talk is a two-minute talk which is a refinement of the material developed in the Bones Exercise. The Laser Talk is taught to newcomers at a RESULTS education and action meeting and is used in conversations with members of Congress, the media, and friends. The Laser Talk is described in detail in Chapter 25.

dogged stick-to-itiveness were to show up in my own persistence during years when citizen advocacy was the last thing most people wanted to do.

My father's other activities showed additional connections to my founding of RESULTS and our political action to end hunger. He wrote a column in a community newspaper and went to city council meetings every Wednesday night. In his retirement, he wrote, typeset, and delivered his own community newspaper to several thousand homes. Each year he dressed up as Uncle Sam and rode in the Memorial Day Parade. My father ran for mayor of West Miami, Florida, several times. The link to my own political action is clear, but none of this civic action was what he did for a living. He was a food manufacturer.

My mother's work was in the home, and the only evenings I remember her not being there at dinner time were when she worked the polls on election day every two years. But most important of all, her gentleness and sense of fairness fueled something in me that longed for justice.

At high school graduation I learned of the death of Ben Rosoff, a fraternity brother one year younger than I. On college graduation day, Robert Kennedy died. These deaths prompted new questions: What am I here to do? What is my purpose in life? As I finally crawled into that pull-out bed in Cleveland, I felt a certain satisfaction with the answers that were beginning to emerge.

My renewed commitment to powerful speaking was given greater impact by innovations developed in the Pasadena RESULTS group and the fourth grade class of Pasadena group leader Dorsey Lawson. When we first met, Dorsey was in her mid-fifties but had the enthusiasm of a 17 year old.

"I was born the day Herbert Hoover was elected president," Dorsey recalled. "The stock market crash and depression were just around the corner. When I was about four years old, my mother had a heart attack and was confined to bed for two years. My father, not wanting to be away from her, left his job in the city, bought an acre of walnut groves in the countryside just outside of Los Angeles, and moved us to the peace and quiet of simple living.

"My father taught himself all he needed to know about small farming, chicken raising and building," Dorsey continued. "By the time I was about six or seven, most of the neighbors were on relief along with the rest of the country. Roosevelt's Works Progress Administration (WPA) projects and surplus food allotments seemed a way of life for the families around us. Luckily, with our chickens, garden, fruit trees, and goats, we had plenty to eat and some left over to trade. The chicken feed sacks were made of cotton cloth with flowers or striped designs. My sisters and I would find three sacks with identical designs and make dresses from them. This is how we expanded our school wardrobes.

"When I was 15, I came across the book *Have We Lived Before?* by Dr. Ernest C. Wilson. It affected me very much. I began to believe that this life was only part of the total picture and that there was more to life than met the eye. When I was in college, I was influenced by the works of Sri Aurobindo, one of India's great sages and an early activist in India's struggle to gain independence.

"In 1952, my husband, sister, brother-in-law, and I headed down to the Los Angeles Convention Center with our hand-painted Stevenson signs," Dorsey recalled. "It was the first time I was interested in politics. Here was a man who spoke like a statesman. His message of bringing people together in peace and justice reached my deepest hopes and dreams. Later that night, when Stevenson conceded to General Eisenhower, Stevenson said, 'It's like when you stub your toe on a chair. You're too old to cry, but it hurts too much to laugh.' I cried a lot that evening. The people had chosen a leader who had spent all his life preparing for and waging war. I think I gave up on politics that night. It must have been 25 years later when my oldest son called, full of excitement, about a presentation he'd been to on The Hunger Project. He spoke about there being enough food to go around and there being ways for people to become self-sufficient. I caught my son's enthusiasm.

"Several years later I met Sam Harris at a briefing at the Bel Air Tennis Club. It was the early 1980s, and a delegation had just returned from Somalia where famine was raging. Sam strolled up to me and said, 'Some of us have been writing letters and making calls to our representatives in Washington, and we were part of an effort led by Bread for the World that got a grain reserve put in place for famines and emergencies.' I was impressed that something concrete and massive could actually be done."

Dorsey invited me to her home to speak to a group of friends. I showed the John Denver film *I Want to Live,* and they wrote letters to their members of Congress. "We were very inspired," Dorsey continued. "We read our letters aloud and cried and laughed. Sam came one more time but said we'd have to lead our own meetings after that. There were six groups in Southern California by then, and he couldn't keep driving to each one."

The Pasadena group led the way in many areas. They were our research and development department in the area of citizen education. "It's funny how our best empowerment tools for RESULTS partners[6] to learn to speak issues came about," Dorsey recalled. "We were trying to master the facts and figures about oral rehydration therapy,[7] and the person who agreed to prepare the

[6]A partner is one of four or more people in a RESULTS group who agrees to participate in three meetings per month: (1) the nationwide telephone conference call; (2) a delivery meeting to learn to speak issues; and (3) the education and action meeting where people gather each month to write letters to elected officials and the media.

[7]In the early 1980s, 5 million children were dying each year from dehydration brought on by diarrhea. Oral rehydration therapy (ORT) is a 10-cent mixture of sugar, salt, and water which, in the right proportion, could save millions of lives each year. In 1978, the *Lancet,* a British medical journal, referred to ORT as "potentially the most important medical advance this century."

talk had been too busy to do a good job. So one of our group members said, 'Let's each write down a sentence or two that we feel describes the problem.' We did that. Then I said, 'Let's each take a turn talking about the problem in our own words so we can get the benefit of each other's ideas.' After each of us felt like we could speak the problem, we went on to do the same thing with the solutions and then the opportunities for action."

It was out of this creative response to the unprepared talk that the Bones Exercise was born. The Bones Exercise provided a simple process for digesting new information and articulating the most important components: the problem, the solutions, and the opportunities for action. The Laser Talk was created when this new information was refined further through the addition of other vital information. Another of RESULTS' innovations, the process of teaching the Laser Talk, came the following day.

"I was working with my fourth-grade English as a Second Language (ESL) students," Dorsey continued, "preparing a school assembly on the opportunity of oral rehydration therapy. The children practiced in groups of four. Each of the group members had a different fact from the talk. They would ask a question and see if the other three in their group could come up with the correct answer. I saw that we could teach the material to anyone if we just broke it into small enough pieces. The children loved it and so did the people who came to our RESULTS meetings."

Peter Rickett, former RESULTS Managing Director, was moved by his first RESULTS meeting and the process by which RESULTS groups taught the Laser Talk. "When I first heard of RESULTS," Peter recalled, "I was a substitute elementary school teacher in Olympia, Washington. I had a teaching certificate from the University of Puget Sound, but a master's degree in cynicism and despair.

"I was an expert in what wasn't working," Peter continued, "and I had an extensive filing system to record all of the major scandals, corruption and decay of the planet. Each day I would scour the newspapers, newsletters and periodicals, joyfully clipping articles documenting my case for despair. I say joyfully, because in between my files on 'Environmental Problems' and 'Iran-Contra' was a big, fat file marked 'Humor.' Humor was the only way to blunt my anger and pain for a world seemingly winding down to a bitter fate.

"The anger and pain were rooted in my own deep caring and concern about people and the planet we inhabit. The despair hatched from a sense of being overwhelmed by the enormity of it all and the feeling that I couldn't do *anything* about it!

"My largest files were about politics—mismanagement, scandals and corruption. Defense contract overruns, Congressional misconduct, devastating environmental policies. They were the largest because I was so political and believed deep down that politics could matter.

"I was politicized in 1968 as a fifth grader. My teacher was 26, passionate and brilliant beyond belief. She believed that anything was possible and believed in us. She taught us about equality, about fairness and justice, about oppression and most importantly love. She valued everyone and taught us about values in the process. So when Martin Luther King and Bobby Kennedy were killed, we mourned and talked and cried together. We watched the news in our classroom. Watched the faces and the words and felt the emotions of those losses. We learned the hard truths about the world.

"But that year the most gripping news event for me was the genocidal war in Biafra. I remember my anger and horror watching the starvation of millions of men, women, and especially children on my classroom television. We wrote letters, we trick-or-treated for UNICEF, we talked. What else could we do?"

Sixteen years passed before Peter met Lynn Walker-McMullen, another teacher. "All she did was invite me to a meeting," Peter recalled. "She claims she asked me three times. All I did was say yes—reluctantly. Secretly I hoped she would forget about it. But she didn't. The last Monday of the month, there I was. Ten, maybe twelve others sitting around folding tables in a stuffy church meeting room. I was nervous. I hated groups (cynics always do), hated speaking in public (even to introduce myself), and it looked like there was a possibility that I would have to do both! Nervous and now sweaty.

"The topic for that meeting was the 'Microenterprise Loans for the Poor Act of 1987.'[8] I didn't start to hear or see anything until we watched a video on the Grameen Bank. I was shocked! They must be mistaken. Here were destitute women, from one of the poorest countries on the planet—Bangladesh—who were given loans to start businesses. But instead of losing the money, they repay the loans 98 percent of the time. They had thriving businesses. Their families were being fed, clothed, and housed. They had dignity. Here was something that worked. Wait, I thought nothing worked!

"Then came something they called the Laser Talk," Peter recalled. "Hear a short talk, answer some leading questions about the talk, pair up, repeat what you heard, hear it again, pair up again. At the end, the group leader, Kristin Blalack asked, 'OK, who wants to give the talk now?' A second went by, then two...

" 'Peter will!'

"It was Lynn's voice, the teacher who'd invited me.

" 'Peter will!' she said again.

"This was the Olympia RESULTS group's idea of offering support. Pushing you out on the skinny branches, where there's some risk. Not physical

[8]The Microenterprise Loans for the Poor Act will be described in Chapter 15. It focused on getting tiny loans ($25 to $100) to destitute women, allowing them to start their own businesses and become self-sufficient.

risk, but risk to who you think you are and what you think you can do. It wouldn't be the last time. 'I can't. No really...I CAN'T,' I told them. But my worst nightmare was realized. What could I do? I stood up, my heart pounding so hard that my chest was heaving in and out. With tremulous voice I delivered the Laser Talk. 'Hey, not too bad,' I thought. But it was still the hardest thing I'd ever done.

"That night I became part of the group and became a monthly sponsor. I had never belonged to a group in my life and had never given money to any charity or cause before that night."

Peter was 26, the same age his fifth-grade teacher had been when she unleashed his passion and his belief that anything was possible.

The move to have people be articulate affected every area of our work. It gave us the skills we needed for the extraordinary success that would come in our grassroots work with the media over the next 10 years.

The ability to speak clearly and compellingly allowed a business machines salesperson to generate an editorial in the *Chicago Tribune* on saving a small UN agency that works with the poor. It helped a preschool teacher convince a *Washington Post* columnist to do a piece on immunizing Third World children. It enabled an executive secretary to arrange a pulpit interview on Dr. Robert Schuller's *Hour of Power* on the World Summit for Children. It allowed a teacher to convince the editor of *Better Homes and Gardens* to write his eight million subscribers, urging them to get involved in seeing that the promises made at the World Summit for Children are kept.

Each of these RESULTS volunteers knew there were things that could be done to make a difference. They studied, they learned to speak the issues, and they took action—always with the support of a group. Each of them made a difference beyond their wildest dreams, and each of them realized that if you can't speak the issues, you aren't dangerous yet.

CHAPTER 4

Our First Victory

The Global Primary Health Care Initiative

We stand by as children starve by the millions because we lack the will to eliminate hunger. Yet we have found the will to develop missiles capable of flying over the polar cap and landing within a few hundred feet of their target. This is not innovation. It is a profound distortion of humanity's purpose on earth.

Sen. Mark Hatfield (R-OR)

RESULTS remained all-volunteer from 1980 through October 1984—a 4 1/2-year period. Our final year as an all-volunteer group was also our first year as the lead private group in a legislative battle to increase child survival funds.

UNICEF had identified several primary health measures which could save some 20,000 lives a day, and we were passionate about promoting them. For us, GOBI wasn't the desert, but an acronym for four life-saving health measures.

Growth monitoring, the "G" of GOBI, allowed parents and health workers to weigh and measure infants, chart their growth, detect dips in growth and the need for supplemental feeding. Malnutrition was often invisible to the eye, but not if the child's height and weight were being charted. It was estimated that half of families with malnourished children actually had sufficient food, but didn't know their children needed extra feedings.

Oral rehydration therapy (ORT), the "O" of GOBI, turned out to be the measure we focused on the most in 1984. That year, more children died of dehydration caused by diarrhea than any other single cause—5 million each year. The normal treatment in a hospital setting was intravenous (IV) feeding which, of course, wasn't available in Third World villages. But a simple mixture of sugar, salt, potassium, baking soda, and water, when taken orally in the right proportions, increased the body's ability to absorb the fluids by 2,500 percent. We learned that the *Lancet*, the British medical journal, had called oral rehydration therapy "potentially the most important medical advance this century." We learned that the mixture cost about 10 cents to prepare.

Breast feeding, the "B" of GOBI, could prevent one million deaths each year caused when infants were fed infant formula that had been improperly measured or had been prepared with dirty water.

Immunizations, the "I" of GOBI, could prevent most of the five million deaths each year from six vaccine-preventable diseases. We learned the six with the help of the mnemonic DPT-MPT. DPT stood for diphtheria, pertussis (whooping cough), and tetanus, and MPT stood for measles, polio, and tuberculosis. We learned that a dose of measles vaccine cost six cents and that measles alone took three million young lives each year.

We also learned that several government programs that could promote this child survival revolution weren't expanding to match the opportunity. UNICEF and the Agency for International Development (AID) Health Account were two examples. The figures below are in millions of dollars.

	1983 Actual	**1984 President's Request**	**1984 Congress' Action**	**1984 Net Change**
AID Health	$133	$100	$125	−$8
UNICEF	$42.5	$26	$52.5	+$10

In fiscal year 1984, UNICEF funding had been increased by $10 million, but AID Health was cut $8 million—a net increase of $2 million. The U.S. defense budget had been increased by $35 *billion* that same year, an increase 17,500 times greater than the $2 million increase in these two health-related accounts.

This defense-driven budgeting demonstrated the need for groups like RESULTS and fueled our work for years. Whenever I spoke, I gave the figures above and then repeated Sen. Hatfield's warning that our will to develop missiles was "not innovation [but a] profound distortion of humanity's purpose on earth."

President Reagan submitted his budget for 1985 at the beginning of 1984. We focused on several accounts including the AID Health Account, UNICEF, and the Child Survival Fund,[9] a new account proposed by a coalition of groups led by Bread for the World. I monitored Congressional action by phone and mail from the RESULTS office, a bedroom I rented from Dorsey Lawson in Pasadena, California.

In a victory led by Bread for the World, a House Foreign Affairs subcommittee agreed to the creation of a Child Survival Fund and recommended $50 million for the new program. The Child Survival Fund would begin to represent the opportunity that had been ignored until now. On March 1, 1984, the subcommittee recommendation went to the House Foreign Affairs Committee, which totaled 37 members that year. But for this vote, only six were present. Rep. William Broomfield (R-MI) offered an amendment to cut the Child Survival Fund in half, to $25 million. The Broomfield amendment passed. I arrived in Washington two days later on the second of my 21-city trips.

"Did Congressman Broomfield know what oral rehydration therapy was—that 10 cents worth of sugar, salt, potassium, baking soda, and water could save a child's life? Did he know that when he proposed cutting the Child Survival Fund in half?" I asked a staff member from Bread for the World and another from the House Foreign Affairs Committee who'd been present for the vote.

"Those are the details," one of them responded, a bit incredulous of the naivete of my questions. "They weren't looking at the details, they were just looking at dollars. You know, 'What's this? A new program? $50 million recommended? Let's make it $25 million.' "

I was still living in Los Angeles, which gave me a better perspective on the nonsense in this thinking. But just having a better perspective was insufficient. It would be the insider strategizing of the House Select Committee on Hunger and its staff, and a powerful television piece which aired 10 weeks after the Broomfield amendment, that would make the difference.

On May 17, 1984, two days before RESULTS' first national conference, ABC's *20/20* aired a segment on oral rehydration therapy (ORT) titled "Next Thing to a Miracle." The segment, which showed children being revived by this miraculous formula, was narrated by Hugh Downs.

Two days later, 95 volunteers from 20 states gathered in Washington, D.C. for RESULTS' first national conference. Up until this point, because of my 21-city trips, I was the only person who knew everyone. The only way people had gotten together before was through our national telephone con-

[9]The Child Survival Fund (CSF) would become an account within the U.S. foreign aid program which funded child immunizations, promotion of breast feeding, oral rehydration therapy, and other primary health measures. It was administered by the U.S. Agency for International Development (USAID) through international organizations such as UNICEF, private agencies such as CARE and Save the Children, and through bilateral agreements between the U.S. and other nations.

ference calls. There was a joke going around before this first national gathering that the people on the calls might be actors I had hired to say at the beginning of each call, "There are four of us here in Brooklyn—there are five of us here in Boston...." At the conference people realized that not only were their RESULTS colleagues real, but so too were our issues. On the second day, "Next Thing to a Miracle" was shown to the participants.

"I have seen something that I would not have believed possible," Downs began after the trumpet fanfare at the opening of *20/20*. "Children, almost at the point of certain death, brought back to health by drinking a simple solution that anyone can prepare who knows the formula....

"This wondrous potion is in this packet," Downs continued, holding up the oral rehydration salts, "and it's about 10 cents worth of simple ingredients, carefully balanced—salt, sugar, potassium, and baking soda. It happened that I saw this almost miraculous revival of children almost halfway around the world. But no matter where you're watching this, you'll rejoice."

RESULTS conference participants were in tears as Downs concluded the 14-minute segment by saying, "...watching those children respond was one of the most moving experiences of my life."

And of ours. We'd studied ORT for some time, but we didn't know in our gut what it could do. The group was energized and decided to try to get the Child Survival Fund back to the original $50 million on our visits with our members of Congress and their staff the following day.

The next segment of the conference featured a panel of hunger and political experts. It included staff from Bread for the World, Church World Service/Lutheran World Relief, and two Congressional aides, one who worked for a Republican and the other for a Democrat. The first questioner said what was on everyone's mind. "We just saw a video on ORT," our volunteer began, "and we want to get an amendment to increase the Child Survival Fund from $25 million to $50 million on our appointments tomorrow. What do you think?"

Marty Rendon, an aide to Rep. Tony Hall (D-OH), urged us to give it a try, but the other three weren't as optimistic. The room was restless and someone shouted, "Let's show them the video." Everyone agreed. The panelists' chairs were turned around, and the video was shown. "Now what do you think?" one of the volunteers asked after Hugh Downs' final words. Rendon still urged us on, but the other three remained skeptical. "First of all," they argued, "members of Congress won't see this video. Second of all, you don't understand the atmosphere here in Washington. We have budgetary constraints."

Telling a room full of RESULTS volunteers that members of Congress wouldn't see the video "Next Thing to a Miracle" was like holding a red cape in front of a bull. The next day, several RESULTS volunteers from Brooklyn left a copy of the video with the staff of the House Select Committee on Hunger. Weeks later it was shown to the Select Committee members as Committee staff poured oral rehydration salts into the representatives' water pitchers and gave them a chance to taste the life-saving concoction. UNICEF Executive Director Jim Grant spoke with members of Congress and met with Tip O'Neill, the Speaker of the House.

Just after seeing the video, Rep. Tony Hall, chairman of the International Task Force of the House Select Committee on Hunger, asked staff director Ernie Loevinsohn, "What can we do about primary health care?"

Loevinsohn had a doctorate in political theory from Princeton and had cut his activist teeth as a staff member of Bread for the World (BFW). As a BFW staff member, he was quoted in that first *Los Angeles Times* editorial I'd generated two years earlier. From that point on, he was a believer in what RESULTS could do.

"Well," Loevinsohn replied to Rep. Hall, "we could ask for new money."

"No, forget that one," Hall responded, hoping to find the resources from existing funds.

"Well, you could shift some military foreign aid over to primary health care," Loevinsohn suggested.

"No, forget that," Hall countered, "We'd lose conservatives on that one."

"Well," Loevinsohn offered, "we could find a large pot of economic aid and earmark some of it for primary health care."

Hall agreed and legislation was drafted that earmarked 5 percent of the Economic Support Fund (ESF) for primary health care. Economic Support Funds were cash grants to countries considered to be of strategic importance to the U.S., such as Israel, Egypt, El Salvador, and the Philippines. It was estimated that ESF would grow to $3.4 billion in 1985 and that 1 percent of it already went to primary health care. The additional 4 percent would add about $144 million for primary health care, nearly six times greater than the $25 million in the newly created Child Survival Fund.

Legislation was drafted. On July 10, Select Committee staff urged us to use the *20/20* video to build support among members of Congress and newspaper editorial writers for an earmark of ESF for primary health care.

Eight days later, on July 18, the first editorial appeared. Michael Squires, a RESULTS group leader who would later serve in the Peace Corps in Liberia, met with an editorial writer at the *Hartford Courant*. Up to this point RESULTS members had generated editorials in Los Angeles and Houston, but only sporadically. Michael's was the first editorial in what was to be our first editorial campaign.

"Although Connecticut Sen. Christopher J. Dodd is sponsoring [an amendment that would create a $25 million Child Survival Fund]," the editorial stated, "it's not expected to pass. The Senate probably won't pass a foreign aid bill at all, and Congress will instead rely on a continuing appropriations resolution for fiscal 1985 as it has for the past two years.

"There are other ways, such as attaching the amendment to another authorization bill or earmarking for basic health programs a bigger percentage of the economic support fund, to get the money through Congress. It should be done.

"There is no defense for the failure of the United States and other governments to commit the modest resources that are needed, when the prevention of hunger for millions of children is within their reach."

Several days later I traveled to the World Hunger Information Center suite at the Democratic Convention. During a news conference at the suite, Rep. Hall described the health measures UNICEF said could cut child deaths in half within a decade. I asked Hall how many of his colleagues (other than those on the House Select Committee on Hunger who'd seen the *20/20* segment) knew what oral rehydration therapy is. "None," he replied.

That wouldn't be true for long. RESULTS volunteers were on the phone to editorial writers and members of Congress. Nancy Taylor, who with her husband Matt owns a business machines company in Chicago, was one of them.

"I was born to an Irish, Catholic, Democratic family," said Nancy. "We considered all three conditions to be genetically coded. In Chicago, all politics were local and of the ward healer variety...'you campaign for our candidates and we'll get your kid a summer job'...'vote Democratic and we'll get your traffic tickets fixed.' It was the world of 'clout' and the little fix. It wasn't pretty or inspiring, but it was the way things seemed to work.

"I carried this cynical view of politics and individual participation to college where I met a truly inspiring American history teacher," Nancy continued. "He presented the birth of our nation as a grand experiment in self-governing. He portrayed our Founding Fathers as real visionaries with a great deal of courage and persistence.

"I left college and, with time, this experience faded into a dim memory. Resignation dulled my senses about the power of possibility.

"Many years later, I met Sam Harris, who was traveling around the country looking for partners in his effort to build a grassroots citizens' lobby to end hunger and the worst aspects of poverty. He explained that the first duty of a partner was to break through the thought that individuals can't make a difference. This certainly rang true for me. As I listened to Sam explain the format, I remembered that college history class and how it excited my imagination.

"For the greater part of my life, I'd lived inside my head, thinking, judging, and evaluating. When I first met Sam, he listened politely to my endless opinions and he gently issued an invitation to take some action in a simple, straightforward way that kept argument and differing opinions to a minimum. The RESULTS format was clear and organized. The action steps were challenging but stunning in their simplicity. It required learning about an issue with universal appeal, such as primary health care initiatives for children, then practicing how to speak about the issues, focusing on the opportunity and solutions available. Once these skills were mastered, the action called for contacting someone who could do something about it, such as a legislator or editorial writer, and convincing them to cosponsor legislation or write an editorial promoting pending legislation. It all sounded so easy, and the preparation was a snap because it took place in my head, my comfort zone. However, when it came time to take action, the panic began.

"There was plenty of reason for action, millions of children were dying and there were simple remedies to several of the causes. Rep. Hall would be introducing a bill to provide a surge of new funding and help alleviate the worst aspects of the suffering. In order to get the legislation passed and implemented quickly, more attention to the proposed legislation was called for."

As Nancy confronted moving from educating herself to action, RESULTS groups all around the country were taking their own actions. On August 6, six partners from the Manhattan RESULTS group met with Rep. Ted Weiss (D-NY). When Weiss told Nick Schatzki, an actor, there was no need to show him the *20/20* video because he already knew what ORT was, Nick responded that knowing about ORT was like knowing about sex; it didn't have the same impact as experiencing it. The congressman agreed to view the video. Showing brief but potent video segments would become a key tool in RESULTS' strategy to mobilize political will. For us, seeing was believing.

That same afternoon, partners from the Brooklyn RESULTS group showed the video to Rep. Steve Solarz (D-NY). Ken Buxton, a building contractor, reported that Solarz favored increasing funds for primary health care but didn't want to use the Economic Support Fund to get the money. He felt the ESF should be used for security purposes, not for development. Solarz asked where the Child Survival Fund came from and who proposed it. Solarz was the fourth ranking Democrat on the House Foreign Affairs Committee, the committee that cut the fund to $25 million five months earlier with only six of its 37 members present.

HR 6117, the Global Primary Health Care Initiative, was introduced in the House by Reps. Tony Hall and Frank Wolf (R-VA) on August 9. The following day Congress went on a three-week recess. All funding bills had to be completed before the fiscal year began on October 1, 1984. If we missed this deadline, we would have to wait until the following year. We had just seven weeks to get the bill through the House and Senate—seven weeks, with Congress on recess three of those seven weeks. The timing was awful, but RESULTS continued to push.

In August, we purchased 21 copies of "Next Thing to a Miracle" from ABC. One of the first groups to show it to a member of Congress was the RESULTS group in Minneapolis/St. Paul. Rep. Bruce Vento (D-MN) saw the video and promised to show it on the House closed-circuit system so that many more members of Congress and staff could view it.

On August 13, four days after the legislation was introduced, an editorial appeared in the *Houston Chronicle* initiated by Newton Hightower, the RESULTS group leader there.

"Recently, a bill was introduced in Congress that would target 5 percent of the U.S. Economic Support Fund for primary health care," the *Chronicle* began. "The bill enjoys broad bipartisan sponsorship that includes Rep. Mickey Leland of Houston, chairman of the House Select Committee on Hunger. One appeal of this bill," the *Chronicle* continued, "is that it would not entail additional expenditures of the taxpayers' dollars. The Economic Support Fund provides assistance to friendly governments. The bill would require a higher proportion of the fund be devoted to health care....New, simple techniques have revolutionized child health care in developing countries. Their worth and effectiveness have been proven, and, in these times of budgetary pressure, the price is right."

Effectiveness as a RESULTS volunteer was something that could be developed in a matter of weeks. Jack Waters, an insurance salesman in Milwaukee, would prove this in a meeting with his representative after being in RESULTS no more than a month. His congressman, Rep. Gerald Kleczka (D-WI), hadn't been in Congress much longer.

"I grew up in Philadelphia," Jack said, recalling his path to RESULTS. "My grandfather was a staunch Republican and was very involved politically. The family joke was that if Chiang Kai Chek ran on the Republican ticket he'd get my grandfather's vote. He taught me I had to do other things for the community, aside from my work. I enjoyed the passionate discussions at the dinner table and found myself passing out flyers before the election to get people to the polls. I knew that someday, one day, I would get really involved—maybe even be in Congress.

"Watergate left me very cynical about politics, however....I felt that Nixon had betrayed the trust of people who'd believed in him—people like my grandfather. I watched the hearings and read everything about it. Underneath the cynicism, I still felt I could have an impact and that someday I would be active.

"In 1976 I went to Shippensburg State College in Pennsylvania. The campus was about 40 miles from Three Mile Island. I grew up thinking nuclear energy was a viable alternative form of energy. The guys I lived with came from the Harrisburg area near Three Mile Island. I remember the Three Mile Island nuclear power plant accident vividly. It was a Wednesday. I remember waking up and going down to see a friend of mine. Over the next few days 19 people gathered in that house to get out of the Three Mile Island area. I remember going into Harrisburg on Sunday and it was barren. There was nobody there except the volunteer fire department. It was a ghost town. The next day the situation was declared under control, but I never had the same feeling about nuclear reactors again. There was this feeling that something was wrong here. The last few years of college were eye-opening as far as learning more about issues, but hunger was still not one of them."

That would change two years later when he met Lori, his wife to be.

"Lori was the first person who ever talked with me about ending hunger," Jack continued. "Lori and I were in an insurance class in West Berlin, New Jersey. We went out after school to TGIF for dinner one night. Over dinner, she enrolled me in The Hunger Project and as a monthly contributor. It was in March of 1982. Hunger still didn't have a very big pull for me, but Lori sure did. I went to a hunger briefing she led at the University of Pennsylvania. I remember the page that said 'people thought you couldn't run a four-minute mile—you couldn't put a man on the moon.' I loved those little glimpses into times when some things that seemed impossible were actually possible.

"Lori and I were dating and in September she decided to take a job in Milwaukee. I visited in October, asked her to marry me, she said yes, and two weeks later I had everything I owned in an 18-foot truck with my car attached to the back. After I had moved to Wisconsin, I asked her not to take time to lead hunger briefings, and she agreed."

In July 1984, Jack and Lori went to their first RESULTS meeting, part of my third 21-city trip.

"The thing that struck me most about the presentation," Jack continued, "was when Sam said we got exactly what we asked for from our government. He went around the room and asked who had written their member of Congress in the last year. No one had. Had we met with our representative on a specific issue? Again, no one. Here I was, a person who had known when I was younger that I could have an impact, but I was still waiting for the 'someday, one day,' to get involved.

"I put my hand up to be in the group because of this little glimpse—not from the hunger angle as Lori would, but from the political angle. We could participate together even if for different reasons. We walked out of that meeting and went through the test[10] on the basics on RESULTS, hunger and the legislative process. At the end of the test I asked what was next and Sam said we should call our representative for an appointment. I still wasn't convinced that this was going to work, but I was willing to try. So I called the scheduling person, got her on the line and got the appointment. That hooked me a little more. Sam used to say RESULTS was an experiment and I was

[10]The first thing new partners in RESULTS do is listen to a cassette tape and prepare for a test. I wanted each new partner to have a foundation of information covering (1) the basics on RESULTS, such as the purpose and the activities of a group; (2) the basics on hunger and some of the things we can do to end it; and (3) how a bill becomes law. I often took great pride in testing nine new groups and flunking eight of them. I reasoned that if they did a shoddy job and I passed them, they would know this wasn't for real. With the test I held up a level of excellence I believed to be appropriate for these "community leaders-in-training."

into the experiment aspect of it. The first RESULTS conference call we were on was just before our meeting with the congressman. On the call people were talking about how their members of Congress didn't know about the Economic Support Fund. I couldn't believe it. What kind of bozos did these people have for congressmen and women? Mine was going to know this stuff.

"A few days after the conference call we went to meet with our member of Congress. It was in the middle of the day. I knew the city well but got lost on the way. I was yelling at Lori. I was nervous. Lori and I joined Wendy Sexton and Judy Stevens in the parking lot before the meeting. We brought a TV and VCR to show "Next Thing to a Miracle." The congressman's staff was not happy about that and when we met the congressman he didn't want to see the video—he wanted to talk with us. So right away we were thrown off. The video was supposed to be a major thrust of the meeting. He was in his early forties and had been in Congress for only a few months. The first thing that I said to him was, 'We're here to talk about earmarking 5 percent of the Economic Support Fund for primary health care.' He said, 'What's the Economic Support Fund?' I began to tell him what the ESF was because we had studied it for the test two weeks before. In the course of my two-minute presentation, I watched him lean forward in his chair and found myself leaning forward in my chair. What clicked for me was I could actually tell a congressman something he didn't know and have an impact on him.

"From that point on I was done—I was hooked. He was interested in knowing. He said he'd cosponsor the bill. That was it for me. This was what I wanted to do. I wanted to be able to empower my elected officials. I wanted to be able to have a conversation with my elected officials. Everything I was told was right on track. How to get an appointment and how to prepare for the meeting. From that point forward, anything RESULTS put on the table I pursued. The experiment was working a lot sooner than I thought. My 'someday, one day' was now."

A call went out in an August 28 letter to RESULTS volunteers asking for help in finding a senator to introduce legislation calling for 5 percent of ESF for primary health care. The following week was the most spectacular we'd experienced in RESULTS. There were meetings, like the ones Jack and his partners had, with six more members of Congress. There was an editorial in the *Los Angeles Herald.* There were requests for RESULTS volunteers to write op-ed pieces in the *Chicago Tribune,* the *San Diego Union,* and the *Baltimore Sun.* There were letters published in the *Chicago Tribune,* the *Baltimore Sun,* and the *Houston Chronicle.* There were meetings with editorial writers at the *Seattle Times* and the *Baltimore Sun.*

"A House bill HR 6117," the *Sun* editorial concluded several days later, "would provide $144 million for ORT and other basic health measures in friendly Third World nations, through reallocation of foreign aid funds. If the bill gets enough attention, it might be passed before Congress recesses October

4 and ORT could be saving many more children's lives. It deserves the support of the Maryland delegation."

While there were only four or five partners in the Baltimore RESULTS group and only 10 or 15 people attending action meetings, here was the largest newspaper in the state calling for our action. A letter to the editor or op-ed piece was the opinion of a single person, but an editorial was the opinion of the newspaper. Time and time again, editorials would be the vehicle for shaping opinion in our communities and in Congress. What more could we want, than a thoughtful endorsement to hundreds of thousands of constituents? And what's more, the Baltimore delegation included Rep. Clarence Long (D-MD), in his final year as Chairman of the Foreign Operations Subcommittee of the Appropriations Committee, the crucial House subcommittee for funding Third World health programs.

Nancy Taylor decided to pitch an editorial to the *Chicago Tribune*.

"I can't remember what pushed me past my fear and helped me dial the telephone," recalled Nancy, "but I found myself talking to an editorial writer at the *Tribune*, who encouraged me to submit an article. He explained that this would be the best way to get something printed. Now the heat was really on," Nancy continued. "My action had led to an invitation to take another action. This was getting more perilous by the moment. I wanted to retreat back into my head and turn this one over to a more courageous and capable soul. I got a call from another RESULTS partner and she urged me to accept the invitation and write the op-ed piece. She cleverly pointed out that I was the only one with the opportunity. She also cautioned me that my failure to deliver would be a missed opportunity which might make a difference. I took the plunge and wrote with as much clarity and passion as I could muster.

"After mailing the article, I experienced another bout of panic, but I calmed myself with the thought that it would probably never be printed and I could maintain my anonymity. When nothing had appeared in the paper within two weeks, my panic subsided and my life went back to its normal, safe rhythm.

"My calm was shattered early one morning, however, when my husband thrust the editorial page in my face. There it was, my words and my name. As I read what seemed like foreign phrases, I felt a head rush which was equivalent to an unfiltered cigarette and a stiff martini being ingested simultaneously. I had my first adult experience with getting 'high on life.'

"I was 'out of the closet.' I had thought that reading the newspaper editorial pages was a dead practice, but apparently I was wrong. People I hadn't heard from in years called me and said they had read the article and wanted to know what I was up to. I delivered the message of what individuals can do to impact public policy to everyone who asked and would listen. Each retelling reinforced the validity of what I said. Individuals aren't powerless if they can convert their good ideas into positive actions. The most valuable thing for me about this experience was that I felt alive and full of energy. The creative juices were flowing and I felt an enthusiasm for playing in the game of life. I felt more alive than I had since I was five years old and thought I could sing and dance. And the best part of this high was that it wasn't at anyone's expense, it harmed no one and it might do some good."

"A statement issued by James Grant, Executive Director of UNICEF," Nancy wrote in her *Chicago Tribune* op-ed piece, "estimated that each $1 million in additional basic health assistance, if well managed, would yield the following results: 10,000 or more lives would be saved and an additional 10,000 people would avoid crippling disease; the health status of 100,000 people would be measurably improved; and 10,000 to 20,000 births would be prevented as couples decided to have fewer children."

Members of Congress are able to show their support for a measure by adding their names to a list of cosponsors. Cosponsorship suggests that a member has looked at the measure and supports its basic aims. With thousands of bills introduced each year, and most of them dying due to lack of interest, cosponsorship is an important way to build support in Congress. By September 10, four weeks after introduction of HR 6117 (three of these weeks with Congress on recess), there were 65 cosponsors of the bill. Eleven days later there were 123 cosponsors. Rep. Bruce Vento would demonstrate an even more powerful form of support.

"Mr. Speaker," Rep. Vento said as he stood before the House of Representatives on September 26, "I want to call my colleagues' attention to what I believe is a modern health miracle—oral rehydration therapy (ORT). Recently I met with several constituents from an organization called RESULTS which works to focus public attention upon the problems of hunger and malnutrition. I also viewed a brief film, which was recently broadcast on an episode of ABC's television program *20/20*, which dealt with an amazingly successful treatment for victims of dehydration....This simple and profound discovery," Vento continued, "may save the lives of literally millions of children and adults in the world's developing nations who die from dehydration....Our colleague, the Chairman of the Select Committee on Hunger, Congressman Mickey Leland, and I have arranged for this film to be shown on the House closed-circuit television system on Wednesday, Thursday, and Friday, September 26, 27, and 28, this week at 10:00 a.m. on Channel 6. I urge all of my colleagues to view this brief but highly informative program."

Having a member of Congress speak for your measure before his colleagues demonstrates a higher level of commitment than cosponsoring. Vento would not be the last to do so.

The morning of the House Appropriations Committee mark-up,[11] Houston RESULTS leader Newton Hightower phoned his cousin, Rep. Jack Hightower (D-TX), a member of the House Appropriations Committee, and talked with him about HR 6117. After the call, Rep. Hightower spoke for the inclusion of HR 6117 in the foreign aid appropriations bill. It was included by a vote of 20 to 17. This assured adoption in the catch-all continuing appropriation bill that would pass in the House that year. Attention shifted to the Senate.

Several weeks before HR 6117 was adopted by the House Appropriations Committee, Chris Teal, leader of the newly created Billings, Montana RESULTS group, met in Montana with an aide to Sen. John Melcher (D-MT). The aide, who had worked with the Peace Corps in Africa for six years, was very excited about the Global Primary Health Care Initiative. On Thursday, September 13, Melcher introduced Senate Amendment 4241, which was identical to HR 6117.

The Reagan Administration, jolted into action by the unexpected success of HR 6117 in the House Appropriations Committee, went all-out against Melcher's Senate amendment. Lobbyists from the Agency for International Development visited each Senate office to lobby against the bill. The Administration didn't want to use ESF monies for primary health care, they wanted to use it for security-related purposes.

"We must not let up now," I wrote in my letter to RESULTS leaders on September 14. "Pull out all the stops. No more of this having one person call the senator's office. Have everyone call, but coach them first. We have one week to get the message to the U.S. Senate, especially the Senate Appropriations Committee."

In Honolulu, RESULTS volunteers gathered aides to the entire Congressional delegation in the same room—Sens. Daniel Inouye (D-HI) and Spark Matsunaga (D-HI) and Reps. Cecil Heftel (D-HI) and Daniel Akaka (D-HI)—and showed them the *20/20* video. Senator Inouye, ranking Democrat on the vital Foreign Operations Subcommittee of Appropriations, cosponsored the next day. Sen. Matsunaga cosponsored two days later.

Public opinion grams were sent to senators. Letters to the editor, op-ed pieces, and editorials continued to come in, but perhaps the greatest piece of strategy emerged from seven RESULTS volunteers. Ruth Rosen, Cameron Duncan, Nicholas Schatzki, and Bob Van Olst flew into D.C. from New York City, Bruce Davidson flew in from New Jersey, Barbara Trepagnier flew in from Houston, and Dan Doerfer drove in from Baltimore and showed

[11] After a bill is introduced, if enough support is built, hearings are held. Hearings are followed by mark-up, a time when final changes are made by the committee before sending the measure to the floor of the House or Senate for a vote.

the *20/20* video to the aides to 25 senators. Bruce Davidson was an engineer from Bridgewater, New Jersey. "I'd gotten a call from Cameron Duncan who, along with several other RESULTS volunteers, had been meeting with Senate aides," Bruce recalled. "I arranged to stay with my brother Rick the night before, and on Monday morning I headed for the Select Committee on Hunger for a briefing. After valuable coaching, I walked over to the Methodist Building on Capitol Hill where I had been offered a space to plan my day. RESULTS didn't have an office in Washington yet and was still an all-volunteer organization. I used the phone to call RESULTS partners in the states where the key senators lived and had them set up meetings for me with their senators. When that was done, off I went armed with a VCR and television and a copy of 'Next Thing to a Miracle.' I was about to go head to head with the U.S. Senate.

"Later that day," Bruce continued, "after cordial meetings with aides to three senators, I had 10 minutes with Sen. Jake Garn (R-UT), the first civilian in space. He told me that he couldn't support my issue even though he saw the value of it. He went on to say that the Administration had contacted him an hour before I got there to alert his staff to my visit and to make sure he would remain opposed to the amendment. When the senator told me 'not to worry,' I thought there might be some compromise in the works. I spent another hour with Sen. Garn's staff, showing them the video and talking about the possibility of healthy kids all around the world."

The impact of that lobbying tactic was dramatic. Three weeks after the amendment was introduced in the Senate, there was a vote on it. At 2:30 a.m. on October 3, the Senate defeated Melcher's amendment by five votes: 46 for and 51 against. Instead, the Senate approved a substitute amendment that appropriated $75 million *new* dollars to agriculture and health. Since the House came in with a version that would have earmarked 5 percent of the ESF for primary health care, and the Senate came in with a version that would give $75 million for agriculture and health, they had to go to conference[12] on it.

The House/Senate conferees agreed to $50 million in new money for

---

[12]A conference is when members of a House and Senate committee or subcommittee meet to iron out differences in a bill that has passed both bodies. The version they agree to must return to the House and Senate for final passage before being sent to the president for signature.

primary health and $10 million in new money for nutrition.[13] That was a total of $60 million new dollars that came *directly* out of the work that was done on HR 6117 and Senate Amendment 4241.

"Without RESULTS' lobbying I don't see how we would have gotten more than $10 million for health and nutrition," said Ernest Loevinsohn, staff director of the House Select Committee on Hunger, the day after the decision. In addition, a $25 million Child Survival Fund was created due to the leadership of Bread for the World. The support Bread for the World had built spilled over into our end-of-the-year action, but it wasn't something they worked on directly.

"I want to take this opportunity," wrote Rep. Hall, the lead sponsor of HR 6117, on October 11, "to thank and congratulate you and all RESULTS members across the country who worked so hard on the Global Primary Health Care Initiative....

"Success of the primary health care legislative project would not have been possible without the spirited and persistent efforts of RESULTS workers throughout the nation," Hall continued.

"The work of the RESULTS participants on the Global Primary Health Care Initiative was truly extraordinary, and it demonstrated that concerned and motivated citizens really can have an impact on the legislative process. It was important to the representatives and senators involved to know that they had constituents like the RESULTS participants who were backing the global primary health care legislation and who cared about how they acted and voted. The RESULTS work on the Global Primary Health Care Initiative was citizen lobbying at its best.

"I hope your success on this project will encourage all RESULTS participants to redouble your work to end world hunger in the next Congress. We couldn't have succeeded without you, and we look forward to continuing efforts in the future!"

It was a heady time. We still had no paid staff, and Hall's letter was sent to our office in my bedroom in Pasadena. I was to become RESULTS' first

---

[13]What was particularly impressive was that the House had already agreed to a $48 million increase to AID Health over the previous year. The conferees added the $50 million for primary health to the AID Health account, which created an overall increase of $98 million to AID Health. The AID Health account, which had been $125 million in 1984, would be $223 million in 1985. The numbers (in millions) looked like this:

	1983 Actual	**1984 Actual**	**1985 Actual**	**1985 Net Change**
AID Health Account	$133.0	$125.0	$223.0	+$98
UNICEF	$ 42.5	$ 52.5	$ 53.5	+$ 1
Child Survival Fund			$ 25.0	+$25

full-time staff member a few days later and would move to Washington, D.C. by the end of December. Earlier that year, President Reagan's re-election campaign television ads told us that it was "morning in America." The only thing I could see from my bedroom office perch was RESULTS volunteers awakening to their democracy.

CHAPTER 5

Getting to Our Courage and Action on Ethiopia

*What is required is courage. And courage is one of the easier ones. It's not like you go into a situation where you are essentially weak of heart and afraid and somehow by a great effort of will you screw up your courage and overcome your cowardice to do this thing, even though it is scaring the pants off you while you are doing it—that ain't how it works. Courage comes from 'heart'—*coeur *in French,* corazon *in Spanish—and courage means you see the importance of this thing in front of you so strong and so seriously, and you have so much heart and you care about it so much that you are single-mindedly intent on doing it, and you don't even consider whether you are afraid or not. If your knees are knocking together like castanets, it doesn't matter because what has to be done has to be done and you don't consider that other stuff. You love somebody enough, or you love everybody enough, that it is worth your while to do it.*

Stephen Gaskin, Mind at Play

RESULTS' description of courage was often less eloquent than Stephen Gaskin's. I would refer to my "nausea quotient" when my insecurities loomed larger than what I perceived to be my ability. But for everyone in RESULTS, it was the vision of eradicating hunger and poverty that allowed us to enter the ring and take actions that often seemed too daunting.

By the mid-1980s, RESULTS was still at the beginning of its experiment to discover how ordinary citizens could become community leaders. The most prevalent model for citizen lobbying had donations flowing to Washington, D.C. from around the country with the bulk of the advocacy done by paid staff based in the nation's capital. The unspoken assumption was that because the issues were so complex and the public too busy to learn the details, the organizations would lobby on behalf of their members. RESULTS worked to shift to a model that realized that the best lobbyists were the people themselves working in their own communities around the country.

Groups like CARE, Save the Children, Oxfam, and Christian Children's Fund worked directly with the poorest people in the developing world. RESULTS had a different mission; we immunized no children, we trained no farmers, we opened no village health posts. Instead, we lobbied the Congress for policy changes and for funds that would do these things and much more. But to accomplish this we had to develop community leaders, which required moving into areas where failure was always a threat. If we wanted to grow as leaders, if we wanted to demonstrate courage, we had to move out of our comfort zones.

Dorsey Lawson, volunteer Assistant Executive Director of RESULTS, wrote group leaders about these forays outside our comfort zones while I was on my fourth 21-city trip. "Greer Malone, Secretary of RESULTS, called for an appointment with her congressman, Glenn Anderson of Long Beach, to show him the *20/20* video," Dorsey wrote. "Rep. Anderson's office said the aide had seen the video and told the congressman all about it and he wholeheartedly supports the program. Greer said she wanted the *congressman* to have a personal experience of what is possible. They gave her the appointment! She and her partner Peggy Brutche showed it to him. He was excited about it and said, 'What other congressmen have seen this? I want all of them to see it! I want everybody to see this video!' Greer is following up with him on that.

"Shirley Williams called the editor of the local Pasadena newspaper," Dorsey continued, "to request an appointment to discuss an editorial and to show the video. After four calls she reached the editor. No, he didn't want to see the video. No, he didn't want to write an editorial. No, he didn't have someone to write an op-ed piece. YES, he would print one if she would write it, get it to him in two days, and he would publish it two days after that. She did. He did. You have the brilliant results enclosed, 'End of World Hunger Within Our Grasp.'

"If you're scared to do this kind of stuff, know that we are too. Greer got nauseated writing her op-ed piece for the *Long Beach Press-Telegram*. Shirley got a splitting headache before she finally got through to the editor. I felt flushed and feverish driving off to the reception for 40 people with Rep. Matthew Martinez. If you don't have any discomfort, look at what would be a stretch for you. RESULTS is people breaking through the thought, 'I don't make a difference,' to emerge as community leaders. Those who have pressed themselves to new heights of participation know the joy of this. What's next for you?"

As always, she signed the letter, "Love, Dorsey."

After our Global Primary Health Care Initiative victory, we focused a great deal on the famine in Africa. Attention to the famine exploded when Tom Brokaw began his coverage on *NBC Nightly News* in October 1984. My first conversation with an editorial writer on the famine in Ethiopia was in June 1983, 17 months before the NBC broadcast. As was usually the case in my Los Angeles days, I got my information from Bread for the World. The *Los Angeles Times* editorial finally appeared in September 1983, 13 months before the NBC broadcast. Later we would realize the importance of having an item covered as a news story in the newspaper or on television. But for now, our expertise would be generating editorials on issues that were *not* in the news.

The famine touched people around the world and, for some in the U.S., served as their path to RESULTS. Mark Toogood, who works for the Peace Corps in Minnesota, was one of those people. "My father was a social worker and my mother a nurse," said Mark, reflecting on his earliest influences. "I can recall my father frequently discussing the civil rights movement and protecting the well-being of children. There was a strong emphasis on service in my Catholic education. You could say there was a seed-bed of compassion that had been cultivated in my upbringing. But somewhere along the way," Mark continued, "I grew convinced that it was hopeless to try and actually do something, in the real world, to make a difference for others. I really don't know if it was from coming of age in the cynical Watergate years, or the bitter political disillusionment in the wake of Vietnam—but somehow I had (albeit unconsciously) concluded that I could not make a difference."

This was to change as Mark saw the first film clips of the famine in Ethiopia in 1984.

"I was drinking a beer and planning an evening with my girlfriend," Mark continued. "I remember vividly, setting my beer down and watching with horror the stark imagery of emaciated mothers cradling their wasted children in their arms. The shock of their reality in contrast to my own was a turning point in my life. I knew that I had to do something—but what? I had no international background. I knew nothing of politics or fundraising. Moreover, I was a person who *knew* that the 'system' was corrupt and that there was no way one person could do anything to really change the situation.

"But I was committed to doing *something*. I began to volunteer at a place called the Hunger Action Coalition, where I studied the issue of world hunger. I volunteered to help coordinate an 'African Relief Hotline' which helped raise money for famine relief. And I got a job at a local food shelf to try and learn more about hunger in my own community. But through all of this activity my fundamental conviction that the political system was hopeless remained intact—although it was clear that the solution was in the political arena!

"The breakthrough for me came when a fellow named Paul Thompson, a returned Peace Corps volunteer and a member of a citizen's group called RESULTS, invited me to come to an education and action meeting to write letters to our members of Congress, urging support for the African Relief and Recovery Act. After the meeting, which was the first time I'd ever written to a member of Congress, Paul asked me if I'd be interested in meeting with an editorial writer from the *Minneapolis Star-Tribune* to give them information we had learned on this important bill.

"What a concept! 'You mean people can actually do that?!' I said. Paul assured me that it could be done and that he would help coach me in how to place the call and what we would need to do to get prepared. On my first call to the paper it felt like I was calling the President or God—my voice climbed an octave. I spoke rapidly and officiously so as to not waste this important person's time. Then, when I had gotten past the secretary, I really quaked. 'Would it be possible? Could you spare 10 to 15 minutes? We just want to take a few minutes to talk about millions of people dying is all.'

"Amazingly, this somber and very intelligent person, Linda Thrane, said she would give us half an hour. We later met with her after carefully practicing our presentation, and found that once the initial contact was made, this seemingly austere woman was quite generous with her time and very grateful for the material RESULTS provided. Four or five days after our trembling but exhilarating meeting with the editorial writer, we opened the morning paper to find the lead editorial calling for Congressional sponsorship of the African Relief and Recovery Act! Just imagine! In some way we had caused this thing to happen. Just by being willing to go in and take the risk of looking like a fool to this, as it turns out, very decent and caring individual who was really wanting to write something about the African famine to begin with. I learned a very important lesson the day of that meeting, which was that if we all wait until we are experts with 'high-falutin' credentials before we get into action, there is no hope for us to move forward on any of the crucial issues of our time. It is sufficient to the issue to merely be concerned and committed enough to be willing to stick your neck out and study and speak about it. There's no Ph.D. required to exercise one's citizenship."

Mark Toogood spoke for many of us when he concluded, "What RESULTS provided that converted me from a concerned citizen into a 'player' was the structure to learn about the issues, the partnership with other members for encouragement, the research and resources to act effectively, and overall, a shared sense of mission and team (really, family) such that my fear of our political process dissolved."

The sense of family Mark spoke about was especially real as I drove across the country from Los Angeles to Washington, D.C. I had driven across the country five years earlier, in October 1979, on my move from Miami to Los Angeles. On that trip I ate at Pizza Hut salad bars to save money, and slept in my car on the side of the road. As I drove back across the country five years later to set up our first office in Washington, D.C., I stayed with RESULTS leaders each night in towns and cities across America and experienced first-hand the family that had been built.

CHAPTER 6

Moving to Washington and to New Issues

The International Fund for Agricultural Development

Amidst the glut of insignificance that engulfs us all, the temptation is understandable to stop thinking. The trouble is that unthinking persons cannot choose but must let others choose for them. But to fail to make one's own choices is to betray the freedom which is our society's greatest gift to us all.

Steven Muller
President, Johns Hopkins University, 1972-1990
Vice-Chair, Presidential Commission on Hunger

It was 70 degrees in Washington, D.C. the day I arrived, December 30, 1984. Having spent the previous 38 years in Miami and Los Angeles, my first thought was "this winter thing isn't so bad." But 20 days later, it was 20 below zero, and President Reagan's inauguration was moved indoors. This was not the only chill I would feel; soon I would enter the frigid realm of insider politics. But for now, I was still basking in the warm glow of grassroots activism.

"My apartment is directly behind the Supreme Court building," I wrote in a January 4, 1985 mailing to RESULTS groups, "and I'm facing it as I type this letter. I hope to have an office within the next week. I'm 1/2 block from the Library of Congress and about 1 1/2 blocks from the Capitol. I'm pretty sure that Rep. Leon Panetta (D-CA) lives in my building and that Sen.

Hatfield lives on this block, but I'm *very, very* sure that the real untapped power is where *you* are! No kidding!"

While I was still giddy about government and the potential for effective citizen action, a few of the volunteers came to RESULTS with a more seasoned perspective. One of them was Steve Arnold, a clinical psychologist living in Bloomington, Indiana.

"My family had always been political," Steve recalled. "I have a picture of my grandfather at a banquet for Eugene Debs in 1919 in Boston. I remember watching my father go into apartment buildings to get signatures for Henry Wallace in 1948.

"The first thing we did with our new television was watch the 1952 political convention when Eisenhower was nominated," Steve continued. "My parents were very pro-Stevenson. I was only nine, but I was caught up in the excitement. I ran into the street shouting, 'Eisenhower won, Eisenhower won!' A neighbor asked, 'Are you for Eisenhower?' and I answered, 'I don't know.'

"Later I marched for civil rights in Boston and against the Vietnam war in New York. I went door to door in Ann Arbor with a group trying to convince people that we needed to get out of Vietnam. In the late seventies, I stood on Bloomington street corners through heat waves and snowstorms and got thousands of people to sign a pledge that they would help end world hunger. Maybe some of this did some good, but for me, the common denominator was that there was no obvious impact on the real world. It was very frustrating.

"My most ambitious project was a campaign for Congress on the Citizens Party ticket. The party, which had run Barry Commoner for president in 1980, shared large elements of my vision of what the world needed. The local party organizer asked me to run in 1982 after hearing me speak at a world hunger forum I had organized. I jumped at the chance. Maybe now I would finally have a real impact.

"The campaign was grueling. After full days in my job at the Mental Health Center, I'd be out at the mall all evening soliciting signatures to get onto the ballot. It was months before I could set off to get my message out. And when I did, I was armed with $500, a minuscule organization, and zero campaign savvy.

"The southeastern Indiana Congressional district was four hours' drive across, and I spent a half day's travel to meet five ladies at a League of Women Voters lunch in Tell City, or to make a three-minute radio statement in Cornersville, or to address three skeptical voters and a guy trying to sell me radio ad time in New Albany. I marched in a Fourth of July parade, gave out literature at county fairs, bullied my way onto one TV debate with the major party candidates, and fumbled questions at news conferences. I hardly saw my wife and family.

"If I was looking for some positive impact from all this work, the 930 votes I managed to get did not do the trick. The winner, long-time congressman Lee Hamilton, got more than 117,000. The runner-up got 57,000. The only time our party had made the front page was the day, nine months earlier, when some of our ballot petitions were found to have been forged.

"I was crushed. Like many Americans, I had viewed myself as purer and more intelligent than professional politicians. Yet Lee Hamilton had never in his 20 years in the House been touched by any hint of scandal, and his views expressed in debate, though often different from my own, were well reasoned and intelligently set forth. Now that I had tried politics, I had to wonder whether real politicians might not have a lot more on the ball than we give them credit for.

"Meanwhile I was stymied. I wasn't about to run for office again, but what positive action could I take? I retreated from politics for 18 months and felt more resigned than ever. I had a passionate vision of the world I wanted. I saw us daily missing opportunities to move toward that world. But I felt like a helpless spectator.

"In April 1984, I happened to attend one of Rep. Hamilton's public forums. I asked a question about hunger abroad, and Lee responded that while he considered much foreign development assistance useful, there was no effective public support for it. How could this be, I wondered, when I knew from experience that there was a large movement in the United States dedicated to ending hunger in the world? There had to be *something* I could do to give that movement a bigger voice.

"Over the next few days, I devised a plan. I would get in touch with hunger activists in presidential primary states and convince them to follow the candidates and pepper them with questions about hunger. Similar tactics had been used by groups promoting stands on abortion and gun control, so it seemed like a reasonable idea. I contacted The Hunger Project, one of several hunger groups I had worked with, to solicit names of volunteers who had expressed an interest in political advocacy. They sent me 30 names, and I began to telephone.

"The project quickly bogged down. Few on the list lived in states with pending primaries, and only one or two of these had any interest in my idea. What I encountered instead were about 12 people who passionately urged me to get involved with an organization called RESULTS. One, Dorsey Lawson, even tried to get me to agree to start a RESULTS chapter in Bloomington. I was irritated that she used my phone call to try to get me involved in *her* crusade, but I did give her my phone number for future reference.

"A month later, I got a call from Sam Harris. He was doing one of his 21-presentations-in-a-month trips via Eastern Airlines, and Eastern didn't fly to Cincinnati. Would I pick him up in Indianapolis and drive him to a presentation in Cincinnati? Yes, I would. When Sam arrived, I had a strained back, and driving was painful, but I wanted to meet him. During the drive, Sam quizzed me about my interests in hunger issues. At one point, he told me that Lee Hamilton was a leader on the House committee in charge of authorizing foreign aid spending. 'If you got to talk one on one with Lee Hamilton,' Sam challenged me, 'what would you say? What would you ask him to do?'

"I had been involved in hunger issues for five years, so I was amazed to find myself sputtering for lack of a response. The truth was that I had no idea what I'd ask my congressman for.

"That night at the presentation, I learned what I could ask for and how to ask. Sam explained more about how the government really worked than I had ever learned in ninth-grade civics—or in following the news closely in the past quarter century. He laid out the whole RESULTS technology. It was brilliant. He coached us in writing Congress about a specific legislative amendment. I was given all I needed to write an informed, powerful letter. On the way home, I was really excited. I hardly minded driving six hours with a bad back or getting three hours sleep that night. The technology Sam and others had developed had a compelling rightness about it. I knew it would work.

"I asked Sam to come to Bloomington on his next trip (October 1984). Of 66 people I invited through weeks of phoning, writing, and follow-up calls, 22 showed up and 11 answered his call to become partners. We had a developing RESULTS chapter."

Steve's group weighed in on our next big campaign, an opportunity to protect the International Fund for Agricultural Development (IFAD), a small UN agency that helps Third World farmers and the landless poor increase their food production and incomes. RESULTS struggled with the media's tendency to focus on the "loud emergencies" of famine, earthquake, floods, and volcanoes, and ignore the "silent emergencies" of poverty, malnutrition, and disease which take the lives of 40,000 children each *day*, even when there isn't a famine or earthquake. IFAD estimated that it cost $400 to ship a ton of food to the highlands of Ethiopia and that for the same amount, it could train an African farmer to grow a ton of food each year for a lifetime. IFAD's preventive work had to be saved. RESULTS' work with IFAD started with an invitation from Robert Berg, Senior Fellow at the Overseas Development Council, to a breakfast discussion with Idriss Jazairy, the new president of IFAD. The anti-UN feeling within the Reagan Administration had contributed to the United States' departure from the UN Educational, Scientific and Cultural Organization (UNESCO), and now IFAD was also in jeopardy.

The Organization of Petroleum Exporting Countries (OPEC) wanted a 2 percent reduction in their share of funding of IFAD. The change in the funding ratio would bring 60 percent of resources from industrialized countries and 40 percent from OPEC nations. OPEC felt it couldn't maintain the original 58 to 42 ratio. The U.S. wanted to keep them to the original agreement, even, it seemed, at the risk of losing IFAD. All of the other industrialized countries agreed to the change proposed by OPEC. It was estimated that the change would cost the U.S. an additional $3.5 million annually in a foreign aid budget of $15 billion. The stalemate between the U.S. and OPEC, which had gone on for nearly two years, put IFAD's existence in jeopardy.

When the breakfast discussion with Jazairy was over, I followed him into the lobby where he was putting on his overcoat. Jazairy, a silver-haired Algerian diplomat, was distinguished in dress and manner. I introduced myself, and showed him letters to the editor on IFAD written by RESULTS volunteers and published in the *New York Times* and the *Los Angeles Times*. He seemed impressed and I invited him to be a guest on our national conference call a few days later. He said he would be in France by then, but agreed to do it from there.

Jazairy had just been appointed the head of IFAD. Years later he reflected on that first visit to Washington as its president and recalled a warm reception by Rep. Matthew McHugh (D-NY) and by Peter McPherson, the head of the USAID, but a cold shoulder everywhere else. "I just realized how small IFAD was and how big and overpowering the U.S. institutions were," Jazairy recalled. "I wondered how IFAD could make its voice heard under such conditions. I felt it was good to try to see if we could mobilize public opinion."

I remember having difficulty trying to place that first international call to connect us with Jazairy in France. Which was the country code and which was the city code? RESULTS' global expansion the following year, however, would make international calls commonplace. Up to this point, we had felt a connection to the entire country through our conference calls. But now, with Jazairy on the phone in Europe, we felt connected to the whole world.

After the call, an editorial campaign was launched urging the U.S. government to agree to the 60/40 funding ratio. Packets for editorial writers were mailed to all RESULTS groups and the volunteers began practicing the calls they would make about IFAD. We also urged our members of Congress to sign a letter to Secretary of State George Shultz initiated by Sen. Mark Hatfield (R-OR) and Rep. Silvio Conte (R-MA). The letter expressed Congressional support for the 60/40 funding ratio change. Again, the research behind the campaign came from groups such as Bread for the World and people such as Larry Minear at Church World Service/Lutheran World Relief and Vera Gathright at the United Nations Information Center. RESULTS provided the media muscle.

Steve Arnold and the partners from Bloomington were part of this strategy.

"Our first meeting with Congressman Hamilton reflects the power of the RESULTS format," Steve said, recalling their action on the letter to Secretary of State Shultz. "In February 1985, Lee agreed to spend five minutes with us if we would travel to a rural post office where he was making himself available to individual constituents. Three of us took off work to drive through a snowstorm and wait two hours for that brief meeting. I remember that the post office had no rest rooms and that we endured full bladders for fear of missing our chance to meet with him. Finally," Steve continued, "Lee was ready. So were we. We had specific requests, and we were able to speak cogently and efficiently about them. Lee was clearly impressed....He agreed to sign onto a letter to the Secretary of State, urging flexibility in negotiating a funding formula for IFAD.

"The other people who saw the congressman that day presented a real contrast. I remember asking one woman in her thirties who preceded us in the line how *her* meeting had gone. 'Well,' she said, 'I shared my opposition to a PCB incinerator planned for Bloomington.' I asked what Rep. Hamilton had said. 'He told me,' she continued, 'that he too was concerned about the incinerator.' She had talked about the arms race, about overpopulation, and about inadequate funding for anti-poverty programs. Sure enough, he told her he shared her concerns on all of these matters, as well.

"Looking at her face, I could see that while she felt pleased she had the courage to speak up, she was puzzled about whether it had done any good. We differed from her only in that we had spent a few hours reading background papers and practicing Laser Talks. Yet we knew for sure that we had achieved something real because of our specific requests. I wish now that I'd offered her the chance to join our group."

Like Steve Arnold and his Bloomington partners, Bob Van Olst was about to make a specific request on behalf of IFAD. He would be seeking an editorial in the *New York Times*. Bob lived in Brooklyn, and at six foot seven inches, was an imposing figure. He had run for office like Steve, but much earlier in life and with greater success. "I was president of the eighth grade," Bob said, recalling what might be construed as his political activities before RESULTS. "I was also president of my fraternities, in high school and college, and president of the Interfraternity Council. Usually, my platform included getting beyond the beer parties and getting involved in Heart Fund drives and tutoring the disadvantaged. I went to college between 1965 and 1969, in Pennsylvania. One of my best friends went to Princeton. They used to have these colloquiums on the weekends to debate the issues of the day. Those were heady days. The lecture hall was filled with the most privileged kids in the world, and we had a single, unified interest: making the world a better place.

"Then, during the spring of my junior year, the music died. Martin Luther King was killed. A few months later, Bobby Kennedy was gunned down. My senior year went quickly, followed by two years in the Army and then work in New York City as a personnel functionary in a bank. I stayed single, dated and partied a lot. I kept up with the news, but found that none of the people that I worked or socialized with had much interest in changing the world. I think they found me naive and hopelessly idealistic. I guess I began to doubt myself after a while. I felt bitterly jealous about people doing useful stuff but felt too old to start out in a new field.

"Then I saw an article about a school teacher in Los Angeles who was organizing a forum for Congressional candidates on ending hunger. The article said there might be one in New York and gave a number to call."

The number was Cameron Duncan's and Bob worked with Cameron on the World Food Day Forum in 1982 in New York City. During the forum Bob placed a viewer editorial on WNBC with one phone call and tried to have a letter published in the *New York Times.*

"Writing a letter was no problem," Bob remembered. "It was totally safe. I must have written a dozen letters to the *Times* over the next two years. None were published, but I didn't feel bad. I rationalized it. Hey, it's the *New York Times.* Ordinary people don't get published. You have to be some big shot or some expert." Someone suggested that Bob approach Cardinal O'Connor about writing a letter on IFAD, which Bob pursued to no avail. "Then I thought, hey, what if I treat this like a college term paper," Bob continued, "research it, find a few quotes. For a change, I really pored over the RESULTS stuff, did a little extra fact checking, and cranked out a few hundred words on IFAD. I mailed it to the *New York Times.*

"About a week later, to my shock, I got a call from this person saying that he was from the *New York Times.* He asked me if I was Robert Van Olst and exactly how I knew so much about IFAD. At first, I felt as though I had done something wrong. It sort of sounded like he thought I shouldn't know so much about an obscure agency unless I was somebody. I explained that I was Northeast Regional Coordinator of the anti-hunger citizen lobby RESULTS, and a few days later I opened the paper and there it was. Not only did they publish my letter, but they made it their lead letter, added a fabulous drawing to illustrate it, and listed my title in RESULTS. I felt like a million bucks! 'Gosh,' I thought, 'if the *New York Times* printed something I wrote, maybe my ideas are pretty good after all.' "

This feeling was moving throughout RESULTS. It was a magical time for the volunteers. As editorials accumulated they were mailed, three and four at a time, to 19 key officials in the Reagan Administration and on Capitol Hill. The first four were readied amidst a torrential downpour. Charles Beckjord, a volunteer from Minneapolis who had attended our national conference at the end of May, stayed on as a summer intern. I wanted him to hand-deliver the first group of editorials to the Office of Management and Budget, the State Department, and the Treasury Department, but the rain made it difficult.

Just then, Deborah Norton, a two-day-a-week volunteer, happened by on an off day. She agreed to do the driving. Before I sealed the envelopes, Deborah studied the cover letter which ended, "We will send additional editorials under separate cover." She later delighted in confessing, "I thought this poor man is so naive, he really believes there are going to be more editorials!"

As it turned out, there were 38 more editorials over the next five months.

The skills- and confidence-building at the RESULTS National Conference at the end of May caused an explosion of editorials. And it didn't matter that Administration officials don't live in Portland, Pittsburgh, or Seattle—they would see the editorials generated by the RESULTS volunteers there and they'd see all of the others too. But there were several newspapers that didn't really have to be mailed around because members of Congress and their staff saw them every day. One was the *New York Times*. Bob Van Olst recalled how he finally overcame his fear and contacted the *Times* about an editorial.

"Even after my letter was published in the *New York Times*," Bob recalled, "I totally resisted the regular suggestions from Sam to go for the voice of the paper itself, the editorial page. In those days we received weekly calls from Sam or Dorsey. We would do these wonderful little 'mocks,' role-playing a call to an editorial writer, but whenever it came time to do the call something 'seemed to come up.' I think I was so afraid of not succeeding, not doing it right, of getting questions thrown back at me that I couldn't handle, that I just didn't do it. Kind of weird that I was so terrified of that call because, by that time, I was making my living as a corporate head hunter, calling up executives like crazy, interrupting them at their desks and asking them the most personal questions.

"In May," Bob continued, "RESULTS had its national conference in Washington, D.C. At one point, Sam, in what has become a RESULTS conference tradition, asked people to stand who had achieved certain things so that they might be acknowledged for their work. I got to stand during the 'letters to the editor' and 'met with your congressperson' categories. The last category was 'actually got a newspaper to publish an editorial on one of our issues.' I didn't get to stand. But wait, who's that yelling up to the front of the room? No, I thought, it's not my wife. But it was and she was saying that I should stand up with the editorial generators because a letter in the *New York Times* was so special. While I appreciated my wife's love for me and her desire that I be fully recognized, I was primarily mortified. I felt that the distinguishing characteristic of RESULTS volunteers had been that virtual absence of ego on their part. They seemed to do their miracles without desire for personal reward. Now, with this outburst, I was naked. Obviously, there was only one way to set it right. Not long after returning home I went after the big one—a *New York Times* editorial.

"Not that I wasn't still terrified to call—I was—but after the conference, I just had to do it. Turned out, the hardest part was finding the name of the right editorial writer to approach. Once I got that, I sent in some written material and I believe he actually called me."

On June 18, 1985, in the editorial generated by Bob, the *New York Times* said that the United States "is the only holdout against a new funding formula. Other Western donors are even offering a bonus contribution to mollify Washington. Even without that, the OPEC shortfall would amount to only a few million extra for the U.S. By all means keep pressing the oil producers to honor their pledges. But for hungry Africa's sake, don't disable this worthy program with sanctimony."

Ten days later, the June 28 letter to group leaders recounted the exciting buildup of editorials:

> *Saturday*: Editorial on IFAD arrived in the mail from the *Pittsburgh Post-Gazette*, generated by Katy Farrell and Janet Levenson.
>
> *Sunday*: I got a call from Edda Browne saying that there was an editorial on IFAD in the *Sacramento Bee* that morning, generated by her and her husband.
>
> *Monday*: I was interviewed by a writer doing an editorial on IFAD for the *St. Paul Pioneer Press*, generated by Mark Toogood. I got an IFAD editorial in the mail that was generated in the *Seattle Post-Intelligencer* by Dave Cole. I was interviewed by Voice of America....New RESULTS group started in Maryland (10 partners).
>
> *Tuesday*: Got a call from Sunny Yates telling me that there was an op-ed piece on IFAD in the Sunday *Cincinnati Enquirer*, generated by Cincinnati RESULTS and Bread for the World groups. Sunny was completing an op-ed piece for the *Cincinnati Post*. New RESULTS group started in D.C. (7 partners).
>
> *Wednesday*: Got a call from Sara Valk telling me that there was an editorial on IFAD in that afternoon's *Atlanta Journal*, titled, "Ignore OPEC, Save IFAD." New RESULTS group started in Northern Virginia (7 partners).
>
> *Thursday*: Keith Johnson and Dave Cole called to report on the half-hour conference call 17 people from the four RESULTS groups in Washington state had had that morning with Sen. Daniel Evans (R-WA). New RESULTS group started in Topeka, Kansas (6 partners).
>
> *Friday*: Got a call from Melanie Lawson telling me that an editorial writer for the *Orange County Register* was going to write an editorial on IFAD today.
>
> I have in my hands 28 editorials and op-ed pieces on IFAD, generated by RESULTS participants. That number will probably be 32 by the end of next week. This is a real tribute to what Buckminster Fuller called the power of the "little individual." Great job!

A year earlier we'd generated only a total of three editorials and op-ed pieces. Now we'd generated *32* editorials and op-ed pieces on IFAD alone. I continued to ask the volunteers if they realized the level of empowerment that represented. Our achievements were the kind we could only dream about. I felt we needed to keep pinching ourselves to grasp that our achievements were real. The editorials continued to pour in—42 in all. Thirty-nine of the editorial writers had never heard of IFAD before the RESULTS volunteers called. The old adage "information is power" took on new meaning for us. Could it be that the right information in the hands of therapists, head hunters, and business machines salespersons and then delivered to editorial writers around the country could change government policy? We would soon find out.

In July, after five months of deluging the Administration with editorials, I got a call from a State Department official who said, "You can stop the editorials now—60/40 is OK. You can stop the editorials now."

I got chills. It was a victory for citizen advocacy in the U.S. and for the poor in the Third World. And it didn't go unnoticed.

"When I returned to the United States," IFAD's Idriss Jazairy recalled, "people's attitude changed completely and people on the Hill who were very busy the first time suddenly found out what I had to say was very interesting. When I first came, I saw the Capitol and those monuments and those very important people who had no time to receive me...and then, suddenly, everything had changed, and it was like an enchantment. It was as if a fairy waved a magic wand and suddenly everyone was listening....RESULTS had a lot to do with it. Perhaps if we had not succeeded in breaking through those fortresses, IFAD might not be around today. It might just have gone under. There is something extraordinary about this country...through a democratic process the small guy IFAD actually managed to overturn the position of such an impressive and overwhelming power structure, just through the simple act of people across the country writing their senators and representatives [and meeting with editorial writers]...."

The victory belonged to members of Congress, their staff, members of the non-profit community of private groups, and a few within the Reagan Administration who'd worked hard to change U.S. policy. But a broad-based education of Congress could only come from Bread for the World and RESULTS with the added clamor from RESULTS volunteers' work with editorial writers. The International Fund for Agricultural Development's program provided tools and seeds to help farmers who'd been affected by drought. RESULTS provided tools and seeds that helped ordinary citizens out of their civic drought—the drought of their citizenship.

It was during this IFAD victory that an article appeared in Mark Satin's *New Options*, a political newsletter that sought a view beyond left and right, beyond liberal and conservative. Earlier that year several newspapers had begun to comment on our achievements.

"[RESULTS has] a method that sets a staggering example for other grassroots organizations," wrote the *Albuquerque Journal*.

"RESULTS count, and RESULTS knows how to get them....RESULTS is a case study in grassroots lobbying," said the *Baltimore Evening Sun*.

But Satin's comments went behind our methods and attempted to explain what we'd uncovered. "For years post-liberal political activists have been trying to create effective social change organizations," Satin wrote. "Unfortunately, most of our efforts have been so mistrustful of leadership and hierarchy and 'structure' in general that they have been utterly ineffective politically. On the other hand, many apparently 'effective' national organizations have failed to educate or mobilize their grassroots members. In 1985, it is an open question as to which approach is more irresponsible.

"The genius of Harris's RESULTS organization," Satin continued, "is that it has managed to combine effective national leadership and structure with effective grassroots education and mobilization. In fact it has come up with an eminently *replicable* way of organizing around decentralist/globally responsible issues and concerns....

"The strategy of many citizens' groups has been to convince people that government *doesn't* work. The idea is to empower people by making them angry enough to want to take power 'for themselves.' But too often this strategy backfires: leads to feelings of powerlessness or despair. And people are easily co-opted when they discover that, hey, this *is* a democracy.

"Harris's approach is the polar opposite. It's to convince people that government *does* work, but we're too ill-informed or fearful—too caught up in negative self-images or lack of self-worth—to *make* it work. In other words, the onus is on us—rather than our supposedly antagonistic institutions."

At the end of my interview with Satin, I told him about a RESULTS member who met with her U.S. senator on the final day of the 1985 RESULTS National Conference. It was her first face-to-face meeting with the senator, who had cosponsored the Global Primary Health Care Initiative eight months earlier. The initiative gave additional funding for ORT, among other things. She asked the senator if he knew what oral rehydration therapy was. When he said, "No," she said she got goose bumps handing him a packet of oral rehydration salts and telling him what it was.

"Would you exchange that scene for a thousand angry placards?" Satin concluded.

CHAPTER 7

Vitamin A

Believing Is Seeing

In our efforts to find our way toward a new world role, we would do well to revive what made us a special nation long before we became the world's leading military and economic power—our republican tradition that nurtured free citizens who eagerly embraced the responsibilities and pleasures of self-government. With democracy on the march outside our borders, our first responsibility is to ensure that the United States becomes a model for what self-government should be and not an example of what happens to free nations when they lose interest in public life. A nation that hates politics will not long survive as a democracy.

E.J. Dionne, Why Americans Hate Politics

In 1985, another campaign followed our IFAD victory, our second in partnership with the House Select Committee on Hunger. The Select Committee wanted an amendment that would earmark $30 million for vitamin A programs and asked RESULTS to help with some editorials on the issue. We first heard of a breakthrough on vitamin A on a May 31, 1985 RESULTS conference call with John Costello, Executive Director of Helen Keller International. It was already known that vitamin A deficiency led to blindness for 250,000 children each year. New evidence revealed that a large portion of childhood deaths in developing countries could be prevented with vitamin A supplements. A Johns Hopkins study of 420 Indonesian villages showed that 30,000 children given vitamin A had a death rate one-third lower than children in neighboring villages who weren't given the therapy. In addition, nutritional blindness could be prevented with a megadose of 200,000 international units (IU) of vitamin A delivered every six months, at a cost of two cents per dose. The pill was the size of a pea. Later, some would chastise RESULTS for advocating these "golden bullet" responses to hunger and disease. But we were still in the process of finding our political sea legs and besides, how could we advocate more difficult changes if we couldn't win on what should have been the easy ones?

I sent materials to the RESULTS groups on a news conference sponsored by the Select Committee and reminded them that the materials were embargoed until the news conference. That meant the RESULTS volunteers could give the materials to an editorial writer or reporter before that date with the proviso that nothing would be released until the news conference was over.

"[With Helen Keller's birthday June 27]," Select Committee Chair Mickey Leland (D-TX) said at the news conference, "What a birthday present it would be, if this generation ended nutritional blindness forever."

I urged groups to press for editorials on Keller's birthday and asked the groups to help find a representative and a senator on the Foreign Operations Subcommittee of the Appropriations Committee to introduce a bill that would earmark the U.S. share of an effort to end vitamin A blindness in this generation. The money would be earmarked from the AID Agriculture, Rural Development and Nutrition account which totaled $755 million at the time.

The first two editorials on vitamin A were published on Helen Keller's birthday and were generated by Joyce Moore and Shirley Williams in the *Pasadena Star-News* and by Jo Burke in the *Maui News*. Shirley described her route to RESULTS.

"When I was 12," recalled Shirley, a homemaker and RESULTS activist from Orange County, California, "I remember the woman who was cleaning for my mother crying as she told about her child dying from leukemia and about the staggering medical bills she had to pay. She said she wouldn't have minded if they had saved her daughter. I was shaken by her pain and angry at the world for this woman's misery. It was 1940. Today, the image of a mother weeping for her dead child (not from leukemia, but from measles) seems to sum up for me the purpose of RESULTS and serves to motivate my work with the organization."

After attending art school, Shirley worked for six years on the art staff of a small magazine.

"Working in the fashion industry in the 1950s was not very rewarding," Shirley continued, "so I volunteered to teach art classes for the New York City Police Department as part of their program to get kids off the street. This and a short stint teaching arts and crafts in a poor area of San Francisco were the only steps I took outside of my safe, protected world. I taught a bit after my marriage, but mostly I was a housewife raising my four children. I would have liked to have done more, but didn't know how to get started. And then, in 1980, I was invited to attend the Los Angeles World Hunger Event, an all-day program in downtown Los Angeles. I was mildly interested and expected a series of lectures. What I got was much more—a new direction for my life. The morning was spent listening to skits and songs and a few facts about hunger. Then the 200 of us were ushered into the ballroom of the hotel for what we thought would be lunch. The room was divided into 'three worlds.' The First World was represented by a raised dais in the middle of the room. A small group of people were being fed an extravagant meal with waiters, candles, flowers, and music. Surrounding this platform the rest of the participants were either members of the Second World or the Third World, the latter sharing a bowl of rice. Every few minutes it was announced how many people had died around the world during the preceding minutes. At the end of 20 minutes the participants were invited back to the conference room where we discussed our experiences and insights. I remember not really listening to other people because I was so shaken by the clear image of myself sitting on a raised dais eating well while a world of hunger and poverty surrounded me. It was a very powerful image. It stayed with me and still fuels my involvement in hunger and poverty issues. I realized, however, that being aware and actually doing something are very different things, but I wasn't sure how to take the next step.

"Soon after that, I was invited to a RESULTS meeting. I was a marginal member for several months. Then one Saturday, my husband couldn't attend a conference call and asked me to go in his place. I was annoyed, but I went anyway. I sat with a handful of people around a speaker phone as Sam Harris called out the names of cities around the country: Honolulu, Hawaii; Anchorage, Alaska; Miami, Florida; Milwaukee, Wisconsin; Houston, Texas; and several more. 'We're here,' they replied, 'with four in the room.' Chills went through me as I realized that this was a nationwide team of real people working together to impact the political process. That was the day I became a partner in RESULTS."

Shirley would bring her newfound commitment to bear in the RESULTS group headed by Dorsey Lawson.

"Our RESULTS group sat in a living room in Pasadena, California," Shirley recalled. "We had agreed we'd each take a newspaper. I was given the *Pasadena Star-News*. There was a new editor there and I knew I'd have to contact him before the group's next meeting. I went home inventing ways I could get out of doing this frightening task. This time I was to ask for a meeting. What happened next permanently changed the way I thought of myself and my world.

"I paced the house getting up my nerve to make the call. At first I reached a secretary who said the editor would call me back within 20 minutes. I rehearsed my two-minute talk over and over again. The 20 minutes stretched into an hour and a half. I was getting a pounding headache. Secretly I was relieved and felt I had done my duty. It wasn't *my* fault if he didn't call back. But this wasn't about me, I reminded myself, it was about dying children, and I called again. This time I was able to speak with the new editor, Hall Daily, and I delivered my prepared talk carefully. He was interested and said he would call me right back, which he did.

" 'Could you come in tomorrow and talk to my senior staff?' he asked. 'Would an hour be enough?'

"I gulped and said, 'yes!' I had been thinking more along the lines of five minutes. I started going over the material for the presentation with Joyce Moore, another member of the RESULTS group. We studied for several hours and carefully planned what each would say.

"The next day we carried in a VCR and a video tape. In our nervousness we'd forgotten to turn the TV on and couldn't understand why the VCR wasn't working. An editor politely pointed out our omission. From this shaky start we proceeded to talk about vitamin A.

"After the meeting, a science writer stayed to thank us for the presentation.

" 'I should be doing what you're doing,' he said with tears in his eyes. 'I should be out telling people about this.'

" 'No,' we told him, 'You should write about it and you can come to our meetings.'

"As we went down in the elevator, Joyce kept repeating, 'Beyond my wildest dreams—beyond my wildest dreams.' We were ecstatic, and the ensuing editorial was definitely beyond our wildest dreams."

"No one would be surprised if it was reported that the Pentagon has been paying as much for its bullets as it has for its ashtrays lately," wrote the *Star-News*. "But the best weapon available to capture world opinion and protect able bodies may be something called Golden Bullets.

"The Golden Bullet," the *Star-News* continued, "a megadose of 200,000 units of vitamin A that costs only 2 to 4 cents—can reverse the trend of increasing nutritional blindness among malnourished children in the world....

"The megadose is a particularly effective tool since it needs to be taken only twice a year by victims of malnutrition. And the $30 million in seed money for the program supported by Rep. Mickey Leland, chairman of the House Select Committee on Hunger, will buy more productive lives in areas of the world where enough hardships already confront humankind."

As the editorials came in, the names and locations of the newspapers began to have a different meaning for us. *The Burlington Free Press* was in the home state of Sen. Patrick Leahy (D-VT), a member of the Foreign Operations Subcommittee in the Senate. Leahy would become chairman of the subcommittee within five years.[14] The *Maui News* was in the home state of Sen. Daniel Inouye (D-HI), the senior Democrat on the same subcommittee. Inouye would become its chair within a year. The *Herald-Telephone* in Bloomington, Indiana was in Rep. Lee Hamilton's (D-IN) home district. Hamilton was second ranking Democrat on the Foreign Affairs Committee and would become its chair in 1993. The *Pasadena Star-News* was in Rep. Carlos Moorhead's (R-CA) home district. If Moorhead, a very conservative Republican, would support these issues, maybe his colleagues would join him.

Action on vitamin A was delayed as Congress passed a continuing resolution,[15] moving the deadline for completing their work from October 1, the beginning of the fiscal year, to November 14. It would eventually be extended until mid-December. By the middle of December the continuing resolution was completed, and vitamin A was in for the long run too. Congress provided an $8 million earmark for vitamin A which would continue annually throughout the decade. Two cents worth of vitamin A could prevent blindness in a child. Empowered citizens were having the same effect on Congressional vision.

---

[14]Sen. Daniel Inouye was chair of the Foreign Operations Subcommittee of Appropriations from 1972 to 1980. When the Republicans took control of the Senate, Sen. Robert Kasten became its chair and served from 1981 to 1986. Inouye became the chairman again from 1987 to 1988, when the Democrats regained the majority in the Senate. When Inouye moved over to chair the Defense Subcommittee of Appropriations in 1989, Sen. Patrick Leahy became its chair.

[15]A continuing resolution is enacted when there is insufficient time or support for passing appropriations bills before the end of the fiscal year. A continuing resolution may include one, two, or as many as all 13 appropriations bills necessary to keep the entire government running. A continuing resolution may cover a few days, weeks, or as much as an entire year. It often continues funding at the previous year's level but can include changes in funding. During the 1980s, foreign aid was often funded by continuing resolution.

CHAPTER 8

Shots Felt Around the World

The Universal Child Immunization Act

Americans hate politics as it is now practiced because we have lost all sense of the public good. Over the last thirty years of political polarization, politics has stopped being a deliberative process through which people resolved disputes, found remedies, and moved forward. When Americans watch politics now, in thirty-second snatches or even in more satisfactory formats like "Night Line" or "The MacNeil/Lehrer News Hour," they understand instinctively that politics these days is not about finding solutions. It is about discovering postures that offer short-term political benefits. We give the game away when we talk about "issues," not "problems." Problems are solved; issues are merely what politicians use to divide the citizenry and advance themselves.

E.J. Dionne, Why Americans Hate Politics

"In 1936, my father left Germany with his family," said RESULTS leader Michael Rubinstein, who now works for the Maryland Food Committee. "He was 16 years old. His oldest sister had to be left behind. Half of his relatives were killed. While the world watched and—with a few exceptions—did nothing, 11 million people, 6 million of them Jews, were murdered. When I knew that 14 million children were dying each year, mostly from preventable malnutrition and disease," Michael continued, "I could not stand by and watch, as many did 50 years ago when the entire European Jewish community was wiped out."

Michael's comments were not unique to a young American Jew.

"Strange as it may seem, what inspired me to get involved in RESULTS was a TV program in 1983 on the concentration camps during World War II," commented Newton Hightower, a therapist from Houston. His slow Texas drawl conjured up cowboy boots and ten-gallon hats, but there was seriousness and heart beneath the "good old boy" twang.

"After the end of the program," Newton continued, "I realized that I was sitting by while children died of starvation needlessly, much as the German community had sat by while Jews died needlessly in the gas chambers. So my inspiration to take the risks necessary to start Houston RESULTS came from the view that knowing what I knew about world hunger and how it could be ended, it was indeed immoral for me to sit and do nothing."

By now, few in RESULTS were sitting and doing nothing. Each of our actions in 1985 pointed to an unnecessary holocaust. We focused on famine relief for Africa, where more than one million persons would die unnecessarily. We focused on saving the International Fund for Agricultural Development when its loss could have put tens of millions of poor families in jeopardy. We focused on the promotion of vitamin A, knowing 250,000 children were blinded every year from vitamin A deficiency. And we focused on hunger in the United States where millions of children lived in poverty. A luncheon speech in March 1985 by UNICEF's Executive Director James Grant turned our focus to a campaign to immunize children in the Third World where 3.5 million died each year from *vaccine-preventable* diseases. Grant, an American, had been born in China in 1922, where his father had worked for the Rockefeller Foundation training "barefoot doctors." Now, as UNICEF Executive Director, Grant carried a 10-cent packet of oral rehydration salts in his pocket along with other props which he used to show how the lives of children could be saved inexpensively. Grant's boundless energy and natural salesmanship could have made him a fortune in advertising and promotion. Luckily for the children of the world, he worked for them instead.

I sat through Grant's luncheon speech inspired by his vision. He spoke of 80 or 90 heads of state coming to the United Nations in the fall to celebrate the UN's fortieth anniversary. He laid out a plan to have the heads of state target universal child immunization (UCI) by 1990, which meant immunizing 80 percent of the world's children by the end of that year.

This upsurge in immunizations could make a lifesaving difference for millions of children, as a four-part series in the *Washington Post* in 1986 titled "Africa's Children" showed. Child immunization levels in Africa were the lowest in the world. "The [World Health Organization] says that only 35 percent of children are immunized against measles," the article stated, "a disease doctors call a 'disaster' for even mildly malnourished children...."

During Grant's luncheon speech, he told about "days of tranquility" in El Salvador in which the fighting was to be stopped so the children could be immunized. The first two "days of tranquility" had been completed, and the third was just weeks away. In 1984, many more children died of measles, polio, and other immunizable diseases in El Salvador than all the civilian and military deaths in the country's civil war that year.

The lack of news coverage on life-saving stories like the days of tranquility was a constant source of frustration and discouragement. We realized, however, that a world without a sense of purpose would always produce a great deal of meaningless news. The tabloids, and increasingly the talk shows and local television news, focused on items with the greatest shock value. Titillation was an understandable substitute when it seemed that nothing made a difference.

But we weren't satisfied with substitutes and began our work on the "days of tranquility."

"Sunday, the war in El Salvador will stop for a day," wrote the *Baltimore Evening Sun* on April 19, 1985, in the first RESULTS-generated editorial on the topic. "In a remarkable arrangement, government forces and guerrillas are cooperating in a campaign to immunize young children against childhood diseases. This Sunday is the third such cease fire since February. The truce days have given 20,000 health workers and volunteers an opportunity to complete the series of three vaccinations that will save thousands of young lives....

"If El Salvadorans can set aside their weapons long enough to make this kind of commitment to their children," the *Evening Sun* editorial continued, "perhaps there is hope that the country can create a political climate that will spare their lives from bullets as well."

Six days later I met with Rep. Mel Levine (D-CA), a member of the House Foreign Affairs Committee from Los Angeles, who had known RESULTS from the end of his State Assembly days. He attended our World Food Day Forum on Ending Hunger in 1982 as a candidate for Congress and was honored at an event two years later for his leadership on hunger issues. His office was typical of other House offices—leather couch and chairs set apart from his long wooden desk. When he stopped to take a call before our meeting began, I noticed photos of him with Menachem Begin and Golda Meir. I knew of Mel's commitment to Israel, the specter of the holocaust and the "never again" resolve it called forth. I'd come to talk about a current holocaust that could be prevented, and prayed I would be able to speak powerfully enough to have him take it on.

I asked Mel if he knew that UNICEF was pushing the goal of immunizing 80 percent of the world's children by 1990. I wasn't surprised when he answered "no."

"Did you know," I continued, "that 3.5 million children die each year from six vaccine-preventable diseases?"

"Yes," he answered.

"Did you know," I asked, "that more children die *each day* in India from *measles* than the total number of adults and children that died in the Bhopal tragedy?"

His eyes began to light up when I asked this question. He answered, "No!"

"Did you know," I continued, "that more children died of vaccine-preventable diseases last year in El Salvador than the total number of civilian and non-civilian deaths in the civil war?"

Mel was involved in the Salvadoran issue, but this was one aspect of it that he didn't know about. This time his eyes really lit up as he exclaimed, "No!" "Given the volume of issues that you and your colleagues face in Congress," I continued, "it's really possible for the next five years to go by without the opportunity to immunize 80 percent of the world's children being noticed. Would you be willing to get groups of your colleagues together for a briefing on this program?"

"Yes, I want to do it," he responded. "Maybe my wife would get involved, also, but even if she doesn't, I still want to do it."

I was ecstatic. It was as if an electrical jolt had gone through me. I'd been in Washington less than four months and had left my job as a substitute teacher only six months earlier. I believed that most members of Congress were people of deep commitment and when it was sparked, as it had been here, miracles were possible.

"As a graduate student at Princeton," Levine related years later, "I had spent a summer in Central America and written a master's thesis on Central American economics in 1965. That was the height of the flowering of the Peace Corps and the Alliance for Progress and it was shortly after President Kennedy's assassination...in every mud hut that I visited, there were two items you would find in every single place in the midst of utter squalor and poverty. One was a straw crucifix and the other was a newspaper photograph of John F. Kennedy, which represented what America meant to the people of Latin America at the time. I ran for Congress 17 years later in large part to be involved in American foreign policy."

But one month after Levine agreed to host the briefing, only Rep. Carlos Moorhead (R-CA) had joined him as co-host. I urged the volunteers to push for additional conservative co-hosts because I felt the liberals would be easier to secure. One week later the list included conservative Rep. James Sensenbrenner (R-WI), as well as more moderate Reps. James Jeffords (R-VT) and John Miller (R-WA) and the more liberal Rep. Tony Hall (D-OH).

The briefing was led by Dr. Stephen Joseph, Special Coordinator for Child Health and Survival for UNICEF. Joseph was one of two officials who resigned from the U.S. Agency for International Development at the beginning of the decade to protest the U.S. vote *against* an infant formula marketing code before the World Health Assembly, the *only* country to do so. Several years after this briefing, Joseph became New York City Commissioner of Health.

"There won't be more than 30 Congressional aides in the room," one Hill staffer predicted. But RESULTS volunteers moved into action and there was a standing-room crowd of more than 70 aides.

Our most dramatic action on immunizations in 1985, one that would play a central role in setting the stage for the legislative campaign in 1986, was to come from a second meeting with Jim Grant. Several RESULTS volunteers in New York City had decided to prepare a video program on opportunities to end hunger, and they invited Grant and me to be part of it. After the taping, Grant handed me several documents on the upcoming fortieth anniversary of the UN.

I sent each RESULTS group the materials Grant handed me, which included a letter from the Secretary General of the UN to all heads of state, urging them to commit to the goal of universal child immunization and to address it in their prepared remarks at the Fortieth Anniversary Commemorative Session. I urged the groups to get the materials to their editorial writers immediately and have editorials begin appearing on October 14, the week before the UN session. "I feel like that time in June when IFAD editorials were flying in here left and right," I wrote in a letter to RESULTS volunteers in late October. "As of today, I've received 29 editorials and op-ed pieces on UCI by 1990. These 29 pieces have *all* come in within the last four weeks. You are doing a brilliant job!"

One more action in 1985 set the foundation for our legislative work in 1986: news conferences on the release of *The State of the World's Children 1986* report from UNICEF. More than any other activity, hosting a news conference was the work of a community leader—calling the local media together in order to make an announcement. The *State of the World's Children* reports were a source of inspiration for our work, and the 1986 report was to be released in December 1985. It focused on achieving universal childhood immunization (UCI) by 1990 and was written with and for James Grant by Peter Adamson, a British journalist and activist. The writing was visionary and poetic and the report concluded with the words of Maria Auxilia Paja, a mother from a rural area in South America. A trained health worker arrived in her village, but only after two of her children had already died—one from a respiratory infection and the other from measles.

"For the baby boy, I tried to get help," Maria said. "But as I was carrying him for help, he just died in my arms.

"My daughter was older," she continued. "I had got used to playing with her, being with her. It's difficult...it's sad to remember those times with my children. She was alright when she went to bed. By midnight she was sick. She died just as day broke.

"I am not alone. It's happened to a lot of women."

"Maria Auxilia Paja is indeed not alone," the report concluded. "In the last 12 months, approximately 15 million mothers like her have been forced to watch their children die."

The U.S. Committee for UNICEF agreed to have RESULTS groups co-convene news conferences on the release of the report. In the cities where there were no U.S. Committee for UNICEF paid staff, RESULTS volunteers would take the lead.

No one in any of the groups had experience in hosting news conferences, so a major effort was made to coach the 17 groups that took it on. Timmie Jensen, press secretary for the Select Committee on Hunger, was interviewed on organizing news conferences, and a cassette tape of the interview was sent to all groups. Coaching calls, special letterhead, sample news releases, and checklists were also provided. To make sure that the message was communicated fully and accurately, I arranged for one segment of the news conferences to include a nationwide telephone hookup with James Grant taking questions from members of the news media. Actor Raul Julia, who joined the RESULTS Board of Directors several years later, served as moderator for the conference call with Grant.

Raul took a train down from New York City for the Washington-based telephone conference call. I cleaned up my apartment, all 400 square feet of it, and had Raul stay there. It wasn't the Ritz, but it was all we could afford.

I usually get nauseated when going beyond perceived limits—stepping out on the thin branches. These news conferences kept me nauseated for 2 1/2 weeks because this time we could fail publicly. If you write a letter to the editor or call an editorial writer and you're turned down, who knows? But if you invite community leaders to speak at your news conference, spend five weeks organizing the event, and none of the news media comes, it can be debilitating—especially for a volunteer. But the 17 news conferences were attended by 30 TV stations, 29 radio stations, and 23 newspapers. It was a victory of ordinary people, and Chuck Woolery's story of the San Francisco news conference tells it as well as any.

"I was the exhibit technician at the petting zoo at the University of California at Berkeley," Chuck recalled. "Just as I was checking one of the cages, a page came over the public address system. I put down my screwdriver and went to my office to take the call. I wondered, 'Was it my wife or a coworker?' No, it was the President of Stanford University, Dr. Donald Kennedy, who was calling to say he would serve as moderator of our news conference.

"We decided to have children pour 40,000 pennies into a big metal container to show that thousands of lives could be saved each day for a matter of pennies. Mayor Feinstein gave an oral polio vaccine to a child, and of course Dr. Kennedy was our moderator. All five local TV stations were there to cover it."

Chuck's story was not unique. These news conferences, and the ones that followed each succeeding year, sent RESULTS volunteers out into their communities seeking support and coverage. Very often they came back with something more—a boost in self-esteem.

RESULTS volunteer Steve Dewhurst had moved from Nebraska to do post-doctoral work at Harvard. "Working as a junior scientist with a world-renowned AIDS researcher at the Harvard School of Public Health, my first year in Boston wasn't easy," Steve recalled. "Fresh from graduate school in the Midwest, I'd had little training in molecular biology and now I felt like I was suddenly back in my first year in the lab. Everything I touched was a disaster. One day the phone rang in the lab, and my boss happened to pick it up. 'It's for you,' he said, adding, in an ironic but impressed tone, 'It's *Harvey*.'

"Harvey Fineberg, the Dean of the School, isn't ordinarily concerned with junior scientists," Steve continued, "but on this particular day, he was returning my call to say that he'd be pleased to have the school host a news conference for the release of UNICEF's annual *State of the World's Children* report. It was the first big thing to go right for me since I'd moved to Boston almost 12 months earlier. Organizing the conference began to restore my confidence and self-esteem. It was something I *knew* I could do well, working with the RESULTS office and the other members of the Boston RESULTS group. It was something I could build on."

The U.S. Committee for UNICEF sent RESULTS press kits for the media and 400 copies of the report. The news conferences and the distribution of *State of the World's Children* reports to the groups became an annual ritual and a key component of the education of RESULTS volunteers.

The day before the December 1985 news conferences, the Universal Child Immunization Act of 1986 was introduced in the House by Reps. Tony Hall (D-OH), Ben Gilman (R-NY) and Chris Smith (R-NJ), and in the Senate by Sen. Bill Bradley (D-NJ).

At the RESULTS education and action meetings in the following two months, we wrote members of Congress, urging them to cosponsor the legislation. The legislation sought to increase the Child Survival Fund by $50 million to a new total of $75 million. The additional $50 million would go to the UCI goal.

As with the IFAD editorials we'd generated, we had a mailing list for the editorials on universal childhood immunization (UCI) by 1990. Our editorials on UCI by 1990 went to 62 leaders including members of Congress and officials of the Reagan Administration. By February 1986, we'd sent nine mailings with editorials focusing on the days of tranquility in El Salvador, the special UN session, the *State of the World's Children 1986* report, and on the legislation itself. In response to these editorials, Brad Morse, head of the United Nations Development Programs and coordinator of the UN's African famine relief effort, wrote, I have been closely following the tremendous coverage the [immunization] program has been receiving due to the absolutely outstanding effort of RESULTS."

Over the succeeding six years RESULTS and Bread for the World had different major focuses, but not this year. Bread for the World's large membership base and RESULTS' success with editorial writers were a powerful combination. Our goal for the Universal Childhood Immunization Act of 1986 was to get support from half the House (218 cosponsors) and half the Senate (50 cosponsors). On January 24, 1986, there were 49 House cosponsors and 10 Senate cosponsors. Two months later those numbers had more than doubled and tripled, respectively, to 121 House cosponsors and 31 Senate cosponsors.

As the 1986 RESULTS National Conference approached, I wrote the groups, again trying to give voice to the challenge they had taken on.

"When we attend our first RESULTS presentation and sign up to be partners in a new RESULTS group," I wrote, "we do so in the glow of inspiration and new awareness. And, despite all of our good intentions, we go out and bump up against the things that slow us down, if not stop us altogether: (1) a general apathy among many people; (2) disdain for getting involved in the political arena; (3) our own lack of experience in speaking, organizing, inviting, and leadership skills; and (4) more than anything, our inexperience with keeping a vision alive and the sense that 'someone else should be doing this' or 'I'm not the one.'

"But when you want your life to be of service, an offering of courage and love," I continued, "and you know that the atmosphere around you is not always rooting for you, it's important that you put yourself in environments that renew you and reconnect you with your commitment. I can't think of any better environment than the RESULTS National Conference. Just meeting each other and going home would probably be enough."

"I have to admit, during my first year in RESULTS, I wasn't particularly effective," commented Michael Rubinstein. "Then I attended my first RESULTS conference. It was tremendously empowering to spend three days singing, talking, and learning, with about 300 people sharing the same vision—a world without hunger.

"The most impressive moment in the conference," Michael continued, "was when we had a panel of Hill staffers discussing our attempts to get increased funding for the Child Survival Fund. This was the summer of 1986, the first year of Gramm-Rudman, and the foreign assistance budget was being cut. The Hill staffers told us that we shouldn't ask for more money. We were lucky, they told us, if we even got a slight increase. If we asked for the full $50 million increase, we would just alienate members of Congress.

"The message that the Hill staffers shared with us had no impact whatsoever. The 300 RESULTS partners in the room listened carefully, asked questions, were polite and respectful—even enthusiastic—but they were completely unmoved by the discouragement. Nothing was going to stand in the way of our vision. Children were dying and they needed vaccines. The politics were irrelevant. I have seen too many starry-eyed, pie-in-the-sky dreamers. But this was different. Behind the vision was a hard-nosed practicality. What everyone wanted to know from the Hill staffers was not why it *couldn't* be done, but how it *could* be done. I had never been so inspired in my life."

The 1986 RESULTS conference was our third national conference. The following year we were joined by RESULTS volunteers from Australia, Britain, and Canada, making it our first international gathering. If there could be only two words to describe the 1986 conference, they would have to be "working celebration." With the singing and sharing, the workshops and connecting, more than anything it was a celebration of the human spirit.

By June 27, our work and that of Bread for the World took us past the halfway point with Senate cosponsors of the UCI legislation and five short of the 218 cosponsors needed to exceed 50 percent in the House. Four weeks later, 55 percent of the House was cosponsoring the Universal Childhood Immunization Act, HR 3894, and the House Foreign Operations Subcommittee agreed to increase the Child Survival Fund to $50 million, *not* the full $75 million. I urged volunteers to meet with senators on the Foreign Operations Subcommittee during the August recess.

We urged Rep. Tony Hall to introduce an amendment in the full House that would increase the appropriation by $25 million to the full $75 million originally called for and told the groups to start preparing for an editorial campaign. The Washington staff of most of the other hunger groups wanted to accept the $50 million. They were concerned about angering House subcommittee chair David Obey (D-WI) by pushing for more than the $25 million increase he approved. They also believed that the hundreds of cosponsors weren't that committed—that they wouldn't vote for an increase if it came to a vote on the floor of the House. I wasn't sure they would either, but I always believed members of Congress should have to stand up and be counted.

During the six years spent working with RESULTS, I continually pushed myself. I felt that with each new level I moved to, I brought with me my vision and commitment and also my anger and fear. With most other groups wanting to accept the $50 million, my anger raged. I was furious with what I perceived as a sellout, a Washington insiders' decision that was a slap in the face to grassroots advocates who had worked so long for the much-needed $75 million funding level.

The aides to members of Congress on some of the key Congressional committees weren't happy with our pressure. Months earlier one aide had commented, "This immunization thing is snowballing too fast."

What did that mean? Was it that the move to stop unnecessary deaths from measles and other preventable diseases was moving too fast? Or did it mean, we don't have room in our current thinking to expand funding too much this year? Either view was unacceptable, especially with the wasted billions in foreign aid that could be shifted to programs that saved lives, and there were too few groups working forcefully for this change.

I got permission from the bill's lead sponsor, Congressman Tony Hall, to mount an editorial campaign that would push for the full $75 million. I stayed up until 1 a.m. several nights in a row producing the new editorial writer packets. The night the packets were mailed to the groups I had difficulty falling asleep. Eventually I crawled out of bed and jogged around the Supreme Court building. It was 2 a.m. The run seemed to release some of the fury.

The editorials began to pour in—30 in 30 days. Bob Van Olst called the *New York Times*. The resulting *Times* editorial stated, "It should not be beyond Congressional wit to find the money already authorized."

Newton Hightower met with the *Houston Chronicle*, and they wrote, "When Congress returns to Washington on Monday, it must deal with a host of appropriations bills, including the massive $13 billion foreign aid package. Buried in that mound of money is a relatively minor sum for the Child Survival Fund which deserves further attention."

Jack and Lori Waters joined their partners Wendy Sexton, a nurse, and Julie Hochman, a cellist, in a meeting with the editorial board of the *Milwaukee Journal*. Their senator, Robert Kasten, was chairman of the Appropriations subcommittee that would make the decision on child survival funding. Would the board of the largest newspaper in the state write an editorial with power equal to their senator's position? Would they urge him to increase funding for child immunization?

For the first time ever, the board's comment was in the form of a memo. The day the editorial was published there was a day-long conference in Washington, urging a more humane foreign assistance program. During an end-of-the-conference reception, we got the reception room quiet, leaned a microphone as close to the speaker phone as possible, and had one of the RESULTS partners in Milwaukee read the editorial to the gathering:

> MEMO TO: Wisconsin Sen. Bob Kasten
> From: The Journal Editorial Conference
> Re: Human Suffering
> Dear Bob,
>
> Within the next few days you will have the opportunity to make a real difference in the lives of needy souls all over the globe. As chairman of a Senate subcommittee that makes hard decisions on doling out foreign aid, you set the tone for the panel's reactions to 1987 budget requests: whether to commit more of America's largess to military assistance abroad, as the Reagan administration wants, or to aid for struggling nations. May your heart and mind incline toward the latter....

We know the administration wants you to press for the full $6.7 billion it requested for foreign military aid, at the expense of programs that would vastly improve child survival and increase worldwide food production. We are confident, though, that you can turn your back on such a cynical request, and fight hard for the lives of the poorest of the world's poor.
Sincerely,
Sig, Dave, Leon, Dick, Whitney, Sue, Dick and Bill

There was a stunned silence throughout the room after the last name was read and then a cheer. I felt like a proud papa ready to hand out cigars. For RESULTS it meant special attention for our campaign to increase the Child Survival Fund to $75 million, and the only committee that could do it was chaired by Sen. Kasten.

The pressure that was being generated was felt on all sides. "When we were going [to] the Senate to increase what we'd been given in the House," Rep. Tony Hall, the bill's lead sponsor, recalled, "I remember having some heated words with Rep. Obey about it. It was like, 'Don't rock the boat, we've already done you a great favor, done the issue a great favor. You're rocking the boat, don't mess with it.' There were starting to be some articles in the paper, in [his home state of] Wisconsin and he was starting to feel some heat about it."

But Hall wasn't complaining about the editorial support. "Those things helped," Hall recalled, "because my colleagues would come back from being home over the weekend and [those editorials] helped to educate them and give focus to what we were talking about...."

Newspaper editorials weren't the only tool of our campaign. Michael Rubinstein used a different medium to get the message out. "Shortly after the RESULTS conference in 1986," Michael recalled, "I became the group leader of my local Maryland RESULTS group. Cameron Duncan was my regional coordinator. He called me weekly to support me in managing my group and keep us up to date on what needed to be done.

"I was very fortunate to have Cameron supporting me," Michael continued. "Better than anyone I knew, Cameron could hold the vision and inspiration in one hand and the nuts and bolts and the how-to's in the other. He had a way of looking deeply into your eyes as if to see the very core of your being and to support you with love and appreciation."

Cameron left the RESULTS staff at the end of 1986 after being diagnosed with AIDS.

"In one of our weekly conversations, Cameron asked me to call the local Washington, D.C. television affiliates and to try to get myself a viewer commentary. I said, 'Gulp.' I was familiar with the idea. I remembered an episode of *All in the Family,* in which Archie did a viewer commentary opposing gun control. It had never occurred to me that I could do such a thing. The idea terrified me. It took me about three days to screw up the courage before I called the three stations. Amazingly, the NBC affiliate accepted my script.

"The next step was to make myself look presentable," said Michael, who graduated from college four years earlier. "At the time, I was never much into looking good. I was young and never took myself very seriously. I looked into my closet and found a navy blue blazer that had been lent to me by an acquaintance in college. He had never come back to pick it up. I noticed that I had a pair of blue pants that matched the color perfectly. I now had a suit. I had just gotten a haircut for the occasion, cutting my 'Jewish Afro' really short. I put on a necktie, a very rare occurrence for me, and made myself look as good as I could.

"I went in to the station at the appropriate time, sat down in the chair, my throat dry, looked in the camera, and said, with all the passion and emphasis I could muster, that the needless deaths of 3.5 million children each year due to vaccine-preventable diseases 'is a holocaust of staggering proportions.'

"The editorial director told me she really liked my script. She was also impressed that I got it in one take. A year of practicing RESULTS' Laser Talks paid off. It was easy for me to write it and to memorize it after having done countless other similar talks.

"Then they flashed my completed viewer editorial up on the television monitor. I saw my name and my town on the screen below a face that I didn't recognize. There was this respectable young man, a community spokesman, up there on the screen, speaking in strong terms about an important issue of the day. I had never seen myself in that light before, and I have never been the same since." While Michael's TV editorial was aired in the D.C. area, the first five newspaper editorials were delivered to all 535 House and Senate offices. Then the next 17 were delivered. The Senate subcommittee agreed to the full $75 million. We were ecstatic! They went into conference with the House and both agreed to $75 million. We were delirious—another victory for grassroots action and for the poor. Again we had gone against the conventional wisdom. We had kept pushing when others wanted to stop. Our work, especially our grassroots media work, was helping create what I would later call "a mini-sacred cow."

What did the additional $50 million mean? At the time, UNICEF estimated that it cost $5 to fully immunize a child from manufacture of the vaccine to injection. Now 10 million children would be immunized, saving, by UNICEF's conservative estimate, 125,000 young lives.

"It is clear to me," wrote Rep. Hall after the campaign, "that the success achieved in the 99th Congress on global immunization and related funding for international health and hunger programs simply would not be possible without the persistent, dedicated work of RESULTS members across the nation. These victories are really theirs, and they deserve to be commended for their efforts."

"I want to convey my heartfelt thanks," wrote UNICEF Executive Director Grant after the victory, "for the unflagging and satisfyingly successful efforts of RESULTS on behalf of vulnerable children and mothers everywhere. I thank you in my mind at least weekly, if not more often, for what you and your colleagues are accomplishing—but I thought I should do it at least once this year in writing."

But this did not represent everyone's opinion. There was bitterness building in some corners of Capitol Hill. At the end of the campaign, in discussions on an upcoming piece of RESULTS-initiated legislation, an important Congressional staffer asked sarcastically, "Are you going to insist on getting it *all* this time too?"

CHAPTER 9

Raising Money

Fundraising Was a Slower Breakthrough

A vision without a task is but a dream. A task without a vision is drudgery. A vision with a task is the hope of the world.

From a church in Sussex, England

Slowest among RESULTS' projects were breakthroughs in fundraising. In our first year, people were asked to contribute a dollar at each meeting to help pay for stamps, envelopes, paper, photocopying, and phone calls. Between the end of 1981 and the end of 1982, we raised $11,000 for our three candidate forums through a variety of low-cost fundraisers—mostly potluck suppers. Concerts at St. Augustine-by-the-Sea, an Episcopal church in Santa Monica, raised enough to keep us going for three to six months because we had no staff and no office. Perhaps most telling, however, was a conference call in early 1983. A guest, not actively involved in RESULTS, was so inspired after the call that she made out a check to RESULTS for $100. Within minutes, six more of us wrote checks for the same amount—more than any of us had ever given to RESULTS.

Most Americans aren't involved in fundraising, and when they are, it's through a rummage sale, pancake breakfast, walk-a-thon, or some other more indirect way of asking for money. When we first sought monthly sponsors, RESULTS volunteers were saying, in effect, "here's the work we're doing, it's very powerful, won't you fund it monthly without a tax deduction?"

Without a tax-deduction?!

After facing the fear of rejection, the second toughest part was the lack of a tax deduction. Internal Revenue Service (IRS) regulations state that if you are primarily a lobbying organization, contributions are *not* tax-deductible. Most groups choose to have contributions be tax-deductible and are therefore limited in how much grassroots lobbying they can do. These groups are 501(c)(3) with the IRS. RESULTS, while being a non-profit organization, is *not* tax-deductible because we are a citizens' lobby—501(c)(4) with the IRS. There are very few groups in this category.

It always seemed to me that an unspoken deal had been struck between the government and tax-deductible organizations which went something like this: "In an attempt to make it easier for *you*," the government says to the tax-deductible organization, "we will allow you to raise money that is tax-deductible. But in an attempt to make things easier for *us*," the government continues, "you will be allowed to do only a very limited amount of lobbying."

I've yet to find many people excited about starting an organization to which contributions are *not* tax-deductible. Foundations run for the hills when 501(c)(4)s like RESULTS come around. So do corporations and many major donors. As I see it, you gain a tax deduction and lose your voice, or at least you're required to lobby with your hands tied behind your back. So much for helping people reclaim their democracy. RESULTS volunteers learn early that if they want a voice in public policy, they can't depend on foundations and corporations—they have to learn to ask their friends for financial support. This was a lesson Newton Hightower learned when he set out to enlist our first $100-per-month donor.

"One of the important things for me," Newton recalled, "was to have a sense that I was contributing my money as well as my time in making something significant happen in the world. It was a sense that I grew up with as a boy in my church, feeling the importance of contributing my money and having it do good in the world. When I began in 1983, RESULTS had no paid staff. It was exhilarating to find an organization that was so conscientious about money that its only expenses were photocopying costs, telephone calls, and bus and airfare for Sam to travel from city to city.

"One of the things that had to happen," Newton continued, "was for Sam to quit his substitute teaching job in L.A. and move to Washington. In order to do that, we were going to need more money in this organization. I suggested that we start a $100-a-month club and call it the Century Club, and I agreed to try to enroll the first person in it.

"My first and only prospect was George Davis, a Houston industrialist. He had attended two RESULTS meetings. I talked to Sam about this, and he gave me the OK to approach George. I talked to a lot of people to get ideas and encouragement. I called George and told him I wanted to come and tour his factory...and also to talk with him about contributing at a larger level to RESULTS.

"At the time I was a social worker at the VA hospital, and I didn't have a lot of contact with wealthy men who owned factories, so it was more difficult for me to call on George than it was to meet my congressman or editorial writer. I remember waiting in the reception area, and there was a phone there, so I started calling people again to ask for support and get some last-minute coaching from people locally. When I met with George, he was doing what a good, wealthy Texan was supposed to do—chewing on his cigar and leaning back in his chair behind his desk. I talked to him about the vision of RESULTS, told him about the importance of Sam going to Washington, and I talked about leveraging his money."

RESULTS' work over the previous year had begun to demonstrate that relatively small amounts of money for citizen lobbying could leverage much larger amounts of government spending on lifesaving programs.

"I told George that I would like for him to begin contributing $100 on a monthly basis and there was a new Century Club," Newton continued. "He started a bit when I mentioned the number, and he asked me how many people were contributing $100 a month at this time. I told him that he would absolutely be the first person in the country to do this, and I was surprised how I turned this into something positive rather than something I was actually embarrassed about. I said that we needed to break new ground nationally, and I thought he was the man to do the job! People were thinking too small about money in this organization, and we needed to blow the lid off these nickel and dime contributions and have people start thinking in larger numbers. I asked him to lead the country....I pushed the monthly sponsor card across the table, which only had up to $50 at the time. He commented there wasn't any room for $100 on the card, and I told him he could write it in. He said he only had one question, 'This is tax-deductible, isn't it?' I so much wanted to say yes, but I told him no, and he dropped the pen and looked at me in shock.

" 'You mean you're asking me to contribute $100 per month to an organization that doesn't have one employee and it's not even tax-deductible?' George asked in astonishment. "That's right, I said. It was the only thing I could think of to say. He laughed and we talked a little bit more, and I asked him again if he would be willing to do it right now. He paused, then agreed he would. He filled out the card and then I did what I always do, I asked for the first check. He laughed and wrote me out a check for $100.

"After I left there, I stopped at the first convenience store and started putting quarters in the phone to tell people that George had signed up to be a monthly sponsor and the first member of the Century Club at $100 per month.

"At the next monthly RESULTS meeting, I made the announcement that Houston RESULTS was the first group in the country to have a $100-a-month sponsor, and I wanted to acknowledge George Davis. There was much applause. George's response, though, was the biggest surprise. He said that he was glad to do this and that he really wanted to thank me for having the guts to come into his office and ask him to do it. He said he was initially shocked and in disbelief at my nerve and that had inspired him to write the check. He said with a big laugh, 'I can't believe I'm paying out $100 a month to an organization that is not even tax-deductible.' I turned bright red at the front of the room with the acknowledgment, and there was a lot of laughter in the group at me being praised for asking people to do things that were quite out of the ordinary. I was surprised as well that George realized how difficult this had been for me and what I had gone through in asking him. I also learned that being bold and asking outlandish things of people worked a lot of the time, and some people were inspired by the requests. So with a support system I had the courage to ask outlandish things with the idea that I knew that I wasn't doing this for myself but out of my strong belief that lives were at stake." Newton was ahead of most of us in RESULTS. I'm sure our avoidance of major fundraising during the early years of RESULTS was propelled by my insatiable need to salve personal unworthiness with action. Maybe one more legislative action would salve it; maybe one more candidate forum would salve it. It was hard to tell where Sam Harris ended and where RESULTS began. I'm sure I related funding RESULTS with funding me—something my insecurities couldn't justify.

Clarity on my insecurity came years later from the most unexpected place—television. I was flipping channels on a Sunday afternoon and came upon John Bradshaw and his *Homecoming* series, part of a PBS fundraising drive at the end of 1990. I tell it now because it offers insights into another part of what fueled my founding of RESULTS.

After flipping to the program I felt a strange pull to its message. Bradshaw talked about addictions including my personal favorite, work, and about their origins. I watched the first hour, and then the second and the third. I seldom did things half-way. Bradshaw was about to lead a guided meditation and asked the studio and the viewing audience to close their eyes. I moved to a large blue pillow on the hardwood floor of my Washington, D.C. apartment six blocks from the Capitol. The theme "Going Home" from Dvorak's New World Symphony played in the background. Bradshaw asked us to picture our childhood home—whether it was a house, a trailer, or an apartment. Mine was a little three-bedroom cinder-block house built in Miami just after World War II. It was pink with a lush green front lawn lying just over the septic tank.

Bradshaw asked each of us to walk inside and see ourselves as a child. I did. My image came from a picture that hangs on the wall in my office. I'm a well-tanned Alfred E. Newman without the freckles. I have Spock's ears from *Star Trek* and a toothless smile that could light up the world.

"Ask the child if you can pick him up or pick her up," Bradshaw continued. "Now tell the child, 'I'm here to take care of you. I'll never leave you again.' "

When I first looked at the child, I felt a warmth in my chest. But with this instruction I started to cry. I was a little unsure where this exercise was going, but I stayed with it anyway.

"Ask your parents to come into the room," Bradshaw said. "Tell them, 'I'm giving you back your pain. I've got my own pain to carry. I'm giving you back your pain.' "

I sobbed uncontrollably. I experienced a sense of abandonment by my father from his incessant work and difficulty with intimacy. I was in touch with a deep emptiness inside and grieved this loss for the first time, at age 44.

Bradshaw spoke of intergenerational pain—pain handed down from generation to generation. My great-grandfather, Rabbi David Schlossberg of Lithuania, moved to Israel around the turn of the century with his daughter, Rebecah Schlossberg. At 16, she was sent to America to marry Samuel Harris, a frame maker and a man twice her age, in an arranged marriage. Becky Harris had three sons—the oldest, Ben; the youngest, Leonard; and the middle son was Morris, my father.

Whenever we looked at a picture of my great-grandfather there was always the comment, "Look how stern he looks." What was my great-grandfather's pain that showed as this sternness in the picture? What was my grandmother's pain, sent to America at age 16 to marry a man she'd never met who was twice her age? And what was my father's pain, covered by a workaholism which I emulated to cover my own pain?

When my grandfather, Samuel Harris, lost his job during the Depression, I'm told that he used to dress up every morning and sit in the corner "davening" (praying). Sometimes he would just sit in silence. Because he was so smartly dressed, the kids used to call him "the Senator." Sometimes I wonder if one of the reasons my father dressed up each Memorial Day as "Uncle Sam" was to reach for his own father, Sam Harris.

Before these realizations, I used to speculate that my passion to create RESULTS, an organization that would allow people to make a difference, came out of a sense that I didn't make a difference myself. What I didn't realize was that its origins went deeper than that—to my core sense of my self and my worth.

Eventually, my passion for action overtook my insecurity, and between October 1983 and February 1985 our fundraising was fueled by my five 21-city trips. It was easier for me to ask for money at the end of a three-hour RESULTS presentation. Surely people could see the power of our work by then. The funds paid for our expansion, and it was more important to cover additional Congressional districts than it was to cover my sense of worthlessness.

In 1986 we launched our first "RESULTS 100" campaign. During the campaign 100 volunteers wrote and spoke to friends in order to generate three new monthly sponsors each. We invited our friends to contribute a set amount each month, usually $10. It was the first time we brought all of our groups into a major fundraising drive.

"RESULTS is growing very rapidly now," I wrote in the letter to my own list of friends, "and I want to invite you to invest in our dream....Our budget in 1984 was $53,000, in 1985 it was $120,000, and is projected at $220,000 in 1986. We are *not* in a financial crisis. We are simply doing powerful work that must continue to expand. We are funded currently by 1,200 individuals and families who contribute $10 or more per month as RESULTS Monthly Sponsors. They do so without a tax deduction because we are a nonpartisan citizens' lobby. They do so out of their commitment to a world without hunger. I invite you to become a RESULTS Monthly Sponsor....I will call to see if you have any questions. I cherish your love and support."

I asked the volunteers to send me copies of the letters they sent to their friends.

"I want to use the word *courage* again," wrote Steve Arnold to his friends. "Most of us get real scared going into the offices of senators and representatives. We feel like someone else should be doing this. Most of us are scared to ask our friends, colleagues, and relatives for money. Most of us are scared to walk into a newspaper office and tell journalists that we have information they ought to be printing. Yet it is our willingness to keep going in the face of our fear that will end hunger and needless disease on our planet and set new precedents for worldwide cooperation."

"On her death bed," Barbara Dunlap, RESULTS leader in West Los Angeles, wrote in a letter to 39 of her friends, "Margaret Mead said to her friend Jean Houston, 'Forget everything I've been teaching you about the governments and about the bureaucracies.'

"Jean replied, '*Now* you're telling me this?'

" 'Yes,' Margaret continued, 'I'm just realizing that if we are to survive and really create the world that we could have—it's a question of citizens' volunteer groups; citizens getting together, deepening, growing, expanding their capacities, and then going out and making a difference.'

"I am privileged to be doing just that—with RESULTS," Barbara continued.

For many, asking for money was more difficult than meeting with a member of Congress or calling an editorial writer. Perhaps Anna Amarandos, a scientist and RESULTS leader in Thousand Oaks, California, expressed the discomfort best.

"This RESULTS 100 Club," she wrote me, "is the most confronting thing I've ever done. Your proposal to call all 138 of us to encourage our fundraising calls jarred me into action, so I've been writing all weekend. I'm writing my friends and family long-hand. Each letter has been about four pages long, so it's quite an undertaking. I'm hoping it'll be more effective than a xerox master. We will see. With each person I write, I become clearer and clearer about the opportunity, but the fear of rejection hasn't gone away....Well, it's time to write another letter."

"Most people," I wrote in a February letter to group leaders, "wear a quiet armor that says, 'I don't make a difference.' Every time you invite a friend to become a monthly sponsor you are taking off the armor. So too with calling your representative or editorial writer. Taking off that armor is an act of courage. It goes against the status quo."

On February 28, the final day of the RESULTS 100 campaign, 272 of the targeted monthly sponsor cards had reached the office. By our conference call eight days later, the goal of 300 was surpassed. And if you listened closely, you could hear the clanging sound of RESULTS volunteers dropping their armor of despair and hopelessness all across the country.

CHAPTER 10

Starting a RESULTS Group in Albuquerque or Any City

If at First You Don't Succeed

The American beacon helped to teach people everywhere to aspire to self-realization and to rebel against powerlessness. Now, it seems, the former students must re-educate Americans in the meaning of their own faith. Perhaps that is when the American moment will begin: when Americans find the courage to speak honestly again in the language of democracy.

William Greider, Who Will Tell the People?

Sara Keeney lives with her family in Albuquerque, New Mexico. When she first heard about RESULTS, she was "clear that it was a waste of time and energy to try to influence politicians," a belief that is not uniquely her own.

Whenever I led a RESULTS presentation I'd say to the host, "I'll either start a group, or I'll plant a time bomb—and I'll take either." Well, Albuquerque seemed like the slowest time bomb I'd ever planted. After two visits, there still wasn't a group. On a third visit, this time by Dorsey Lawson, a group was started, but it died eight months later. The fourth visit to Albuquerque was the charm, and its story could be any city's story. We have to push through our failures to find our success.

"I was raised in an activist tradition, a tradition of Christian conscience," Sara Keeney explained. "My parents became Quakers during World War II when my father was a conscientious objector. My upbringing was steeped in

Quaker values of peace testimony, equality of all people, and respect for differences. But at the same time, the gap between what was and what could be was so large that it was difficult to see how to make a bridge in any way, other than as an individual living the most peaceful and fair life possible. That is the path my parents took.

"By the time I went to college I'd made the decisions that I live by as an adult....I would try my best to live a peaceful life and influence people around me to do the same. Outward forms of activism like demonstrating and protesting didn't suit me. For me, shouting angry slogans did not fit my image of a world where people lived out of an inner peace that inspired them to treat others well. There were times when I marched, but without fully believing it was the most effective action. I also decided that life was a sweet gift that I didn't want to waste in sadness over things I couldn't change. In the end I gave my service in a psychiatric half-way house and eventually as a teacher on the Navajo reservation. I believed that the work I did in education could have an effect in the world.

"The first time I heard of RESULTS was from an old friend who had become a Hunger Project staff member. He told me in 1983, 'There's this guy, Sam Harris, who's getting people to write to Congress and work on ending-hunger legislation. He's traveling around starting new groups and he'd like to come to Albuquerque.' He asked if I'd be interested in getting something going. My answer was an emphatic 'No!' I was clear that it was a waste of time and energy to try to influence politicians. I knew people who had been writing to Congress and the president for years and none had ever claimed success for their endeavors. The whole idea felt like a heavy weight.

"A year later Sam did come to Albuquerque at the invitation of a friend of mine," Sara continued. "I was one of only three people who attended that first meeting. Two things moved me that afternoon. One was the way Sam spoke to us. The audience of three could have been 50 for the effort and power he put into his presentation. It was clear to him that we were the ones who could generate the political will that would end hunger. Another part was his story of how an extra $60 million was generated in 1984, against the advice of other hunger groups. I said I would host a second meeting. Four months later there were seven in the room, but there still weren't four who would become partners."

A third visit was made to Albuquerque, this time by Dorsey Lawson, and this visit marked the start of the first RESULTS group. Sara didn't become one of the partners. The group disbanded eight months later. RESULTS still returned for a fourth try at getting a group established. It's so important to realize how persistent and committed we had to be to allow our grassroots structure to grow. This fourth visit was two or three more than many other grassroots lobbying organizations would bother making.

" 'Admit it,' Dorsey Lawson said to me at the end of that fourth RE-

SULTS presentation, 'you are the leader,' " Sara continued. "I was, and a flourishing group was born. I started out tentatively, but got a lot of encouragement and support. There was a seed of hope, Sam's stories of past successes, that counteracted the sadness and resignation I was used to feeling.

"That summer, I traveled to Washington, D.C. on a family trip and decided to visit my congressman, Rep. Manuel Lujan (R-NM), who later became Secretary of the Interior in the Bush Administration. I had never heard of Rep. Manuel Lujan supporting anything I believed in, and I was sure that I would meet with a flat no to any request. At the RESULTS office, Sam and Cameron gave me lunch and handouts, made sure I was clear on the requests, increased funding for the Child Survival Fund, took me through the labyrinth tunnels to the House Office Building, and pointed me toward the directory of offices. Rep. Lujan was ready to meet me at the appointed time. I was nervous and when I opened my mouth to tell him about the 40,000 children dying per day and how measles killed two million a year, yet a simple vaccine could stop the dying, my voice trembled. I talked in a flood of words for several minutes as he listened. My hand shook as I handed him a copy of a bill that would increase funding for child immunizations. He looked quickly at the material I handed him, and to my utter astonishment turned to me and said, 'Yes, I'll cosponsor this.' My mouth flew open, but I had no words to say. Eventually I managed a thank you.

As I walked back to the RESULTS office I noticed that I was hooked, completely swept up with the influence I could have, one lonely citizen who could ask her congressman to help fund child survival and he would. The James Joyce quotation, "Yes, yes, and yes again yes," spun through my mind. I noticed a difference between me with my business dress, shoes and briefcase, walking around the Capitol and the tourists in shorts, taking snapshots of the dome. I was thrilled to the core of my being to be an active participant in my democracy. I would return home with more than just a photograph."

CHAPTER 11

Expanding RESULTS Beyond the United States

Starting RESULTS in Britain

The problem is that for every thousand exhortationists there's only about ten organizers. And that's not going to do it. There's just too many people exhorting and throwing the caveats all over the place and not enough rolling up their sleeves and organizing, or training organizers. That's what does it.

Ralph Nader

"RESULTS won't work here," I heard from people in Britain and Canada, "Parliamentary governments are different." They were right about Parliamentary governments being different, but what *was* the same was people's discouragement, their loss of connection from government.

By our own expansion standards, RESULTS exploded in Britain during the last half of 1986 as eight groups were started during my first two trips there. That same year, groups were started in Australia after Karen Cloud, a RESULTS leader from Seattle, moved to the capital city, Canberra. The year before, I'd tried to start groups in Britain by leading transatlantic meetings over the phone. When it became clear that wasn't working, I began to plan a visit. I'd anticipated starting three groups in Britain on that first trip, but there was so much interest that an unexpected fourth group was started.

On that first transatlantic flight, as my airplane approached London's Heathrow Airport, I remember closing my eyes and taking a deep breath before touching down, unsure of what lay before me. Soon after entering the baggage area, I piled my luggage on a cart and pushed it toward the customs window to face a question that I would have to answer on each subsequent visit. I often worried that my response might get me detained.

"Are you here on business or pleasure?" the customs official asked.

"Business," I replied, unsure how I would explain my work. Would he question my mission, to coach British citizens on pressuring their government more effectively?

"What kind of business are you in?" he asked.

"I head an organization on ending world hunger," I blurted out.

Luckily, Band-Aid and the Live-Aid concerts were both still fresh in everyone's mind, and I got a reassuring look from the customs official, who stamped my passport and sent me on.

"I couldn't have been older than four when I began to wonder why Tom, the black servant who prepared and served our meals, was never invited to join us at the table," commented Jessica von Boeventer, the original leader of the RESULTS groups in the United Kingdom. "It bothered me. It was not fair, but that was the way things were when I grew up in South Africa in the 1940s and 50s."

I felt an instant rapport with Jessica, a craftsperson who made pottery and jewelry. From the moment I met her, it felt like I was greeting a long-lost cousin.

"The Second World War still created shock waves for just about everyone," Jessica recalled, "including those of us born during or after the war. For South Africans there was the added dilemma that the government was pro-Nazi and a later prime minister was interned for his German sentiments at the time. My teenage years in Habonim, the Jewish youth movement, reinforced my understanding of what was right and wrong as did guidance from my parents.

"But as things grew worse and the Nationalist party became stronger and more outspoken in its ghastly racist policies, I came closer to doing what I always knew I would do—leave. This was not my home. I found Israel exciting, but I would continue on to England, the land my parents' families had set sail from for South Africa.

"Years later, I was feeling particularly open and at peace living with my husband Matthias and children Louella and Nathan in Wiltshire in the quiet West Country of England when I was persuaded to attend an Ending Hunger Briefing sponsored by The Hunger Project. It was 1984, and the African famine had hit the headlines. After that briefing, my first thought each day was, 'How am I going to contribute to the end of world hunger today? What can I do?'

"I raised some money, organized briefings on hunger, spoke to anyone who would listen and many who didn't. I led a local Oxfam Hungry for Change group, and went to the Mass Lobby of Parliament organized by the World Development Movement in 1985. That was when I first met my member of Parliament,[16] Dennis Walters. About 40 of us went by coach to meet four members of Parliament (MPs) from our area. We were joined in London by thousands of others coming to meet their MPs. It was the largest mass lobby in history. Somebody on the coach had a few questions for us to ask which were handed out at random.

"My real sense in the meeting was that our member of Parliament hadn't been briefed at all. It seemed he didn't exactly know where Africa was on the map. I asked when the government would reach the UN target of 0.7 percent of GNP for development aid and got more blank looks. By the end of the meeting I remember Dennis Walters throwing his pencil on the table and saying, 'I'm only a back-bench MP. There's really nothing I can do.'

"I thought, 'Here I am thinking *I* can do something, and he doesn't even feel the same way, and he's the MP.' I walked out feeling that a door had closed. I was despondent and didn't know where to go from there.

"Later that day, I wrote down, 'I need more guidance.' I wanted someone to teach me what I needed to know to have more than a four-year-old's 'It's not fair!' outrage. A short while later, an acquaintance telephoned to ask if I'd host an evening for someone coming from Washington, whose organization had something to do with politics and ending hunger. At the time, anyone saying that there was something I could do to help with ending hunger always had me say 'yes,' although I was beginning to question the relevance of politics.

"I called my friends and said, 'This guy is coming all the way from America, it's about ending hunger and I don't quite know the direction. I'll prepare a buffet before the meeting, so just support me and come along."

Jessica's husband Matthias, a native of Germany, picked up the story from there. As with many of the couples I met, it was the wife who did the hunger work. But Matthias was open to new ideas and soon joined Jessica's passion.

"My diary," Matthias von Boeventer continued, "says for Saturday, July 5th, 1986, 'Sam Harris arrives. Good meeting in the evening.' We had been in our new home only a few months and just the day before, the carpet had gone down in the lounge. Sam arrived in the afternoon and became part of the family within five minutes. I remember something he said before the meeting, 'If I'm brilliant this evening, we'll start a RESULTS group in Bradford-on-Avon. If I'm good, there's still a chance. If the meeting is so-so, then please take any of these ideas and use them any way you'd like.' It was as if

---

[16]In the Parliamentary system, members of Parliament are elected in much the same way as members of Congress. The leader of the party that wins the majority of Parliamentary seats becomes the prime minister, and the prime minister selects all of the other government ministers from that party's members of Parliament. In the U.S. system, our ministers are the cabinet officers, appointed by the president, who have no constituency back home. If the U.S. had a Parliamentary system, the Speaker of the House would likely be the prime minister, and he or she would select the other ministers from among the members of his or her party who are serving in Congress.

he wasn't totally sure RESULTS would take root, but he was convinced he had something very valuable to share with us. There were about 21 people in the room that evening," Matthias continued. "It was a three-hour tour de force, and I have rarely come across someone speaking with such clarity, gentleness, conviction, and sense of purpose. At the end of the meeting Sam asked us all to write letters to our local newspaper, the *Wiltshire Times*, about key primary health measures and increased funding for UNICEF. When I'd written the letter, and even addressed the envelope, it occurred to me to ask Sam, 'We're not really sending these off, are we? This is just a practice session, isn't it?'

" 'No, no,' Sam replied, 'these are for real.'

"While I wasn't sure about the letter I was going to post, I remember feeling really exhilarated by the meeting itself and about becoming a partner."

"I was keen to be a partner too," Jessica added, "because I wanted to work on a team with others, rather than scrambling around on my own every day."

"I didn't think much about my letter to the editor," Matthias continued. "But a week later, my stepdaughter Louella came home from school and told me her teacher saw my letter in the paper. I ran out the door and bought a copy. I ran back home, opened the paper and read it with Jessica. Opening the paper and reading my letter was like opening a door to a world that was very closed to me—the world outside. It was at that moment that I began to feel part of the whole world. I thought, 'this is good stuff and I'm prepared to do it again.'

"Sam continued to make outrageous requests of us. No sooner were our letters published and our replies from our member of Parliament in hand, then it was time to make an appointment to see him. A call was made to set the meeting with Dennis Walters. We went over the meeting several times. Seven of us went and all seven met at our house so we could go over together.

"The Bradford-on-Avon venue for the rotating circuit of surgeries[17] is right in the middle of town in an 18th-century house overlooking the park and river. We had a 15-minute appointment, the first one of the afternoon. It was raining as I carried the TV up some flights of stairs and as someone else carried the video machine. The TV was a cast-iron one they used to make in the early seventies and was very heavy. We were shown in and the seven of us waited. As we sat there, I had this feeling of despair because the time was ticking away and I kept thinking 'we won't have time for anything.' Dennis Walters was 10 minutes late," Matthias continued, "and apologized profusely. After our introductions and how-do-you-do's, and establishing there wasn't

---

[17]A surgery is the session set aside, usually weekly, for a member of Parliament in Britain to meet his or her constituents.

enough time to show the video or use the TV I'd dragged up the stairs, Mr. Walters assured us he had done all he could by forwarding our letters to the minister who handled the issue. He got up to shake our hands goodbye, and it was only because we kept talking that he sat back in his seat. I think he was very uncomfortable. For a start, I don't think he'd had seven people in his surgery before, and it was obvious that the topic of Third World hunger was quite unfamiliar to him. He felt as a constituency MP it was out of his scope.

"In that first meeting we moved him from 'who *are* these people, and what do they want,' to 'these people are OK...and I wonder if they'll come back?' "

"We came back to our house after the meeting," Jessica remembered. "We were really pleased. I definitely felt that after that meeting Dennis Walters saw some possibility of what he could do. He said he'd look at the video we'd taken along and would be in touch with the minister about increasing the funding for UNICEF. At the mass lobby the previous year, my feeling was that of an end point; I didn't see where we could go from there. This time the feeling was one of a beginning...When Dennis Walters retired six years later and we met with his successor David Faber, Faber said to us, 'This bulging file has been passed on to me by Sir Dennis with glowing recommendations.' "

"I think we were on the right track," Matthias concluded.

Four U.K. RESULTS groups were started in July 1986, and they all wrote to their newspapers and wrote and met their members of Parliament. Our policy focus on that trip was increasing the British contribution to UNICEF. More than 40 people wrote to 15 MPs who forwarded these letters on to Chris Patten, the newly appointed Minister for Overseas Development and the MP from Bath, a town next to Bradford-on-Avon.

Four months later, I visited the original four groups and started four more. Now 120 people were writing to more than 30 MPs who were forwarding the letters on to the minister. On the second trip, we focused on Britain's contribution to IFAD's[18] Special Program for Sub-Saharan Africa.

"If I were to pinpoint a moment when my perception of myself and my relationship with my government shifted," Jessica recalled, "I'm sure it was the first time I met Chris Patten, the Minister for Overseas Development. Sam had returned to Britain and led the meeting in our home on IFAD the night before. The next afternoon, I met Mr. Patten at a fair in our town. At the last minute, Patten decided that instead of speaking he would just walk around and meet people. If Sam hadn't been at the fair I might not have gone

[18]The difficulty on IFAD's funding formula had been resolved, but overall funding was at a lower level. To help make up the difference, IFAD's donors created the Special Program for Sub-Saharan Africa to which donors could contribute.

up to the new minister. I was afraid he might ask questions I couldn't answer after I finished the Laser Talk on IFAD that I'd just learned at the RESULTS meeting. I asked if, when, and how much our government would give to IFAD's special appeal for Sub-Saharan Africa. I told him what I knew, and he gave me a peculiar look. I interpreted it as 'even in a small, seemingly sleepy town like Bradford-on-Avon, people are telling me what they want.' I was really proud to have gone up to him."

Jessica wasn't the only one getting the Overseas Development Minister's attention.

"After my first letter was published in the *Wiltshire Times*," Matthias recalled, "I had another published, this time on IFAD in the *Bath Evening Chronicle*, Mr. Patten's hometown newspaper. The letter prompted a comment from the local editor. Then, about a week later, an open letter from Chris Patten was published with the headline, 'I obliged.' By this he meant that he had announced a contribution to IFAD and therefore obliged my request for a government contribution," Matthias concluded.

"When we met at a surgery many months later," Jessica remembered, "Patten said that our conversation at the fair had influenced his decision. He announced an extra 7 million pounds days after our encounter. I was *sure* at that moment that I had made a difference."

The seven other fledgling groups across Britain were having their own impact.

"I am extremely encouraged and have no doubt," said Robert Smith, Director of the U.K. Committee for UNICEF, on a RESULTS U.K. conference call, "that RESULTS groups have played a significant part in the increased pressure that there seems to be already on members of Parliament and the minister." Smith was talking about the letters and meetings on increased funding for UNICEF during the first six months of RESULTS' existence there. Two weeks after Smith's comments, the British government announced an unprecedented 5 million pounds to UNICEF for immunizations and other primary health measures. This was equal to about 7 million U.S. dollars.

On my second trip to Britain, I had an encounter that would clarify for me what it was RESULTS had to offer. It was a presentation in a sitting room in Leeds. We'd spoken a bit about government, politics, and hunger when a woman's hand shot up. It seemed she'd heard quite enough and had something she needed to say. I pointed to her and what followed was a simple declarative sentence.

"I've never been *behind* my government's policy," she asserted.

I thought for a moment and asked, "Have you ever been *in front of* your government's policy? Rather than saying, 'my government did this and I didn't like it, my government did that and I didn't like that either,' have you ever decided where you'd like your government to be and pulled it up to where you are?"

In that same room I met Sheila Davie, who started a group near Manchester four months later and became RESULTS U.K.'s first full-time paid staff member. Sheila carried the vision presented that evening to communities throughout Britain.

CHAPTER 12

Going Down Under

Starting RESULTS in Australia

We who lived in concentration camps can remember the men who walked through the huts comforting others, giving away their last piece of bread. They may have been few in number, but they offer sufficient proof that everything can be taken away from a man but one thing: the last of the human freedoms—to choose one's attitude in any given set of circumstances, to choose one's own way.

Viktor Frankl

" 'Peter, would you like to come to a meeting that has the potential to save 40,000 children's lives a day?' " Jim James, a co-worker at the Australian customs service, asked me.

"I groaned inwardly," recalled Peter Graves at the odd invitation. "I thought, 'what *is* this about?' Only the fact that it was Jim James calling on the phone stopped me from saying 'no.' It was 1986, and we had worked together for some time. Jim told me about the meeting that was to start RESULTS in Canberra as the preliminary to other cities around Australia," Peter Graves continued. "It was a meeting that would eventually crystallize my commitment to children—and my effort to make a difference.

"While Jim was talking with me, I thought about an incident the week before when my blood had helped save the life of a newly born child in Canberra. I have a rare blood type that can be used to transfuse newly born babies when their mothers have Rh negative blood and their fathers have Rh positive. Otherwise, those babies can die. On Saturday night, one week earlier,

I and a few other similar donors had been called out at 10:30 p.m. for an emergency transfusion which had been ordered by the court. For religious reasons, the parents had been willing to allow their child to die. After that night, the child was to live.

"After listening to Jim, I thought that there had to be a connection here—from a dying child in Canberra to the dying children of the world. From the micro to the macro—what could I do that would make a difference? So I went along to that first meeting and still wasn't particularly convinced. Jim and his wife, Karen Cloud, were persuasive speakers, but politicians do not rate very highly in the esteem of the average Australian, and I was very dubious about being able to affect Australia's foreign aid policy. What did I know, and why should a politician listen to me anyway?"

Karen Cloud had been in the RESULTS group in Seattle, Washington. She'd moved to Australia, married Jim James, and they'd begun to study the Australian Parliamentary system to understand how RESULTS could be successful there. "As I said," Peter Graves continued, "I was skeptical about the worth of writing letters to members of Parliament. I had worked in the federal public service for many years and seen how so many letters to ministers were in fact answered by bureaucrats, with pat and repetitive phrases. So the first thing I did like was RESULTS' strategy for ensuring a minister did see my letter by using my local member of Parliament as a trimtab and writing through him or her to that minister. At the first meeting, Jim had mentioned how ministers do give first priority in their correspondence to letters from other members of Parliament and personally sign those replies. It was quite a thrill to see those first series of letters coming back signed by ministers and to know that out of all of the many letters sent, ours were the ones receiving the minister's personal attention."

In 1986, the RESULTS group in Canberra met with three members of Parliament over a five-week period. This is how Jim James described one of those meetings with his member of Parliament, John Sharp, and an important follow-up 12 months later.

"I visited my rural conservative member of Parliament at his electorate office," Jim James recalled. "John Sharp was a surprisingly young man from a family of pig breeders, I believe. His office was one room in an old row building in the sheep city of Goulburn. An enterprising local had erected the Big Sheep—a 40-foot-tall tourist attraction replica of a Merino sheep that symbolized the source of local wealth.

"My hands sweated so much," Jim continued, "that my notes were drenched and totally illegible. I swore that I'd never do this again as I sat in his only visitor's chair, waiting for him to finish a conversation about mutton exports to Saudi Arabia. He apologized for keeping me waiting and asked what he could do for me. I blurted out the whole story in one long sentence. Heaven only knows why he didn't turn me out on the spot. To my astonishment he too deplored the conditions of poverty in the world....I learned later, after scores of such conversations, that many politicians enter Parliament out of a sense of battling injustice and working for a better world for their constituents. Pretty soon, however, they are beaten down by the fierce cynicism that prevails and by the entrenched interests that seek to concentrate power and wealth in the hands of the few."

A year later, Jim James made plans to see Sharp again, this time on universal child immunization by 1990.

"This time I went to see Sharp in his Parliamentary office," Jim continued, "a broom closet really, tucked between a printing room and a staircase. He actually had to stand up from his desk to let me reach the only visitor's chair. I briefed him on cuts that had been made to the UNICEF budget and on the low-cost, successful work of the agency. By this time, I had become sufficiently confident to draw breath during conversations and could bring handouts without needing a plastic bag.

"John cut me off just as I was asking him what he thought we could do about the cuts and grabbed the telephone. 'I know who would be the perfect person for you to talk with,' he said. 'Andrew,' Sharp said into the phone, 'I have someone here who needs to talk with you.' I realized that he was giving me the brush-off and I would have to start all over with some office gofer. A few minutes later, Andrew Peacock, the longest serving Minister of Foreign Affairs in Australian history, walked in. We all stood up to let him into the office. John moved aside to let him sit down, saying, 'Andrew, this is Jim; Jim, Andrew,' and Sharp left the room. My palms turned to water and my heart started pumping wildly. Never again I muttered....

"Peacock was now the shadow minister[19] for foreign affairs. What surprised me, however, was that he wasn't familiar with the goal of immunizing 80 percent of the world's children by 1990," Jim continued. "He didn't know about it at all. Mr. Peacock listened to my story and immediately said that it couldn't be done. Even as he said it, he checked himself and said it could be done and it should be done.

"And it was," Jim James concluded. "The government reversed cuts in the aid budget with increased funding for UNICEF and a $22 million primary health initiative. Somehow it never got any easier to go see representatives, senators, editors and the like. I certainly never would have kept coming back for more without the support and companionship of everyone we worked with."

[19]The party or parties that do not achieve a majority in the Parliamentary elections select their own list of ministers who are responsible for overseeing and criticizing specific ministers. The party with the Parliamentary majority selects the ministers. The parties in the minority select what are called "shadow ministers."

CHAPTER 13

Starting RESULTS in Germany

To believe we can put democracy on automatic pilot and just cruise into the third millennium is to fall into The Democracy Trap.

Graham E. Fuller, The Democracy Trap

With expansion to Germany, we entered our first non-English-speaking country where there were important adjustments to make. My three-hour presentation had to be done in half the time to allow for translation, and the Action Sheet and other materials had to be translated before the meeting.

My initial host was Rudy Vietz. Rudy had a twinkle in his eye that was part prankster and part visionary. He played guitar and enthralled Germans as he sang humorous songs. Rudy, a German leader of World Runners, an anti-hunger running club, hosted the first RESULTS meeting, stayed with the group the first four months, and drove me to four cities on my return visit. There were two leaders, Martin Delker and Nancy Wimmer, who took over and guided RESULTS Germany over the first two years.

Martin was born in Munster in 1958, the middle of five children. He had the discipline of the athlete that he was, having trained for the Pentathlon, and a deep sense of caring.

"When I was five or six," Martin recalled, "I visited my grandparents who also lived in Munster. There was a Catholic missionary staying in their home, whose work in Africa my grandparents had supported for many years. I walked over and sat and listened to his stories. I told him I wanted to be like him, going to foreign countries and working with the poor. When it was time for him to leave he said, 'I need to take down your name in my notebook if you are going to become a missionary.' I was very proud that he took me seriously, and I was very proud that my grandparents were there to see him take down my name."

Martin's childhood commitment didn't find expression until he became involved in The Hunger Project some 20 years later. After several years as an active volunteer, Martin decided to take a break.

"I felt for the first time a little tiredness," Martin remembered, "and I enjoyed that they didn't ask me for participation right in the beginning of the year, as they usually did, leaving me a little time to rest. At that time I got a phone call from a friend inviting me to a presentation of a group with similar aims. I remembered that I had already heard of the group. They had this pretty self-confident name—RESULTS. I attended the first RESULTS presentation in Germany with no other intention than learning about what they planned to do in our country.

"It turned out to be an extraordinary evening. More than a dozen German participants had some difficulty listening to a former music teacher who could only speak in English. Sam Harris provided information on an important issue and then dared to ask us to write a letter to our members of the Bundestag (MdB)[20]—in German and right there on the spot.

"Before I had talked a lot about how politics would need to change before hunger could be ended. And until then it was clear to me that we would first need to have a very large portion of the voters on our side before the politicians would change their minds. Therefore, I'd been busy with much more important things than writing a personal letter to someone I didn't know and for whom I would have been nothing more than a single voice. I didn't even know the name of my member of the Bundestag! But somehow Sam Harris knew even that, and so I decided to take it as an amusing experiment—why not try it once!

"About 20 minutes later I was deeply impressed how really doing it, taking myself and my MdB seriously enough to write him a letter, changed my way of seeing politics and the issue of hunger. And when the other participants read their letters aloud, I couldn't believe what that short meeting and letter-writing session produced, how each one of us had found our individual expression for a common concern.

"When it came to the point that Sam asked for the first four partners to start RESULTATE[21] in our country, I was convinced that we would need such a group here in Germany and I couldn't wait to see who would declare to be a partner. It took only moments for the first three hands to go up, but then followed this little silent eternity, when it looked like this whole meeting was in vain: no one else raised their hand! I don't know how long Sam really

[20]In Germany, the parliament is the Bundestag and an MdB is a member of the Bundestag.

[21]One of the issues we had to face in Germany was what to call RESULTS. The literal translation would be Ergebnisse, but we decided to go with RESULTATE, which was less literal and less German but worked.

held this tension, but at least it was long enough for me to realize that it would take me to start this group. So much for my vacation.

"I left the meeting as a RESULTATE partner, really interested in finding out whether politicians answer letters from ordinary citizens because I still had my doubts.

"A few days later 'my life changed.' There was this letter in the mailbox, signed by Dr. Kurt Faltlhauser, my MdB, saying he would like to discuss my questions in his office and that I should call his aide to set a date. I remember those evenings, with Sam Harris on the phone, practicing with the partners for our first meeting with an MdB. And I remember Dr. Faltlhauser's first words when we met him: *'Was die Entwicklungspolitik angeht, bin ich blank und offen,'* which meant, 'Concerning development issues I'm blank and open.' It was totally unexpected for me. I assumed he already knew about these issues and would be opposed to our requests. I now get more letters from him than he gets from me! Whatever passes his desk and seems to be of interest for me gets copied and sent to me, sometimes with passages underlined and a few handwritten margin notes."

This was what we found everywhere—our members of Congress and Parliament knew everything we'd asked them to know, and we hadn't asked them to know very much. Martin's surprise with his own member of the Bundestag would be topped by an encounter with Rudy Vietz's member, who held a position of greater influence.

"A couple of weeks later I accompanied Rudy to a meeting of the Christian Social Union (CSU) Party," Martin continued. "Rudy's member of the Bundestag was Minister Hans Klein, a member of this party and the Minister for Economic Cooperation, the ministry on foreign assistance. We planned to meet Klein before the meeting. Rudy had spoken with a party leader who promised to introduce us to Minister Klein. We arrived early, but the meeting had already begun. Klein arrived late, ordered a meal, and started eating as the meeting continued. We saw there wouldn't be time for an introduction and when the woman sitting next to Klein got up, Rudy and I walked over and sat next to him. Rudy introduced himself as Klein continued to eat. There were only two or three minutes before Klein was to give his speech, and we were concerned that he would leave immediately afterward. Rudy asked if we could talk with him when his speech was over. He said, 'Yes, yes, I think so.' But we weren't sure it would really happen." Klein gave a speech about development and the arms race and then took questions from the audience, three or four at a time. Martin described Klein as looking very angry as he answered many of the other questions, but after taking several questions, one of which was Martin's, he smiled and answered that one first.

"What can we do as citizens to help you get more for your foreign aid budget?" Martin asked.

"When he finished his speech, he came down from the stage, walked in our direction, and the most amazing thing happened," Martin continued. "He took our hands and thanked us for the questions we were asking. Rudy hadn't introduced me when he introduced himself originally, but when Klein came down, Rudy introduced me and Klein said, 'I knew from your questions that you both belonged together.' *Sie beide* is the formal form of the phrase 'you both.' But Klein said *Ihr beide*, which is the informal form and the one you would use with a close friend. I was shocked. He didn't even use the informal with many of his party colleagues—but with us he was already using the informal form."

Martin and his partners spent their first four months in meetings like these, learning the issues and working on translations of RESULTS materials. On my return visit in June, Rudy took me to four new cities, including my first visit to West Berlin. My most vivid memory of the Berlin Wall would come four months later, in November 1988, one year before the Wall would fall. We'd driven to a friend's apartment, two blocks from the Wall, in order to change for the evening's meeting. Because I had a little extra time before the presentation, I walked to the graffiti-filled wall and climbed up to a perch. For the first time I realized there was a wall on the West German side, a grassy area in the middle, and a wall on the East German side. At that moment, a U.S. helicopter flew along the walls, the East German guards tensed, and as I watched this deadly game the thought that came to mind was, "Boys will be boys." A moment later I noticed rabbits eating in the grassy area between the walls, oblivious to the human folly on either side of them.

The night before my visit to West Berlin, I led my second presentation in Munich, a meeting attended by Nancy Wimmer, an American who had lived in Germany with her husband Klaus and daughter Stephanie for more than 20 years. After working with Martin for two years, Nancy would become the first National Manager of RESULTS Germany.

"I had been interested in politics in the U.S.," Nancy recalled, "but when I went to Europe, married, and settled down in Germany, American politics were no longer of special interest to me. I know it's odd, but I wasn't particularly interested in German politics either. I was much more concerned with integrating into German society. This meant not only language, but 'thinking' differently: a new profession, people with a different past and mentality, and bringing up a child in a foreign environment. At that time I was concerned with creating a kind of 'movement' in the German neighborhood: Why don't mothers help each other? If there are 13 kids playing in the sandbox, there are 13 mothers watching them and defending their kid's rights! Why not choose two to watch and let the other 11 take some time off? I put my energy into bringing families together, sharing concerns, and just having fun together. Gradually we developed into a real community.

"It was May 1988 when Heide and Bill Craig came to dinner in Munich," Nancy continued. "Heide, my husband Klaus's cousin, lived in the United

States, and I had been hearing about this woman for years. We celebrated with a sumptuous dinner and were well into it when Heide began talking about the problem of hunger and a lobby called RESULTS. 'Would you like to hear about it?' she asked in the middle of my salmon with champagne sauce! She went on to explain that it was a citizens' lobby dedicated to creating the political will to end hunger. And by the way, did I think I could influence political decisions? I hadn't thought about this in years! Me, make a difference in politics? I'm in Germany! 'Yes, and that's the point,' she told me.

"A month later Klaus and I were listening to Sam Harris in Munich. We sat there examining our concept of political will when the past caught up with me. All of a sudden I was back in Cleveland, Ohio. I was 15 when my mother suggested we visit an old age home at Christmas. I had been busy preparing a visit to an orphanage as part of the Christmas program for an organization I led at school. I still remember my mother's words: 'Lots of organizations visit children at Christmas. Old people are forgotten.' We went to the old age home and were welcomed by a room full of smiling, spirited older people who had gathered a full two hours before our arrival. Their joy was palpable. They applauded almost every move we made during our skit, were visibly moved by our small presents, and ate my mother's freshly baked cinnamon cake like champions. Voices were strong and laughter almost boisterous. 'Loud enough to wake the dead,' an elderly lady said to me and then winked. I flushed and fortunately was too embarrassed to speak. 'You've made us feel alive today, like people who really matter.'

"Later that same year, I was in church listening to the sermon when ideas in my head seemed to shift. Our minister was again describing a typical event in our small suburb: A black family had been to the town hall, requested residence, and was refused. I had heard this dozens of times in and out of church—our minister was my best friend's father. But this time I heard his words differently. 'These are not second-class citizens,' he said. 'This is a family with three young children. They're people just like us.' Thoughts and images started to interconnect in my head. What makes people *people*? Knowing that they exist? Having the right to buy a house in a white community? Pleading their case in a half-empty church whose congregation is getting tired of this 'civil rights stuff' again? This was all rather confusing for me at 15! Who was responsible? It couldn't be the friendly people I knew by name in church. Was it the people in the town hall?

"These human questions took a more political dimension when, as a student of political science in the sixties, one of my professors asked me to be his assistant. He was working on a book on interest groups and lobbying in the U.S. I had just finished a year of Constitutional law under his tutelage, and the power of one Supreme Court decision was still imprinted in my brain: *Brown v. Board of Education of Topeka* had ruled that separate educational facilities are inherently unequal, thus putting a legal end to segregation in schools. Weren't our democratic institutions the principal force in affecting change? The events we examined proved otherwise. Over 2,000 school districts, including all in the deep South and Virginia, remained segregated almost a decade after this decision, and drastic measures had to be taken both to maintain and overcome it. President Eisenhower had to send federal troops to Little Rock, Arkansas, to maintain order when several black children tried to enter the high school. President Kennedy had to protect a black man with federal marshals when this man chose to enroll in the hitherto all-white University of Mississippi. What injustice. History seemed to be moving backward and forward at the same time. Arguments going back to slavery days were being used 100 years later to prevent black children from mixing with whites in classrooms.

"But it was what happened in Georgia that had its greatest impact on me. There, Rev. Martin Luther King, Jr. was addressing this injustice with a new approach. Borrowing the tactics of Gandhi, he began schooling his people in non-violence, starting with a bus boycott in Montgomery, Alabama. Soon thereafter people began to "sit in" at lunch counters in drug and department stores. Within a few weeks the sit-in movement had swept the South, whose authorities retaliated with sweeping arrests. The Supreme Court responded with decisions that voided these arrests on the ground that merely to sit unserved at a lunch counter was no breach of the peace.

"For the first time I was struck not by the decisions and the legislation, but by the people who had created the conditions for it to be addressed! The sit-in movement had made it unmistakably clear that blacks intended to claim their legal rights, to claim their democracy! Like Gandhi they had exposed injustice—they made it visible. And they were prepared to use economic and political as well as legal weapons in the struggle that lay ahead. I began to really grasp that it was these *people* who were creating political will, the political will to remove the obstacles which kept them 'in their place.' "

These memories and experiences rushed through Nancy's head as she sat at her first RESULTS meeting.

"Yes," Nancy continued, "I had a vivid idea of what political will was and who created it. And I wasn't doing a thing. I had chosen to treat politics academically, like the rest of my friends; and like them, had a host of reasons. Sam confronted us with the question of whether we had ever written to our member of the Bundestag. Now this would be a step I could take, but what should I say? We were introduced to a two-minute Laser Talk and the fact that there were six vaccine-preventable diseases which could save thousands of children's lives. And now the real shocker. The German *people* contributed more to UNICEF than the people of any other country in the world, but the German *government* ranked 13th among donor nations.

"We were moved by the facts and relieved that we didn't have to take on the problems of humanity all at once. We could actually begin. I became a partner and Klaus a participant. We both became sponsors. Neither of us had any idea who our member of the Bundestag was. We found out and started to write. In fact *everyone* was writing! There was an atmosphere of confidence and community in the room; we were relying on ourselves to take this step. You could *feel* the determination which was intensified as we read our letters out loud. How different from the endless discussions which left everyone almost anesthetized. And I remember thinking, 'The RESULTS approach is so focused, so unspectacular, it could work.'

"Months later I was addressing these issues in Germany's first press packet. I still remember how this came about: I had been reading about RESULTS' successes in the U.S. and was intrigued by how partners used the press to impact policy. I conveyed this to Sam with the familiar 'Wouldn't it be effective in Germany if...,' and he answered by faxing me sample press packets so that I would know how to begin. That's the way people get results in this organization, you just start. But was I the one to do this? I had never worked with the press. My only experience up to now was an article about oral rehydration therapy in a local newspaper which was stuffed without charge into people's mailboxes. I picked up the telephone and called a senior editor at Germany's most widely read daily newspaper on politics and economics, the *Süddeutsche Zeitung*. I had learned to start with the most formidable from my husband Klaus. His way of teaching me to ski was to send me down the steepest slope I could manage. After that everything was a piece of cake. 'Good morning, Dr. Schütze,' I said in my first call. 'I read your leading editorial today in which you pointed out again how sound political solutions had been ignored by the government. Do you have two minutes to hear about sound programs that could save millions of children's lives?' He said, 'yes,' and the article appeared on the editorial page in March 1989 with the title: 'Survival at the price of 10 airplanes; only every second infant can be immunized for lack of funds in the UNICEF budget.'

"Three months later articles demanding an increase of government funding for UNICEF had appeared in a total of 15 German newspapers, but it was never really a piece of cake. Every single call was standing at the top of a steep slope, and it sometimes took hours before I 'pushed off.' What did change with time was my attitude towards success. Success was to make the call and communicate the issue to the media.

"In September 1989, the German government responded with a 1 1/2 million mark increase in UNICEF funding. It appeared in our brochure as our 'first' success. And it no doubt did spin a few heads that a dozen partners had succeeded in making it good politics for the German government to respond to our request. I was touched more by the fact that so few people could initiate such a process. Thousands of German people had learned of the interconnections between needless children's deaths and population growth; between disease and hunger; between hunger and poverty. And *all* of the editors who wrote those first articles in 1989 are still writing them now. We had begun something in 1989 which is a driving value in the organization of RESULTS; we had begun to build lasting relationships."

CHAPTER 14

Starting RESULTS in Japan

I can no longer protect myself from the reality of starvation by pretending that people who starve are nameless, faceless strangers. I know now who they are. They are just like me, only they are starving. I can no longer pretend that the collection of political agreements we call 'countries' separates me from the child who cries out in hunger halfway around the world. We are one and one of us is hungry.

Marilyn Ferguson

After starting more than 20 RESULTS groups in Britain and Germany and additional visits to Australia and Canada, it was only natural to continue my expansion frenzy with trips to Japan, a nation that would surpass the U.S. as the world's largest foreign aid donor. But while we had been invited by Canadian, British, and German citizens to bring RESULTS to their countries, we had no such invitation from a Japanese citizen. I cashed in some "frequent flyer" miles and got tickets for myself and my assistant, David Schnetzer, who had studied Japanese in college. We stayed in the Tokyo home of Chris Malone (the brother of RESULTS leader Greer Malone), ate mostly soba and ramen (noodle dishes for the bargain hunter), and had the most inexpensive 10-day exploratory visit to Japan imaginable.

My trip to Japan brought a startling discovery. When I stood in front of groups in Britain, Germany, or any of the other countries I'd visited and said that RESULTS is committed to healing the break between people and government, there were always a few nodding heads—always some air of recognition. When I'd lead people in writing letters to their members of Parliament, it was an action they felt they should be doing. But the Japanese I met didn't seem to recognize a break between people and government. Perhaps, more accurately, they believed that they weren't supposed to be connected to their government in the first place. They would do their jobs and good leaders would take care of them—just as Japanese corporations would take care of their employees. However, my plane touched down the day the latest political scandal had hit the news. It turned out that constant political turmoil and the ensuing loss of trust would do more than anything else to awaken some of the Japanese I met to the need for RESULTS-style participatory democracy.

When I arrived in Tokyo, I set about arranging a RESULTS meeting in Chris Malone's apartment for the last day of my visit. Using leads from friends in The Hunger Project, I called Toshihisa Nagase (Toshi), who taught English in a Japanese high school. We arranged to meet at a railway station near his house. Over the phone he said, "I'll be the one with a mustache, most unusual for a Japanese man."

Toshi was unusual. In a society that puts a high priority on conformity, he was willing to step out in ways many Japanese would find too difficult. "When I was a small child," Toshi recalled, "I loved TV heroes like 'Superman' and 'The Thunder Birds.' I especially liked 'The Thunder Birds' because they were courageous, had high technology, and loved justice. These heroes had a big impact on me and convinced me I would be a man who would help save the earth and help bring a peaceful world order. Later I realized that communication skills were the most crucial thing for making a difference. I majored in English at the university where I met Prof. Ouchi, the National Manager of The Hunger Project Japan.

"In 1985," Toshi continued, "I was invited to an international telephone conference call led by The Hunger Project and was very shocked to find that there were so many hungry, dying people around the world. I was also very glad to know that there were so many people who were fighting this tragedy and that we had enough food and technology to solve this problem.

"In 1986, I was on the plane for Hawaii to take part in the Briefing Leader Training prepared by The Hunger Project. I became the first Japanese briefing leader.

"In March 1989, several weeks before Sam Harris came to Japan, I received the call from Washington, D.C. and heard Sam's voice for the first time," recalled Toshi. "Sam explained what RESULTS was doing. This was the very first time that I heard the expression 'political will to end hunger.'

"At that time the Japanese prime minister was in another big bribe scandal, so most of the Japanese, including even small children, were discouraged about politics and politicians. The sound of 'political will' gave a sense of something fresh and new to Japanese people. Sam visited Japan three more times. During his visits, I found out the real power of RESULTS—the power which takes back the democracy to people—the power which gives us the opportunity to make Japanese politics better."

Toshi's first big experience with reclaiming his democracy took place in a phone booth at the high school where he taught. RESULTS had an op-ed piece, signed by members of Congress and Parliament from six countries, on issues surrounding an upcoming World Bank meeting. Toshi called the *Yomiuri Shimbun*, a newspaper with a circulation seven or eight times larger than that of the *New York Times*.

"One day in September 1989, I was standing in front of the pay telephone at my high school," Toshi continued. "I was going over what I would say to the operator of the *Yomiuri Shimbun*, one of the major newspapers in Japan. I was sweating because it was my first experience calling a reporter to ask about publishing an op-ed piece. After a short ring, the operator answered and suggested that I talk to a reporter at the commentary department. I was a little surprised, because I didn't expect such a positive reaction. I talked with a reporter, Mr. Sugishita, and told him who I was and what I wanted him to do. Mr. Sugishita listened and asked me to fax the information as soon as possible. I was surprised a reporter from a major newspaper welcomed information from a stranger like me and responded so positively. There was no fax machine at school, so I ran to the fax service after school. A few days later, there was an article in the morning paper.

"My first son, Takao, was born in 1989," Toshi concluded. "He gave me courage to get into RESULTS as the National Manager. I love him very much, so I can understand the desperate feeling of the parents who cannot give adequate nutrition to their children. 'This is my job,' I thought."

Over a four-year period I traveled out of the U.S. every four months. These 12 overseas trips helped start RESULTS in five other countries, but they were also the cause of a new strain in the organization—the strain that comes from expanding too fast. The constant pressure for Action Sheets, conference call guests, editorial writer packets, issues research, and conference planning in six countries meant we weren't serving anyone as well as we had. I made a conscious decision to curtail international expansion and to focus more of my energies on the United States. But the World Summit for Children Candlelight Vigils kept me from my intended U.S. focus, and the determination of RESULTS volunteers in the U.S. and Canada overcame my call for no more international expansion.

CHAPTER 15

Banking on the Poor

The Microenterprise Loans for the Poor Act

If you follow your bliss, you put yourself on a kind of track that has been there all the while waiting for you, and the life you ought to be living is the one you are living. Wherever you are—if you are following your bliss, you are enjoying that refreshment, that life within you all the time.

Joseph Campbell

"I went to my first RESULTS Regional Conference in 1984," recalled RESULTS volunteer Ron Fischman, an analyst with an investment banking company in Cleveland, Ohio. "I learned a lot about ending hunger and how a bill becomes a law, but I still didn't see where *I* was making a difference. Then, a guy named Ernie Loevinsohn spoke about a draft piece of legislation. For a young guy, I thought the list of titles Loevinsohn held was as improbable as the spelling of his last name.

"The bill was to be known as the Self-Sufficiency for the Poor Act of 1987. It contained a simple premise: if the world's poor were given access to enough money to do for themselves what they already do in near slavery, they would prosper. Since there is already a market for their products, services, and labor, Loevinsohn declared, a poor person, newly empowered with a little credit to buy her own tools and to reach a market, would raise herself out of poverty. This dramatic change could be achieved with no dumping of Western largess on the infrastructure which serves only the wealthier classes.

"The power of the ideas he presented was so compelling to me that I suspended my disbelief, held my breath and blurted out, 'I promise that Congressman Ed Feighan will introduce this bill.'

"Having made this promise to have Feighan introduce the bill, and having done so in the inspiration of the moment, I was confronted with a dilemma. I didn't even *know* Ed Feighan. I had no idea where to start. So I did something I did know how to do, I volunteered in his campaign. I was 26 at the time and I'd only been a RESULTS volunteer for four months."

Ron described his volunteer work in Feighan's campaign as helping to "get out the vote." Afterward he would ask for Feighan's help in introducing the legislation. The appointed time for making the request was the victory party on election night, after a difficult day in front of a polling center.

"It was a typical November day on Lake Erie," Ron recalled. "It was the kind of day the world came to know from Gordon Lightfoot's song, 'The Wreck of the Edmond Fitzgerald.' The rain alternately froze in the air or on my hood, and the wind whipped right through my rain-drenched overcoat. It was clear to me that working the polls was not among my 35 favorite things to do that day. Every voter who braved the weather, whether for Feighan or his opponent, got a big 'Thank you for coming!' from me as I handed out my Feighan poll leaflets. My rediscovered sense of mission in my citizenship was affirmed by each soggy, shivering voter.

"The moment the polls closed, I rushed downtown to the Feighan post-election party, which I fervently believed would be celebratory. Congressman Feighan tells me that we first met in the elevator, and that I said something about empowering the poor. I was too frozen to remember the encounter. I was only slightly warmed up when, a few hours later, the close race had been decided and the Congressman was walking up to the podium to give his acceptance speech. I decided this was my moment. I crashed his line, slipped my hand through some others, and said the words which will live in my memory forever. 'Congressman, congratulations on the tough win! I was out there today. I have a bill which could really make your next term. When can we talk about it?'

"I had gotten this far and hadn't been whisked away to the 'Big House' by stone-faced security guards. So I was not surprised to hear him say, 'For the next two weeks, I'm going to go into a hole and rest. But talk to my aide about it and she'll get something started. And, thanks for your help.' I became delirious—I still don't remember one word from the Congressman's acceptance speech which followed."

Ron's excitement ran throughout the organization. To this day, fighting for programs like the Grameen Bank in Bangladesh has been the volunteers' way of following their bliss.

After three years of following the lead of the Select Committee on Hunger, we embarked on having our own piece of legislation introduced. RE-

SULTS hired its first legislative director, Michael Rigby, a key RESULTS volunteer who had joined us from Search for Common Ground, a group that worked to find win-win solutions to issues like the arms race. Michael was a dazzlingly brilliant guy who'd never finished high school. Born in Great Britain, he'd been in the U.S. for less than five years and had not yet received his U.S. citizenship. Citizen or not, Michael helped lead the new legislation through the Congressional maze, inspiring the volunteers with his commitment and humor every step of the way.

Our awareness of poverty lending had its roots in RESULTS' work on IFAD in 1985. We were first introduced to these programs through a video of one of the projects IFAD supported: the Grameen Bank in Bangladesh, a rural bank for the poorest of the poor. In 1986, Dr. Muhammad Yunus, the bank's founder, spoke before a joint session of the House Banking Subcommittee on International Development Institutions and Finance and the House Select Committee on Hunger. He told of the founding of the bank and of a woman he met in 1976, in a village near Chittagong University, who would be its first borrower. She worked all day making bamboo stools but made only two pennies for a full day's work.

"My trained mind in economics could not accept the proposition that one could work all day to build bamboo stools and make only two pennies," he told the Congressional panel. "On closer scrutiny, I found that it was because she did not have the small amount of money to buy the bamboo to make the bamboo stools, so she borrowed the money from the trader who would buy the final product, the bamboo stool, from her. As a result, the trader dictated the price, which barely equaled the cost of the raw materials."

Yunus decided to make a list of the people in that particular village who borrowed from the trader and how much money they were borrowing.

"I had a student of mine with me," Yunus continued, "and we prepared a list of 42 such persons. The total amount they borrowed from the different traders totaled 856 taka, which is barely a total amount of $26. I felt extremely ashamed of myself for being part of a society which could not provide $26 to 42 able, skilled human beings...trying to make a living."

At first Yunus considered taking the money out of his own pocket and having his student lend it to these destitute women so they wouldn't have to borrow from the traders and so they'd be free to sell their products to the highest bidder.

"The next question came to mind," Yunus continued, " 'Why should I be the one to do it?' So, I went to the bank, which is located within the campus. I talked to them...Giving money to the poor people is not their cup of tea. So, anyway, [the bank officer]...said, 'I do only things which my head office asks me to do.' So I persuaded his senior officer later on to give loans to these poor people, taking me as the guarantor, and I took the loan from the bank and gave it to the poor people in this village. I wanted to make sure the recovery was 100 percent. I got myself involved in taking the money back to the bank. And it worked very well."

Yunus expanded the program of making very small loans to very poor women, hoping the banks might take it over. The premise was simple, but profoundly life-altering. Five women formed a borrowing group. The first loans went to the two who needed the loan the most. If they made their loan payments each week for the first five weeks, the next two women received their loans. If the four of them continued to repay over the next five weeks, the fifth received her loan. These destitute women, who had no collateral, served as each other's collateral. But the more the program was expanded, the more the banks said it couldn't be done on a wider scale, that very poor women were bad credit risks and would not repay their loans. Yunus continued the expansion until his lending program covered the whole district with a loan recovery record of nearly 99 percent, far higher than the repayment rate for other banks in Bangladesh.

In 1983, after the bank had been expanded to several other districts, it was converted into an independent bank called Grameen Bank. A decade later, the 1993 statistics tell of its extraordinary success. The bank has 1.5 million borrowers, 93 percent of them destitute women. It lends $20 million a month in loans averaging $75 each with a default rate of less than 3 percent.

After a trip to Grameen at the beginning of 1990, Peter C. Goldmark Jr., President of the Rockefeller Foundation, spoke about the numbers and history of the bank. He described it as having no marbled entryways, no tellers or white-shirted loan officers, no blue-shirted security guards, and no number-crunching machines.

"The local Grameen Bank Center is a hut," Goldmark said, "about 15 feet by 7 feet. It holds 35 women who sit on the floor in rows—five to a row. Each five-person [borrower] unit represents the primary group for planning and critiquing business ideas. Each five-person unit must approve a loan for one of its members before it is submitted to a larger group. Most important, each five-person unit is—as a group—the guarantor of the loan.

"On the day I was there, the women were...sitting, reporting to a loan officer, jumping to their feet, reciting their 16 'decisions,' or pledges.

"As I watched, I could see something else. I could see the smashing of ancient rules, the shattering of a traditional canon. I could see subversion. Here's what was being subverted:

The belief that poor people are helpless people.
The belief that women are the most helpless of all.
The belief that poor landless people are terrible credit risks.
The belief that poor people cannot cooperate, cannot plan ahead, cannot decide for themselves, cannot manage or service a loan.
The belief that a lot of credit is always better than a little credit.

The belief that the best form of economic development is aid for massive, centralized projects undertaken by the state.
The belief that you can build the economy by destroying the earth.
If the old beliefs were made of pottery, the floor of the Grameen Bank would be littered with broken shards.

"The Grameen Bank is not based on transactions. It is based on commitment. It deals in something more than contracts. It builds on a compact. And business sense.

"It is the only bank in the world with its own birth control policy. Its members make this pledge: 'We shall plan to keep our families small.'

"It is the only bank in the world with its own marriage policy. Its members make this pledge: 'We shall keep the center free from the curse of dowry. We shall not practice child marriage.'

"It is the only bank in the world with its own sanitation policy. Its members make this pledge: 'We shall build and use pit-latrines.' Do you begin to see how much can be accomplished if we choose to look at the world in a different way?"

My own visit to Grameen in 1990 was awe-inspiring. But it wasn't until a conversation with Yunus several years later, in which he described the bank's methodology for finding the *poorest* women, that I really understood exactly how revolutionary this program was.

When the Grameen Bank wants to expand into a new village, one of its 12,000 staff members visits with the women in the village to introduce the bank and explain how it works. Women will come forward and say, "I am poor, I can use the loan." The staff is told that they can listen to these people, but they are not the borrowers.

"After awhile," Dr. Yunus says, "they will see that nothing is happening, and they will get bored and go away."

After many, many weeks of these visits, it's time to identify the first borrowers. The bank tells the staff that the first borrowers aren't any of the women with whom they've talked. The first borrowers are the women they haven't talked to, the women who were too timid to come forward, the poorest women. When the bank worker goes up to one of these women to discuss giving her a loan, she will usually respond by saying that the worker must have made a mistake, the bank worker must have meant to speak with her husband. The woman will be told that no mistake has been made and that they wanted to talk with her about the possibility of taking a small loan to start a tiny business. Often she will say that there is nothing she can do and that she doesn't need the money.

"If the woman says she does not need the money," Dr. Yunus continues, "we have probably found the right person. The woman has been so beaten down that she doesn't think anything good could come her way."

Sometime later, the woman will see one of her neighbors receive a loan and start a successful enterprise—husking rice, weaving baskets, buying a cow and selling the milk, etc. Then she will be willing to try herself. She will form a group with four other women, study for and take the test, and eventually qualify for her first loan. Dr. Yunus says that the night before a woman receives her first loan is "the worst night of her life." She spends the night tossing and turning, unsure if she will be able to repay the loan. The next morning she has almost decided not to go through with it, but the other four women in her group come to her, offer their support, and accompany her to the bank. When she is finally given the money, her hands are trembling because she has never seen $30 in Bangladeshi currency before.

It turns conventional wisdom on its ear. I might seek the most aggressive women, women who seem more likely to repay their loans, but Yunus is looking for the most timid. I would think the night before she receives her first loan is the "best night of her life." But no, it is the worst night of her life. From such trembling hands come miracles. Women who have been living at the edge of survival can now feed their children, can now ensure that their children go to school, can now begin to plan for the future. These are the women for whom we advocate.

Despite the success of the Grameen Bank, we met tremendous resistance from the Reagan Administration to the whole concept of microenterprise poverty lending. In a February 1987 meeting with senior officials at the Agency for International Development (AID), we were told "AID doesn't work with the poorest of the poor. We work a few rungs up, with people who can hire poor people." The women who qualified for a Grameen loan would be disqualified by AID's definition—a perversion of what was possible. AID's resistance was also expressed in a statement by an official who was central to Administration policy on this proposal. Nine months after the bill was introduced, the official was quoted anonymously in the *Christian Science Monitor* as saying, "A lot of people are poor because they don't have the talent, skills, or IQ to get out of poverty."

"I've sent him a condolence note," remarked Margaret Goodman, an aide to Rep. Dante Fascell, about the comment by the not-so-anonymous AID official.

Any employee at an agency whose purpose was to fight Third World poverty who would say such a thing should either be fired or asked to apologize. And the choice would say much about that agency. Weeks after the comment, this official was given a promotion to a position of greater influence.

Anytime I saw the IFAD video on the Grameen Bank I thought, "If I could just get Ronald Reagan in a chair for five minutes to see this thing, I know he'd stand up and click his heels." But I couldn't get the president's attention, and all we got from his administration was opposition.

Years later, I often used a quote from an Israeli diplomat that always brought a laugh and tapped the frustration most people felt about government and its bureaucratic wrongheadedness: "Governments can be counted on to do the right thing," remarked Abba Eban. "But only after they've exhausted all other possibilities."

From RESULTS' perspective, the 1987 campaign was a perfect example of this axiom. And it was our job to press the government to do the right thing without wasting time, money, and lives. Initially, attention to microenterprise lending on Capitol Hill began with a Select Committee on Hunger briefing in 1985 and hearings in 1986. Legislation was introduced in 1986 by Rep. Ben Gilman (R-NY). We supported Gilman's 1986 legislation but also researched another bill that would slowly shift tens and eventually hundreds of millions of dollars in foreign assistance to these microenterprise poverty lending programs. It was RESULTS' work in 1987 that blew things wide open. Our bill required that 10 percent of the U.S.'s $4 billion in economic assistance given to foreign countries be converted to loans, repayable in local currencies. The local currency repayments were to be used for loans to people in those countries whose income was $250 per year or less, with special attention to women. The local currency lending would be channeled through U.S.-based and indigenous private voluntary groups, the Peace Corps, and UN agencies such as IFAD and UNICEF. We urged our groups to look for a Congressional sponsor on the House Foreign Affairs Committee.

Ron Fischman left the election night celebration, determined to have Rep. Feighan introduce the bill. Ron spent the next three months writing economic analyses and sharing the information with George Stephanopoulos, Feighan's legislative director and chief of staff, who would later become a senior aide to President Clinton. Ron called friends and family, urging them to write letters to Feighan, and made sure RESULTS legislative director Michael Rigby kept working with Feighan. Ron later confided that he was "deathly afraid that someone else's member of Congress would get there first."

Others in RESULTS were bringing the draft legislation to their members of Congress. The Bloomington RESULTS group drove two hours to meet with Rep. Lee Hamilton (D-IN), the second ranking Democrat on the House Foreign Affairs Committee.

Reps. Feighan and Hamilton urged members of the House Foreign Affairs Committee to join them in signing a letter to AID administrator M. Peter McPherson, asking for his comments on the legislation. Three weeks later, the letter was sent to McPherson with 27 signatures, two-thirds of the committee.

"Finally, on January 10, 1987," Ron continued, "I was getting the RESULTS conference call connected to our living room, and wound up speaking to Michael Rigby. He spoke in a hush in order to avoid disturbing the rest of the staff on the call. Yet the excitement in his voice carried over the phone and leapt into my ear as he whispered, 'News flash: Your man, Ed Feighan, has agreed to introduce the Self-Sufficiency for the Poor Act this week!' I felt in that moment that my life was complete."

Feighan would later describe his sponsorship of the measure as quite a departure for him.

"I was very much a mainstream Congressional thinker on American development aid until that time," Feighan recalled. "The concept of putting American development aid, not just small amounts, but *minuscule* amounts, in the hands of individuals was as foreign a concept to me as proposing that we earmark a portion of development aid for extra-terrestrial life!

"There obviously was a lure in the beauty and simplicity and common sense approach that the microenterprise proposal had," Feighan continued, "and it certainly wouldn't have been incorporated without the success story of the Grameen Bank. Having the power of that story and the visual of the video was invaluable. [But] there was an enormous institutional resistance to as dramatic a change in policy as this was....That was, to my recollection, the biggest challenge: not allowing the institutional forces in the Congress and in the Administration to co-opt us by saying, 'We're going to try it, we're going to do a few pilot programs and if it works well, someday, this is going to be a significant dimension of foreign development aid.'

"My most vivid recollection of interacting with my colleagues on this was not their resistance to it," Feighan recalled, "but their commentary about being under the gun from a constituency group. RESULTS as an organization didn't mean anything to them, to be honest. It was unprecedented during my 10 years in Congress. I have never encountered an issue that had as many members massaged into place by constituents in such a timely fashion. It didn't spring out of some great spontaneous combustion....It obviously was the result of some serious planning."

That planning was grounded in the volunteers and the actions they took.

"Thirty-two members of the House have signed on with Feighan as original cosponsors of the bill," announced an editorial in the *Fort Lauderdale News* three days after the legislation was introduced. "Among them is U.S. Rep. E. Clay Shaw (R-FL), who says the bill 'hits at the basis of Republican philosophy...to give people a hand up rather than a handout.' The bill has won both Democratic and Republican support for its simplicity, its economy, and the successful history of similar loan programs. An official response from the Reagan administration is expected within a week or two through the Agency for International Development, which is responsible for U.S. economic and humanitarian assistance in less developed countries. That response should be a resounding endorsement of the self-sufficiency bill."

It wasn't! The response from AID administrator Peter McPherson arrived the same day as the editorial was published, and he expressed strong reservations about the measure. By the time McPherson's letter was received, there were 59 cosponsors of the legislation. Cosponsor number 47 was Rep. Pat Swindall, a very conservative Republican from Georgia. Steve Valk, who designs features sections for the *Atlanta Journal-Constitution*, described his road to RESULTS and to seeking Swindall's support.

"As far back as I can remember," Steve recalled, "I've always had an affinity for the underdogs of the world. This probably came from being a Mets fan in the early sixties, but whatever the cause, there has always been within me a deep desire for social justice, to make what was wrong in the world right. I couldn't go by a crooked picture without straightening it out and I couldn't go by a problem without wanting to fix it.

"With this desire to make the world a better place pushing me, I embarked on a career in journalism. I truly believed, and still do, that solving our problems is simply a matter of getting the right information to the right people at the right time. But whether the media could actually play a role in solving societal problems was another thing altogether. Within a few years of graduating from college and going to work for the Atlanta newspapers, it slowly seeped in that newspapers weren't in the business of solving problems, they were in the business of making money. Working at a publication that employed thousands of people, I felt pretty powerless to alter that purpose."

Steve would eventually find RESULTS through Sara DeMent, a woman he met in 1980 and would marry years later. Sara lived in the apartment above a friend of Steve's who worked with him in John Anderson's presidential campaign. Steve and Sara shared an interest in music but would not meet again until 1984.

"In 1984 I was an angry young man who wanted to change the world but couldn't see how," Steve recalled. "I was getting more involved with music and songwriting and wasn't particularly interested in some lobbying group that my friend Sara was involved with that was trying to do something about ending hunger. I thought it was nice that she was trying to do something, but I really didn't want to waste my time on a hopeless cause. I would take her to her meetings and then pick her up afterwards. It wasn't until six months later that my curiosity got the better of me and I decided to go to a RESULTS meeting.

"Being a journalist, I'm inclined to approach most things with a skeptical nature. Being a journalist, I was also not sure how deeply to get involved with political causes, but I couldn't just leave that crooked picture alone, and when I realized that nobody else was going to straighten it out, I took a deep breath and dove in. Over the years I've come to terms with this because my position at the newspaper is one where I have absolutely no influence about what goes into the paper or how it is written. I design pages for the features sections, but it's somebody else who assigns and edits the stories, and it's somebody else who writes the stories and takes the pictures. As I began to get involved with RESULTS, I saw myself as a link between people who had important information that could save lives and the media that could make that information available to the public.

"In 1985, there was a conference call with Idriss Jazairy, President of

IFAD. At the time the U.S. was threatening to withhold funding to IFAD over a disagreement with OPEC countries. Listening to the roll call, I became keenly aware that I was no longer alone with my vision of a better world. I felt as though I were part of a conspiracy, and it excited the hell out of me. I made calls to the Washington bureau of Cox newspapers and laid out the IFAD story for them. On Sunday, June 9, 1985, the *Atlanta Journal-Constitution* ran a news article headlined "Funding Squabble Threatens Aid Program for Poor Nations." Sara visited the newspaper and talked with Cynthia Tucker, who was then on the editorial board, about the IFAD issue. Within a few weeks there was a Cox wire story in the news section and an editorial, and for the first time in many years, I started believing that I could make a difference. I've always been the kind of person who likes to 'get involved' with causes, but until RESULTS my involvement always seemed to have a Don Quixote-like quality. I dreamed the impossible dream only to be rudely awakened at some point."

Steve was elated to be using his contacts with the newspaper to get the right information to the right people, but his greatest thrill with RESULTS was the conversion of Congressman Pat Swindall, a conservative Republican from Georgia's fourth district.

"In January of 1985, within a week of Pat being sworn into office," Steve continued, "four RESULTS volunteers, myself included, met with the congressman to request that he cosponsor and vote for the Famine Relief in Ethiopia bill that had just been introduced in Congress. One of the volunteers, who did not meet with us for a breakfast practice session before the meeting, wound up being a loose cannon of sorts, insisting that we cut military spending to feed the hungry, putting the conservative Swindall in a defensive, so to speak, posture. Swindall made it clear that he didn't think the government should be involved in humanitarian aid, and that it was something best left to the churches and private sector to take care of. A few weeks later, Pat was one of only 15 or so congresspersons, out of more than 400, who ended up voting against the famine relief bill, and he made headlines by giving a big speech about it on the floor of the House."

Steve spoke about the shame he felt over Swindall's vote.

"Have you ever seen the fans of a really bad sports team," Steve continued, "who sit in the stands with bags over their heads because they're ashamed to be seen rooting for such losers? If politics were a sport, and we were sitting in the stands watching our congressman playing on the field, we would be wearing those bags on our heads over the shame we felt for having Pat Swindall as a representative. Our thoughts and discussions about him were very negative, and we pretty much wrote him off, figuring our best chance was that maybe he would be defeated in two years.

"But at Sam's suggestion, we began to shift our thinking on Pat. There was this prayer Newton Hightower had written to his member of Congress,

Rep. Bill Archer, someone he had similar difficulties with two years before. We adapted it to Swindall. We added Swindall's name and it went:

> Thank you, God, for Pat Swindall. We know he is a good man who wants to do right in the world. We know he struggles with the same problems we do: closing our hearts to those who don't agree with us. There are no thoughts or feelings that he has had that we haven't had and vice versa.... We pray for all of us to learn compassion for people in our country and far away, for rich and poor. We pray that Pat and we will be less frightened of each other. We pray our focus will be more to love and appreciate him and less to change him. Help us to remember that sharing love with the world is the highest contribution we can make and will lead to children being fed and the planet surviving. Forgive our righteousness and anger. Open our hearts and minds to find the next expression of love for Pat that he can receive.

"We eventually let go of our negative attitude toward Pat. Instead, we began to see him as a human being who, just like us, did not want to see people dying in the world from hunger and disease. All he needed was a little education. We began to show up at "Chat with Pat" sessions around the district. There were other people with other issues in the district who had bones to pick with Pat (we jokingly called the sessions "Spat with Pat"), and whenever they did, they didn't get anywhere. If anything, he stiffened his resolve and defended his position. When he got around to us, he was visibly relieved to see us greeting him with a handshake and a smile instead of a scowl and a sharp tongue. Then we would give him a two-minute briefing on an issue such as IFAD. And when we started talking about enabling a farmer to grow a ton of wheat a year for the same amount of money that it would cost to send one ton of wheat one time, well, he started listening a little closer. Gradually, a relationship of trust and respect was built.

"In the spring of 1987, RESULTS launched its microenterprise legislation with the Self-Sufficiency for the Poor Act. We decided it was time for an office visit with Pat, and four of us took off time from work to go see him. It was late afternoon, and we must have been a sight sitting in his waiting room with a TV and a VCR to show him the Grameen Bank video. Earlier in the day, feeling very confident, I told Sara that after Pat agreed to cosponsor the legislation I would ask him if we could write an op-ed piece in support of the bill to appear under his name.

"'I don't know, Stephen,' she said. 'I think you'd be pushing it.'

"But I figured once he's committed to the bill, what did I have to lose?

"The four of us piled into a small office and set up the TV and tape. We all took a deep breath and the congressman joined us. Everyone spoke brilliantly in the meeting. As we were showing the video, Pat was sitting on a desk, knees drawn under his chin, staring intently at the screen. We told him about the tremendous opportunity of the Self-Sufficiency for the Poor Act and asked him to become a cosponsor. 'I'd be delighted to be a cosponsor,' he said.

"Sensing we were on a roll, I began to ask about an op-ed, but before the words were even formed in my mouth, the congressman spoke: 'You know, I think it's important on an issue like this that we try to build public support in the media. I have a column that appears in the local paper [*The DeKalb News-Sun*], and I'm thinking maybe you could write a piece about this bill, and we could run it in my column. Do you think you could do something like that?'

"I glanced over at Sara with a smile so wide it hurt. 'Pat, I'd be more than happy to do it.' I was now ghost-writing for a man who two years earlier voted against famine aid for Ethiopia. We were probably the only lobbying group in Georgia that could get Pat Swindall and liberal Congressman John Lewis to cosponsor the same legislation.

"That experience changed me. I now see that everyone has the potential to do the right thing if given the opportunity. It's refreshing to see people as possibilities rather than obstacles."

With Swindall and 58 other members of the House as cosponsors, we moved into high gear, crafting a response to USAID's opposition with Rep. Feighan and his staff. As we put the final touches on Feighan's answer to AID's February 5 letter, World Bank President Barber Conable, speaking in Africa on February 10, gave us just what we needed.

"Our assumptions have been imperfect," Conable said at the launch of a World Bank "Safe Motherhood" initiative, "our results uneven. Macroeconomic planners have slighted the growth that comes from the bottom up. In too many nations...too many women are at the bottom. Their arms hold the family together. Their hands build the foundation of stable, growing communities. But development efforts have not lent enough strength to those arms, have not entrusted enough resources to those hands. And along with women, development itself has suffered."

His statement was a gift from heaven and was used to close Rep. Feighan's response to AID.

On March 3, while I was in Britain starting new RESULTS groups, hearings were held before the House Foreign Affairs Subcommittee on International Economic Policy and Trade on the Feighan bill and the one by Rep. Gilman. The two measures would soon be merged. RESULTS Legislative Director Michael Rigby was among the last panelists to testify before the subcommittee.

Rep. John Miller (R-WA) had to leave early, but not before commenting to Chairman Don Bonker (D-WA), "Mr. Rigby's Puget Sound operatives have already talked with me at length, and based on what we've heard so far, I'm very supportive of the approaches of Congressmen Feighan and Gilman."

"Mr. Rigby's operatives are also in Olympia, Washington," Chairman Bonker responded, "which is why we're having this hearing today."

Just then, Michael Rigby smiled because he knew he was not alone. He knew the RESULTS groups in Seattle and Olympia had done their job and had made his infinitely easier.

There are two ways change is made in Washington. One is rabble-rousing from the outside and the other is the insider decisions made by members of Congress, their staff, and others able to get close to them—lobbyists, large contributors, and the very large non-profit groups. Because RESULTS pushes hard, frequently for more money or more change than others see as possible, and because of our effectiveness with the media around the country, RESULTS is seen as a group that mostly plays an "outsider," somewhat irritating role. But Bonker balances that view when he says, "Mr. Rigby's operatives are also in Olympia, which is why we're having this hearing today." The relationships these Washington state RESULTS volunteers had built with both Bonker and Miller and the Atlanta partners had built with Rep. Swindall were examples of the relationships being built in communities around the country. Then came another comment from a member of the subcommittee.

"I want to compliment my colleague Mr. Feighan and tell him what unusual lobbying his bill brings about," remarked Rep. Bob Dornan (R-CA). "Sitting at home I got a call last week from a very important television star, Valerie Harper, otherwise known as Rhoda. And she said, 'I just know you're on this bill, Bob.' And I said, 'Well if I'm not, I'm going to get on it.' " Valerie Harper, a member of the RESULTS board, had made this call and others on behalf of the bill.

The hearing was a success, and it brought new light to two aspects of the debate. We began to realize that AID had been using the term microenterprise for years and to them it included loans to firms with as many as 10 or 20 employees. We continued to make the distinction "microenterprise poverty lending": tiny loans to the poorest of the poor for *self*-employment. It was the Reagan Administration's contention that more expensive technical assistance and training were needed in microenterprise lending, and such training was not well spent on someone taking a $50 loan. This notion was challenged, however, by one of the panelists.

"Training and technology frequently come into play only above a certain level of economic activity," said Rupert Scofield in his testimony. "The poorest of the poor can, through their own skill in survival, make astonishingly good use of even the smallest amount of capital without expensive training or technology. While such a discovery threatens the livelihood of consultants such as myself," Scofield continued, "I cannot escape the conclusion that this type of project represents a superior investment—from the beneficiaries' point of view—than many of those much more expensive efforts with which I have been associated in the past."

Scofield was with FINCA (Foundation for International Community Assistance), a U.S.-based private organization which, like Grameen, made $50 to $100 loans to the poor in the Third World. His testimony showed what was behind the intense opposition from many private consultants, people who believed our lobbying might cost them their jobs. But FINCA was on our side. John Hatch, FINCA's founder, called Feighan's original bill "potentially the most important foreign policy initiative since the Marshall Plan." For him the bill meant a decisive attack on poverty in the Third World.

Scofield's testimony was rewritten as an op-ed piece which RESULTS volunteers placed in the *Seattle Times,* the *Tulsa World*, the *Rocky Mountain News,* and two other newspapers.

On Wednesday, April 1, the House Foreign Affairs Committee accepted an amendment offered by Reps. Feighan and Gilman that provided at least $50 million in fiscal year 1988 and $75 million in fiscal year 1989 for micro- and small-enterprise lending. The good news was that the primary emphasis was on making loans to individuals living in absolute poverty. The bad news was that the definition of absolute poverty was weak and hard to measure. During the mark-up, AID tried to have amendments offered that would weaken the measure further, but neither Feighan nor Gilman accepted any further weakening. Both were committed to strengthening the poverty definition as the process continued.

After the amendment passed in committee, I wrote the RESULTS groups that Sen. Dennis DeConcini (D-AZ) would probably introduce a Senate version with a stronger definition of absolute poverty. I told them that if, at the last minute, the strong poverty focus was omitted from his version, we would seek a different Senate sponsor.

It was an unusually strong statement for a relatively small organization (two staffers in Washington, myself and Michael Rigby, and a third in California, Dorsey Lawson), but we were able to make such a statement because of what we brought to the table. We brought hundreds of "unpaid" staff from around the country—the RESULTS volunteers. Feighan's bill was introduced on February 3, with 33 cosponsors and just seven weeks later there were 107 cosponsors, nearly one-quarter of the House, more than 30 editorials and action in the House Foreign Affairs Committee.

Later that year, the assistant administrator for legislative affairs at AID marveled at the speed with which microenterprise poverty lending had become a development priority in Congress. The AID official said that it usually took the Agency three years to get a measure through Congress. We found later that it would take AID at least three years to begin to implement the program properly.

On April 9, Sen. DeConcini introduced the bill we hoped for, S 998. It tightened the poverty definition, saying the loans should be made available to "persons whose income is in the lowest 20 percent of the per capita household incomes in the country...." I made a special call for conservative Republican cosponsors.

The RESULTS group in Denver had worked for 2 1/2 years to get an appointment with Sen. William Armstrong (R-CO), and now they finally had one. They went in with a delegation of six, including a realtor, two computer experts, and a big rig driver for Safeway. Barbara Moore was responsible for the Laser Talk on microenterprise poverty lending. She spent days preparing and memorizing her presentation. Up to that point, Sen. Armstrong, a conservative, had never supported any of RESULTS' issues.

The group sat at a table with the senator at one end, slightly slouched back in his chair. At first he was polite but not very interested. Barbara talked about small loans to poor people with repayment rates of 97 percent. She talked of lives turning around. As Barbara spoke, Armstrong began to lean forward—closer and closer. Just as she finished, he came alive and said, "Now *that* is something I can get behind. I can really support that. Tell me what I can do!" They asked him to cosponsor the bill and he agreed.

Armstrong was the sixteenth Senate cosponsor on a list that grew to 52. His aide reported calls from nearly a dozen Republican Senate offices asking why Armstrong had his name on a bill that was so strongly opposed by the Reagan Administration. This was the beginning of a real partnership between Denver RESULTS and the senator.

On May 29, AID's opposition to Sen. DeConcini's bill was delivered in a letter to each member of the U.S. Senate. The agency asserted that loans to enterprises with four or fewer workers had limited economic viability and impact. Sen. DeConcini responded that 75 percent of the businesses in the world had four or fewer workers.

An article in the *Christian Science Monitor* detailed Administration resistance to having credit reach the poorest of the poor: "Michael Farbman, Chief of AID's Employment and Enterprise Division, says this approach is unsound, and contrary to [AID's] mandate....'We've never been legislated to reach the poorest of the poor,' said AID's Farbman....'The very neediest of the poor means they can't run a business. They're not responsible beyond a visceral response to following the seasons....' "

But even the conservative *Orange County Register* didn't buy AID's line.

"It's difficult to understand why the Agency for International Development is so adamant in its opposition—as evidenced by heavy lobbying of the *Register* and other newspapers—to S 998, the Microenterprise Loans for the Poor Act," the paper wrote in July. "While AID's objections may sound reasonable, incorporating them into the bill would torpedo an innovative, tested way of helping those who most need help." That same month, we made plans for a trip that Grameen Bank founder Muhammad Yunus would be making to the U.S. and Canada. We organized a luncheon for Yunus with members of Congress and a telephone conference call with editorial writers. We'd done a conference call the year before with IFAD's Idriss Jazairy, when he attended the UN Special Session on Africa, and conference calls twice with Jim Grant on the release of the *State of the World's Children* reports from

UNICEF. The former connected 15 editorial writers at their desks and the latter connected news conferences in 17 cities, but neither was in the pitch of a heated legislative battle as this call was. Twenty-eight journalists joined Yunus—two calls, fourteen on each. The telephone, the speaker box, the list of editorial writers, and the tape recorder were set on a long table in our third-floor office across the street from the Hart Senate Office Building. The clock struck 2:00 p.m.—Yunus had not yet arrived. My heart started to beat a bit faster, but he walked in at 2:04 with a beaming smile and the call began.

After months of bureaucratic nay-saying by AID, Yunus's voice was a breath of fresh air. At the end of the first call, Kristen Helmore of the *Christian Science Monitor* phoned the RESULTS office to ask if she could also participate on the second call. I told her yes, but that she'd have to ask her questions last. (It would be one of Helmore's articles on the Grameen Bank that would prompt *60 Minutes* to do a segment on the bank 2 1/2 years later.)

As I listened over and over to a tape of the call, one particular response of Yunus's rang in my ears. The questioner asked about AID's belief that small-scale enterprises aren't the best way to develop because they have limited utility in the long run in terms of developing a nation's economy.

"It all depends what...development means to people," Yunus told the editorial writers. "To me, building a road, building a dam or a huge building doesn't mean a thing....The question that I'll be asking [is] does it increase the income of a poor person? If it does, it is development. If it doesn't, it's not development."

Yunus displayed a deep wisdom, something I saw in people committed to transforming supposedly hopeless situations. It was similar to a time I heard Eugene Lang speak at a ceremony on Philanthropy Day at the White House. Lang was the businessman who offered college scholarships to a sixth-grade graduating class, provided they finished high school. Fifty percent of these students were not likely to do so, but Lang didn't just offer the money, he worked with them over the following six years, and just about all of them made it.

I've come to be intrigued by people like Lang and Yunus. Lang, untrained in education, and Yunus, untrained in banking, developed innovations partly because they didn't know any better. Lang didn't know you couldn't change things and help inner-city sixth graders make it to college. Yunus didn't know that destitute women in Bangladesh wouldn't repay their loans. I'm often grateful that my own training was in music rather than political science. If I had the proper training and had known better, RESULTS would probably never have been created.

On August 5, there was a further blow to the poverty focus of the microenterprise bill in the House. The Foreign Affairs Committee revised its bill and passed legislation at AID's urging which added the words "to the maximum extent practicable." This is a famous bureaucratic phrase that is the equivalent to the insertion of the word "NOT" at the end of any declarative sentence as popularized by the "Wayne's World" sketch on *Saturday Night Live*. It was useful when there was a need to insert a hole in legislative intent big enough for a Mack truck to drive through. The legislation now read, "at least 80 percent shall be used for loans to microenterprises, to the maximum extent practicable, in an amount of $300 or less or, in the case of an initial loan, of $150 or less." As best I could see, AID staff in Washington didn't believe that small loans for the poor were practicable, at all.

In a moment of anger and frustration I dashed off a letter to Rep. Feighan, a friend throughout, and warned, "We know that AID's proposed changes sound reasonable, but such reasonableness has given us the foreign aid program that we have—one that the American public does not support, and one that usually cannot be passed in Congress."

"We found ourselves sometimes lured into the institutional mind-set," Feighan recalled, thinking back on the campaign that year. "Frequently George Stephanopoulos would come into the office and say, 'To get the committee staff on board we've got to back off a little bit on this matter, we've gotta be a little more conciliatory here.' And I would say, 'Fine, let's do that.' Then George would say, 'But then the problem is, we have to deal with RESULTS. RESULTS will never buy it. RESULTS will pound us into the ground.'

"We needed that obviously," Feighan continued. "We needed the sense of pressure on us, even though I was the *sponsor* of the bill. The institutional forces were such that as I got into it, as is always the case, you want the legislation so badly that you are willing to make compromises that you shouldn't be making. And unless there is some force outside of you, carefully watching your every move and insisting that unnecessary compromises not be made, then you don't win the great wars, and this was one of the great wars."

The foreign aid authorization bill was not passed by Congress that year. An authorization bill prescribes policy language and spending ceilings. For example, the authorization bill would set policy such as making 80 percent of loans under $300 with initial loans under $150. It might also say that up to $50 million could be spent on microenterprise loans. The appropriations bill sets spending within the limits agreed in the authorization bill. Another way of saying it is that the authorization bill initiates the program and sets policy and the appropriations bill writes the checks. But the authorization process on foreign assistance had broken down in Congress, and the authorization bill passed only once during the decade. The only thing we could do was to turn our attention to the foreign aid *appropriations* bill, the only bill that would be passed.

Between December 1986 and November 1987, 21 mailings were sent to a list of 120 leaders in Congress, the Administration, the media, and private groups. There were an average of five microenterprise editorials in each mailing. With the focus shifting to the Foreign Operations Subcommittee of Appropriations, I highlighted comments from newspapers in the states and districts of those members of Congress as the editorial comment generated by the Yunus conference call began to pour in.

"The Grameen Bank's example offers a heartwarming case study, which deserves Congressional support," declared the *Honolulu Advertiser* in its August 4 issue.

"We urge you to become involved," the *Maui News* said three weeks later. "Write to Sens. Dan Inouye and Spark Matsunaga, let them know that these measures must be given the highest priority."

"Some pieces of legislation become targets of bureaucratic resistance and test the will of Congress to keep them from being bent out of recognition," declared Rep. Matthew McHugh's *Ithaca Journal* the same day. "Such is the case of a law aimed at helping the world's poorest people become self-sufficient which has been wending its way through Congress this year. Congress should enact this bill into law with firm guidelines and definitions...."

The pounding was as incessant as AID's opposition. One week later, a microenterprise forum on Capitol Hill provided another breath of fresh air. "I'm an economist," John Hatch of FINCA asserted at the gathering. "I look for economic results. I can give you case after case of net income generated of 100 percent, 150 percent, 200 percent from a $50 loan. Yet when you talk with the people, they rarely mention economic benefits. Instead, they say things like 'My family is more united,' 'Our community works together,' and 'I feel like I'm somebody.' Empowering people—that's the real benefit of these loans."

On September 23, eight of the thirteen Senate Foreign Operations Subcommittee members signed a letter to Robert Kasten and Daniel Inouye urging inclusion of the microenterprise provision in their bill. And on October 15, a *New York Times* editorial appeared titled, "Where $100 Goes a Long Way," pitched by RESULTS volunteer Bob Van Olst. "[L]oan amounts proposed under the pending [microenterprise] legislation are too modest to attract the barracudas that usually circle foreign aid," the editorial concluded. "The poor will receive the aid directly and have a chance through their own initiative to become self-sufficient. That sounds a lot like the American way."

RESULTS volunteers generated 100 editorials and hundreds more letters to the editor in support of the legislation. The foreign assistance authorization bill which passed in the House included the weaker microenterprise section. The Senate microenterprise bill, with 52 cosponsors and a tougher poverty focus, languished because no Senate authorization bill was passed that year. But $50 million was earmarked for microenterprise loans in the appropriations bill. The focus on the very poor was not mandated in the bill but was included in the non-binding report which accompanied the legislation. It said that 80 percent of the loans should be targeted to individuals in the poorest 50 percent of the population with special emphasis on businesses owned by women and the poorest 20 percent of the population.

What saved us from a potentially shallow victory was a letter from the head of AID to the lead Congressional sponsors many months later stating, "[we have] complied with, and indeed exceeded, both the letter and the spirit of the microenterprise legislation." It was a strong enough claim to allow us to study AID's implementation of the program.

"I attribute the success of the Self-Sufficiency for the Poor Act almost exclusively to RESULTS," declared Rep. Feighan in a *Christian Science Monitor* interview. "They generated over 100 editorials throughout the country in support of the bill. For a bill that did not have a high visibility on its own, that was a remarkable effort."

Ron Fischman, the RESULTS volunteer who'd convinced Rep. Feighan to introduce the original legislation, put it this way: "I am certain that my work with RESULTS made a difference with my government and in my world. I know that many families have new lives, new futures, and new hope thanks to the Self-Sufficiency for the Poor Act of 1987, a member of Congress, a sleet-drenched volunteer, and an organization called RESULTS."

CHAPTER 16

A Personal Healing and an Organizational Healing

Building Community

I don't know what your destiny will be, but one thing I do know: the only ones among you who will be really happy are those who have sought and found how to serve.

Albert Schweitzer

I made my fourth trip to Great Britain in June 1987, and RESULTS expanded to 17 groups there. Without continuous travel and support, however, the trend was always toward contraction. A year earlier, I welcomed several new U.S. groups and said goodbye to Phoenix and Philadelphia, Billings and Baltimore. I knew they'd be back and I knew we still needed to discover a way to expand and thrive rather than expand and then contract. We continued to search for answers to the question, What inspires an individual to get into action and, perhaps most importantly, *stay* in action? During my 10 days in the U.K. I traveled on Britrail. I loved this time on the train; no phones, no mail, no meetings—just time to read, reflect, and relax. Two years earlier, my 21-city trips in the U.S. often included short legs on the Greyhound bus. I always put my laundry in a pillow case which I'd take out and use as a pillow. I'd prop up this makeshift pillow on the aisle-seat armrest and lay across the seat with my legs crossed yoga-style against the window of the bus. I vowed that my traveling would stop when I was no longer able to take this position. When I wasn't resting Greyhound-style on train travels in Britain, I was reading Scott Peck's *Different Drum*. I was moved by his discussion of community.

Peck asserted that we will never reach peace or an end to the nuclear arms race through arms negotiations, but that our only chance would be when countries (beginning with individuals) reach true community. RESULTS was constantly looking for something that would help groups make it through the difficult times. Perhaps Peck had identified it in his affirmation of the need for community.

Upon my return from Britain, I wrote 300 RESULTS volunteers and told them how Peck described rare moments in his early life when he experienced what he later came to call community. They're times when people from quite different backgrounds and with diverse viewpoints seemed to magically transcend those differences and experience alignment, acceptance, and love.

Peck identified stages a group had to go through to reach true community. He said that most groups assumed to be in community are really in "pseudo-community"—a state where looking good or pretending there are no internal problems is the order of the day. These groups are unwilling to go through the necessary and often painful steps to achieve true community. As a result, they don't reap the benefits and power they could. In pseudo-community, sharing is shallow in order to maintain the appearance of no conflict. The next step he described as "chaos" where differences are present more than alignment or love.

If a group is to make it to community, it must go through a stage Peck called "emptiness"—a kind of emptying of demands. This emptying allows people to reach a real acceptance of one another and one another's differences. If a group makes it through emptiness, then it reaches true community.

RESULTS was always looking for a format, a structure, a message, a something that can empower individuals in their work. I shared all of this on my Saturday call with Dorsey and the 15 regional coordinators. I confessed that I didn't know where to start. I knew we didn't have time for Peck's full weekend sessions on our one-hour call. Dorsey said that on our particular call we were close to community and that, perhaps, all we had to do was to take a minute each and share what Peck called "our brokenness." In other words, we normally shared everything else with one another on the call *but* that.

I started by sharing something I was going through that I would never have shared ordinarily. I talked about my personal relationship and what I had to do to let go of my martyrdom and compulsive overwork around RESULTS so I could have room for the woman in my life. I talked about working seven days a week and about how when I left the office, I switched the phone to my apartment so I could answer it when it rang there. That way I could have RESULTS with me all the time and have no room for my personal relationship. Others shared their experiences on this same issue.

Then one regional coordinator talked about how his Partner Meeting used to be something he loved to go to. It was a session of openness and love, and it really fed his work in RESULTS. He said that now there were many new partners, including some he didn't even like. And he was starting to see his work in RESULTS as a chore—something he *had* to do. He asked how you could create community when you don't even like some of the people.

I told him that Peck said true community is inclusive: if you want to start a community, you should start with a hawk, a dove, a liberal, a conservative, a black person, a white person, a religious person, an atheist, someone wealthy, and someone who is poor. If you can get through pseudo-community, chaos, and emptiness with that group you will have reached true community.

I asked the regional coordinators to get a copy of *Different Drum* and sent copies to the national managers in Britain, Australia, and Canada. We started regional coordinator calls with open sharing, making it a place where we could really talk—especially about the things that discouraged us, be they personal or about RESULTS. We urged regional coordinators to start calls with group leaders in a similar way. We had coaching from Dorsey and others who had successfully brought community into their groups. Some groups brought this into their Partner Meetings—others watched at first.

"Community building has nothing to do with what you *do* to other people," I told the 300 volunteers in a letter, "but has more to do with how you listen and how vulnerable you're willing to be. A group that is in true community radiates aliveness and love. It is a group that others want to be part of. It's a place where people find the support they need to grow as community leaders...."

This quest for wholeness within the organization was preceded by a personal healing I'd nearly missed. My seven-days-a-week work schedule was a blur of compulsion: 9:00 a.m. to 10:00 p.m. on weekdays and eight hours a day on weekends. Work was my priority, and I seldom dealt with my personal life. But at the insistence of a volunteer, herself a parent, I invited my mother and father to come up from Miami to the RESULTS International Conference in Washington, D.C. Up to this point, my father's disappointment in me took the form of a question—"When are you going to lead a natural life?"—which for him meant marriage and children. Neither of my parents understood my work fully until that conference. The time they spent with more than 250 RESULTS volunteers from the U.S., Australia, Canada, and Great Britain; the remarks they heard from Jim Grant, the Director of UNICEF; from their own member of Congress, Dante Fascell; and the other four members of Congress who spoke, changed everything. My sister, brother, and uncle said my father couldn't stop talking about the conference and the work I was doing when he returned home. My father died six months later.

I first received word of his death while I was in Britain on the first leg of an around-the-world trip. On my flight back across the Atlantic for the funeral, I had time to reflect on the importance of my father's visit to the RESULTS conference six months earlier.

In his retirement, my father wrote, edited, typeset, and delivered his own community newspaper, *The West Miami Citizen.* One of the first things I did when I returned to Miami was help my brother and sister finish delivering the last issue he'd published before he'd died. The paper was about 16 pages long and didn't weigh very much. With my brother or sister driving, I'd lean out the window and throw it to someone's front yard. The wind would blow it back toward the car, and I had to get out and throw it again. My father delivered several thousand copies each month by himself at age 76 and with a pacemaker. Delivering those newspapers gave me a clearer experience of who he was, what his commitment to his community was, and where I'd come from. His visit to the RESULTS International Conference and my experience delivering those newspapers were both healings I nearly missed.

CHAPTER 17

Eliminating the Worst Aspects of Poverty

The Global Poverty Reduction Act

The government of the United States is not in Washington, not in the White House, not in the Capitol...the government of the United States resides in us, we the people. What resides in Washington is the administration of our government.

Mortimer J. Adler

For those of us at RESULTS, 1988 seemed like the year to push for dramatic change in our foreign assistance program—no more tinkering at the edges. Working with Bread for the World and others, we had helped save the International Fund for Agricultural Development, pushed successfully for a tripling of the Child Survival Fund, and we were making progress with the microenterprise poverty lending legislation. But no matter how bold our victories, they only dealt with a small percentage of the overall foreign assistance budget.

In search of our next legislative initiative, Michael Rigby and I started interviewing development experts. The initial idea came from the most unexpected of persons, the head of the Agency for International Development, the institution that seemed to be our greatest impediment. Peter McPherson was stepping down as AID administrator, and he spoke at a luncheon of InterAction, a coalition of U.S.-based private groups which worked in the Third World. McPherson reviewed his tenure as administrator at AID and then looked to the future. "One of the things we've been working on," he said, "is performance targets for the Agency."

The idea that grew from Peter McPherson's comments was simple and exhilarating: All foreign development assistance should contribute to *measurable* reductions in poverty. The United States should state, in measurable terms, what we are trying to achieve with our foreign development assistance and be able to see if what we are doing is contributing to getting us there. It was shocking that things were done any other way.

The need to move in this direction was affirmed again, from an unexpected corner. It was October 14, 1987, two days before World Food Day. I went to The World Bank with several RESULTS staffers for the premiere of a new film on Third World development. Bank President Barber Conable spoke briefly before the film was shown. The previous month Conable had given a major speech committing the Bank to "eliminating poverty in the large countries of Asia by the year 2000." At the end of the program, I walked up to Conable, introduced myself, and referred to his comments about overcoming poverty in large parts of Asia by the year 2000.

"What measurements will we use to determine that the worst aspects of absolute poverty have been eliminated?" I asked.

"Well, I don't know," Conable responded.

"Would we know because of specific increases in female literacy?" I asked.

Conable thought for a moment and answered, "Yes."

"Would we know the worst aspects of poverty were being eliminated," I continued, "because of a specific decrease in infant mortality? Is that how we'd know?"

Again, Conable thought for a moment and replied, "Yes."

Then he grabbed my arm—he didn't touch my arm, or brush my arm—he grabbed my arm and said, "We must have goals! We must have goals! You know," he continued, "we doubled the per capita income in Asia over the last decade, but completely passed over entire regions of that continent. We could double per capita incomes in Asia over the *next* 10 years and completely miss entire regions again." He grabbed my arm a second time and said, "We must not let this happen. We must not let this happen."

I left somewhat stunned by the fact that Conable had not had any real idea of how we would determine if the worst aspects of poverty had been eliminated in Asia. I also left excited about the legislation we were developing. Days later, I attended eight RESULTS regional conferences and had a volunteer come to the front of the room to help reenact my conversation with Conable—arm grabbing and all.

We linked our upcoming legislation, the Global Poverty Reduction Act, to our work with presidential candidates. At the end of 1987, we asked each candidate what he would do to eliminate domestic and world hunger. But our campaign wasn't going very well. We knew that *national* coverage was vital, but almost all of *our* coverage was local. We discussed contacting syndicated columnists. Jennifer Robey, an 18-year-old student volunteering in the office over Christmas break, remembered that *Washington Post* columnist William Raspberry had spoken at her high school graduation in Tulsa, Oklahoma six months earlier. She called Raspberry and could hear him working on his computer as they talked.

"Now, thanks to an outfit called RESULTS," Raspberry wrote in his column the next day, "I've got a new [question to ask presidential candidates]. 'What would you do about domestic and world hunger?' All of these questions deal with profoundly important issues," he continued, "and I think any serious presidential candidate ought to have some general ideas for approaching them."

Jennifer's call to Raspberry shattered my notions about what kind of impact an 18-year-old volunteer can have. She joined the staff as college coordinator nine months later.

In January, the groups wrote thank-you letters to 11 Congressional leaders and their own representatives and senators for the most recent increases in funding for UNICEF, the Child Survival Fund, IFAD, vitamin A, and microenterprise loans for the poor. We knew it was important to thank members of Congress when something positive happened. The kudos, however, flowed in both directions. "Thanks for the great winning team you've put together for your—our—cause," wrote Jim Grant of UNICEF. "The results speak for themselves."

Another letter came from Dr. Alfred Sommer, the leading U.S. authority on Third World applications of vitamin A, who would later become Dean of Johns Hopkins School of Public Health. "My sincere congratulations on the successful influence RESULTS has had on the fiscal year 1988 budget," Sommer wrote. "It was another very important tour de force, one much needed by the world's children."

"RESULTS is the most effective lobby working in Washington today," wrote Rep. Ed Feighan. "I only wish I could work with you on every bill I introduce." And, as if to cheer on our upcoming legislative campaign, Feighan concluded his letter by saying, "RESULTS has proven we can use Congress to help end hunger. And I know that with your help, we can make ending hunger by the year 2000 the official policy of the U.S. government." That was what we were about to try with the Global Poverty Reduction Act, a bill that directed the president to devise a plan whereby U.S. foreign development assistance would contribute *measurably* to eliminating the worst aspects of absolute poverty by the year 2000. The legislation specified three targets by the year 2000 and directed the president to identify additional goals.

The first target in the bill was an under-five mortality rate of 70 per 1000 live births which, for most countries, would be a dramatic reduction in child deaths. The median under-five mortality rate for the poorest 33 countries was more than 200 per 1000, which meant that one out of every five children born alive died by the age of five. As I spoke to groups about the measure, I asked them to imagine all of their friends and relatives who had children under five and then imagine one out of five of the children dying. The child mortality goal was obvious. Any attack on poverty that didn't lower the child death rate was meaningless.

The second goal called for increasing female literacy to 80 percent. This too was a dramatic increase because the female literacy rate in those same 33 poorest countries was just over 20 percent. It was hard to reconcile the fact that in the last part of the 20th century nearly 80 percent of women in more than 30 countries could not read or write. In 1985, the female literacy rate in Burkina Faso was 6 percent, and was 22 percent in Bangladesh. Many development experts pointed to female literacy as the single most important intervention for improving the health of children and families. Female literacy always meant more than just girls reading books. It meant lower mortality rates, fewer births, and improved living conditions.

The third goal in the legislation called for no more than 20 percent of the population to be living below absolute poverty.

But the proposed goals were seen as too ambitious by the Reagan Administration. However, the mortality and literacy goals would be adopted at the World Summit for Children 2 1/2 years later.

We looked for lead sponsors for the Global Poverty Reduction Act from among the members of the House Foreign Affairs Committee. We knew there would be a fight and we had to have people on the committee who would carry the water for us. We found them in two old friends of RESULTS: Rep. Mel Levine (D-CA) and Rep. John Miller (R-WA). Miller recalled his first meeting with RESULTS volunteers after he took office in 1985. He was impressed by the fact that they didn't have anything directly to gain from their lobbying and yet they were very committed.

"This set them apart," Miller remembered, "because most people who come to a congressperson understandably have their own direct interest at heart, whether it's their Social Security check, or their business's tax or regulatory problems. There is nothing wrong with it, it's [just] a fact. Here was a group that was interested in how to make U.S. foreign policy more effective and how to help people around the world, and how to attack poverty. This was the first feature that struck me as unusual and I thought, 'These are good people.'

"The second thing that struck me," Miller continued, "was that not only were they good people, they had a pretty good grasp of the political process and they were realistic! They were not asking for the moon, they were trying to work within the political process. I've had plenty of groups in foreign policy who would say that they wouldn't have a direct interest in an issue, but their form of political activity was to throw blood around my office." Miller's comments were prompted by the actions of groups who opposed his support of the Nicaraguan Contras.

"I had pretty much turned off to these groups," Miller continued. "A member of Congress has an obligation to meet with constituents and to be open, but when constituents are non-civil, I think the obligation starts to erode or even ends. The second thing that impressed me was this was a group involved in foreign policy that actually was trying to use the political process in an aggressive but civil way. That combination impressed me. I decided at the first meeting that I was going to work with this group and stay in touch with them."

After this first meeting with RESULTS in 1985, Miller joined in signing the "Dear Colleague" letter on the immunization briefing led by Levine and was an ardent supporter of our legislative campaigns in 1986 and 1987. By 1988, it was time for him to take the front seat, but as Feighan had found the year before, the driving wasn't always easy.

"As we got into this," Miller continued, "we saw there was this vast structure at AID that didn't want to move and there's an inertia on the Foreign Affairs Committee that basic fundamental reforms are hard to push. For a number of reasons, the bureaucracy, the committee structure that wants to get something passed, members who've formed alliances with this group or that group, [there are] all these hurdles you have to get past. You win one victory, and you find you have to win five to win the war. It's not easy to get something substantial done in foreign aid...I think RESULTS was a great example of effective citizen involvement, where no home runs were ever hit, but a lot of singles were strung together...."

Washington Post columnist Colman McCarthy attested to the first dozen and a half singles RESULTS volunteers hit on the Global Poverty Reduction Act. "Eighteen days after the Global Poverty Reduction Act was introduced, 18 newspapers had run editorials backing it," wrote McCarthy in his syndicated column in the *Post.* " 'The bill merits strong support,' wrote the Everett, Washington, *Herald* on April 6. On the same day, the Portland *Oregonian* said the bill's 'great value' was in 'focusing attention on achievable objectives by the year 2000 in combating poverty.' On April 5, *The Salt Lake Tribune* said the bill 'can help ensure that scarce development-assistance dollars are well spent.' On April 7, the Palo Alto, California, *Times-Tribune* urged support for 'this critical legislation.' If all this has an orchestrated sound," McCarthy continued, "the baton leading the editorial writers was RESULTS...."

McCarthy concluded his column by commenting on the mystery associated with generating an editorial. "An anonymous newspaper junkie has said that editorials are important because people who read them think other people are reading them," McCarthy continued. "How to inspire writers to write remains an unperfected art....RESULTS volunteers—professional amateurs—appear to have figured it out. There's not a rich lobby in Washington that wouldn't trade its limos for the group's achievement: more than 300 editorials in three years and a 3-0 record. Nor is there a lobby that has nobler causes: feeding the hungry and self-sufficiency for the poor."

The day the bill was introduced a letter arrived from RESULTS volunteer

Mark Toogood, who was now serving in the Peace Corps in Belize. "I cannot tell you how inspiring (and thrilling) it is," Mark wrote, "to be hunched over a kerosene lamp reading editorials from all over the world in support of programs that my village friends so desperately need. I am not ashamed to say I usually cry from gratitude and love when I read the editorials that my RESULTS partners are working so hard to generate."

At the end of April the groups wrote their senators, urging them to introduce the Global Poverty Reduction Act in the Senate. As our international conference drew closer, finding a senator to introduce the legislation became a greater priority. We went to our grassroots members to find a chief sponsor because they were the ones who had the relationships with their members of Congress.

Sens. Rudy Boschwitz (R-MN) and Tom Harkin (D-IA) had both expressed interest in introducing the legislation, but neither would commit. Helen Samett, a RESULTS volunteer from Los Angeles, arranged a meeting with Sen. Harkin. Helen was executive secretary to a successful Democratic fundraiser in Los Angeles and had access to the senator and his staff. Whenever Harkin or his campaign fundraiser wanted help from Helen's boss, they had to go through her. Helen arranged a meeting with Harkin for Thursday, May 26, two days before the RESULTS International Conference began. As chair of one of the Senate subcommittees of appropriations, Harkin had an office in both the Hart Senate Office Building and in the Capitol itself. Helen and I met Harkin in his Capitol office.

It was an elegant setting, and Harkin was attentive. He admitted to never having heard of RESULTS. His interest grew when I showed him RESULTS' work with the media, especially the editorials on the House bill and the *Washington Post* piece by Colman McCarthy—a liberal soulmate. After hearing a description of the Global Poverty Reduction Act, he turned to Ed Long, his legislative aide, and asked, "Is there anything in the bill that's a problem?" "No, it's fine," Long answered, although I think he believed the bill was a bit pie-in-the-sky.

"Then I'll introduce it tomorrow," Harkin said.

Helen and I were thrilled. With several hundred RESULTS volunteers about to arrive in Washington, D.C. for our international conference, the timing couldn't be better.

What transpired, though, was 24 hours of wrangling between Sen. Harkin, Sen. Boschwitz and their staffs over which one of them would be the *lead* sponsor. When the dust settled, a coin was flipped and it was agreed that Harkin would be lead sponsor this year and Boschwitz would lead if the bill had to be reintroduced the following year. Brad Gordon, Sen. Boschwitz's legislative aide at the time and someone who went on to be an assistant director of the Arms Control and Disarmament Agency under President Bush, recalled the thinking that went on regarding the measure.

"The bill was obviously more comfortable for liberal Democrats than conservative Republicans because for Republicans, Congress is telling its other branch [in this case the Reagan Administration] what ought to be done, and when it's your president's city and they don't want to do it, obviously it's much harder for a Republican to play that game than for Democrats....the bill made a lot of sense to me, and I went in and briefed Rudy on it....He wanted to know how the Administration was going to react and I told him that more than likely the Administration was going to oppose it, simply because it was telling them how to spend their money. Every Administration doesn't like to be told by Congress how to spend its money and that we could expect heat because of that. And he still said, 'OK, let's do it anyway.' "

By July 22, there were 148 House sponsors and 18 Senate sponsors of the Global Poverty Reduction Act with 24 private groups including CARE, Save the Children, and the U.S. Committee for UNICEF supporting the legislation. But, by now, RESULTS' relationship with AID had begun to sour completely. Four months earlier, the day before the bill was introduced in the House, AID administrator Alan Woods sent a letter to each member of four key committees, saying he disagreed "profoundly" with the proposed legislation.

The Reagan Administration's initial concerns centered on language stating that additional goals selected by the president to measure elimination of the worst aspects of poverty "shall be poverty-oriented and directed toward increasing opportunities for the poor, rather than reflecting, or directed toward, overall economic growth." AID interpreted this wording as opposition to the Administration's embrace of "trickle-down economics," a theory that fueled development thinking. The notion was that growth in the overall economy would trickle down to the poor. "A rising tide lifts all boats," its proponents would argue. But the question for us was, "What if you don't *have* a boat?"

The original intention of Reps. Levine and Miller was to measure the elimination of poverty with indicators that were directly related to changes in living conditions for the poor. Using the Gross National Product (GNP), as was always the case, made no sense. There were too many examples of countries like Oman where the per capita GNP was relatively high ($6,730 in 1985), and yet one out of every six children died before reaching the age of five.

The legislative language referring to overall economic growth was removed before the bill was introduced, and the letter from Woods was subsequently withdrawn. For the next four weeks, AID personnel promised to provide the agency's new position in writing "by the end of the week." But eight weeks later, the day the Senate bill was introduced, the Administration still had not presented its position in writing. But while AID failed to finish its position paper, its staff had time to call each Senate office and ask senators to refrain from supporting the legislation until the Administration had an opportunity to present its position.

Reps. Levine and Miller formally requested the Administration's position in a letter dated June 8. On June 14, Senate Foreign Relations Committee Chairman Claiborne Pell (D-RI) made a similar request. All were ignored.

For nearly two years, AID had taken a beating on the editorial pages over its policies on credit for the poor and global poverty reduction. We knew we could embarrass them again, but that wasn't our objective. We just wanted their position in writing. Additional requests were made for AID's written response on July 12, on July 18, and again on July 22. We let them know we were preparing a packet for editorial writers criticizing the agency for its public silence and private opposition. We said we would not send the packet to our groups if AID would respond in writing.

On Friday, July 22, the packets were mailed to group leaders with an unusual request plastered across the top of the cover letter: "PLEASE DON'T DO ANYTHING UNTIL YOU HEAR FROM US." We gave the agency until Monday, July 25 to produce the letter promised four months earlier and set up a hot-line telephone taped message in my apartment that the groups could call for updated information. At the end of the day on Monday, July 25, the groups were given the go-ahead to launch the editorial campaign. But the action was halted six days later when we received word that Democratic presidential candidate Michael Dukakis was endorsing the legislation. AID administrator Woods's reply arrived that same day.

"I regret taking this long to respond," Woods wrote Rep. Miller, "but the complexity of the bill made it very difficult for me to give you a quick response....it is our sense that the operational sections of the bill are too unclear and so ambitious as to require a more extensive look. It is our hope that the authorizing committees will be able to give this bill a thorough review during the next year....The subject of global poverty, which is central to the agency's current mandate, is too important to be treated in an atmosphere of haste."

Haste? Our first reaction to AID's response would have been to laugh if it weren't so sad. We wondered how many bureaucratic hours were spent writing the half-page letter.

Nine days later, the bill's lead Republican sponsors, Sen. Boschwitz and Rep. Miller, urged their Republican colleagues in Congress to join in a letter to Vice President Bush, urging him to endorse the legislation.

As we fought for the lives of our global family, we joined with a member of our immediate family as he faced his own death. Days before the Dukakis endorsement, I wrote the groups that Cameron Duncan, who had left the RESULTS staff at the end of 1986 after being diagnosed with AIDS, was now diagnosed as having cancer and had opted not to undergo chemotherapy. I urged love notes from the 100 groups because phone calls might be too much for him.

Several weeks later I drove to Maine and spent two days with Cameron. He was not able to take solid foods and had been on liquids for many weeks. His emaciated body looked like the starving people we had worked together to help. I remember his gut-wrenching sobs the moment he saw me. We cried together, sang together, spoke and sat in silence. We knew it was the last time we would be together. RESULTS volunteer Jess Regelson Blum and her family had been with Cameron for several weeks, and Jess had been reading the cards and letters sent to Cameron. The pile was very high.

I sat on Cameron's bed, coaching Raul Julia over the phone for a *Today* show appearance with Rep. Miller on the Global Poverty Reduction Act. "Don't let Raul get too caught in the details of the bill," Cameron insisted. "He should focus on the vision." Cameron's coaching, even in his last days, reminded me of the gift he shared with so many in RESULTS.

"Better than anyone I knew," recalled Michael Rubinstein, "Cameron could hold the vision and inspiration in one hand and the nuts and bolts and the how-to's in the other. He had a way of looking deeply into your eyes as if to see the very core of your being, and to support you with love and appreciation."

When Cameron first told me of his cancer and his decision not to have chemotherapy, he let me know he was leaving half of his estate to RESULTS, which he estimated would amount to $60,000. He would leave it to Dorsey and me and the Board to decide what to do with the money. During my visit to Maine, Cameron and I went to a nearby beach and talked about a media award to be presented each year in his name at the RESULTS International Conference.

When it was time for me to leave Maine and Cameron there was a sadness we felt because we didn't want to stop playing and working together, but there was a certain completeness. When Cameron was on staff he often signed his letters "Thrive and Beam." Dorsey and I talked with him on the phone a week after my visit to Maine. He wasn't exactly thriving, but he was still beaming. I don't think he knew any other way.

Cameron was taking morphine to ease the pain, but I could tell he was giving his all to be with us. He shared a memory from Dorsey's visit four or five weeks earlier. After the visit, Cameron had taken Dorsey to the little bus station near his home so she could return to Boston. "Dorsey," he said in our last phone conversation, "I can still picture you standing at the bus station like a little ice cream cone waiting for the bus to come." I didn't really know anyone else who talked like that. His delight in people and in life was obvious and touched us all.

Two weeks after my visit to Maine, I boarded a plane to London en route to a conference on credit for rural women which was held in Bangladesh. This was the second time I tried to get to Bangladesh. I had gone the year before, but only made it as far as London. Upon getting word of the death of my father, I had returned to the U.S. for the funeral and learned several days later that the Bangladesh conference was postponed due to rioting in Dhaka. On this second trip, again I only made it as far as London. This time I was turned around due to flooding in Bangladesh. I slept on chairs at London's Heathrow Airport Saturday night and took a Sunday flight back to Washington. After a hard sleep Sunday night, I was awakened on September 5, Labor Day.

The call I knew was coming, but didn't want to get, came that Labor Day morning about two weeks after my return from Maine. I remember Cameron's father's exact words, "Cameron passed at 7:00 a.m. this morning." Cameron's contribution was the very special light he brought to life. It isn't possible to reconcile that light being snuffed out at age 34. But in some sense, it wasn't snuffed out—it's in each one of us whose life he touched. Perhaps Atlanta RESULTS leader Steve Valk expressed it best.

"I don't know how to explain this, and perhaps it sounds a bit corny," Steve offered, "but my work with RESULTS has played a big part in my rediscovering my faith. A few years ago, Sara and I joined a Catholic Church that is known in the community for its outreach to persons with AIDS. The RESULTS community comes together for a higher purpose: ending hunger. I finally saw the path that I could take to do God's work in the world, and working with RESULTS showed me that I need the support of a community of people who share a similar vision.

"One of those people, especially in the early years, was Cameron Duncan, who supported me with weekly phone calls when I became regional coordinator of the Southeast. Cameron's death from AIDS was a blow to me and everyone in RESULTS. When our first son was born, I thought of people that I'd want him to be like, and Cameron came to mind immediately. Down at our church, everyone is just crazy about our little Cameron, just as everyone was crazy about his namesake."

The day Cameron died, two more editorials were published on the Global Poverty Reduction Act. Support for the measure and reaction to the U.S. Agency for International Development's resistance were both strong.

"Administrator Woods, a Reagan appointee, says only that the act should not be 'treated in an atmosphere of haste,' " commented the *Atlanta Journal* and the *Atlanta Constitution* that day on their joint editorial page. "But each day's delay has tragic consequences: in the Third World, [40,000] children die every day of hunger and hunger-related diseases."

"Alan Woods insisted in a recent letter to Congressional cosponsors that more time is needed to study the issue. Poppycock," wrote the *Santa Barbara News-Press* the same day.

As always, behind each editorial was a story of civic courage. Columbia, South Carolina partner Marjorie Trifon's experience was like that of so many other RESULTS leaders around the country. "I was terrified to call the editorial writer at *The State* in Columbia, South Carolina," Marjorie recalled, commenting on her first action with the media. "Kathy Fitzsimmons, my regional coordinator, supported me over the phone. She told me to call the editorial writer, and even though I was afraid, I said that I would make the call.

"But really, I was terrified that I would say something stupid," Marjorie continued, "and the editorial writer would laugh at me. I sat at that desk and wrote out what Kathy said. I'd pick up the telephone, dial the number, hear the ringing and then hang up as quick as I could. Maybe what I needed was a cup of coffee first. I'd grind the beans, give myself a treat and then study the packet again. Then I would walk into the bathroom, comb my hair and touch up my make-up. Maybe if I looked right the phone call would go smoothly. I'd call Kathy and wait for her to call me back. I couldn't do this alone. I did this routine for a couple of days just trying to build up the courage.

"When I finally called, Barbara Stalnaker answered, said 'editorial desk' and told me the person to talk to was Mr. Krell. I thought, 'Uh huh, he's probably there right now and she's the stone wall I have to get around.' I started doing my Southerner number with her, trying to make small talk. I wanted to win her over and let her know that I wasn't a kook, but someone Mr. Krell would want to talk to. She told me to call back and that the morning was best because he wasn't on deadline. My agony was momentarily relieved, but I still had this black cloud. I knew I had to get through to him and it wouldn't go away until I did.

"The next morning there was more dialing, more coffee, more make-up, and then I finally said, 'that's enough, I'm just going to do it.' I called him up and was reading from this card that I had written from my conversations with Kathy. I remembered to be brief and tried not to bore him. To my great surprise he said yes he would look at a packet. I asked if I could bring it over and he said yes again.

"I decided to put on my navy blue suit with my red silk blouse, my most smashing outfit. When I got to the newspaper, I was struck by the beauty of the building and how plush the offices were. I was very nervous but thought 'this will soon be over.' It was a little like being in a trance. I went in and asked for Mr. Krell. I walked to his office, introduced myself, and handed over the packet I had highlighted for him.

"He had a very courteous way about him. I commented on a newspaper award hanging on his wall. I was trying very much not to be the robot I felt like. The meeting was no longer than five minutes, and he let me know that he would have to discuss the issue with the editorial board. I thanked him and walked down the hall, listening to the castanets in my head which were playing the tune, 'I didn't say it clearly enough; he didn't like me; I wonder if he really will talk to the editorial board; I forgot to tell him some important points; I wonder if he secretly loves AID.' When I got to the front desk, I noticed a candy jar. I decided to treat myself. Did I want butterscotch wrapped in clear yellow paper, the chocolate caramel, or perhaps the M&Ms? I decided to reward myself with all three.

"I went home and waited for him to call. A week went by. The silence was deafening. I wondered if he'd think I was too pushy if I called him back. I wondered if he'd forget if I didn't. Calling back was as tough as making the first call.

"He answered the phone, and I asked if he remembered the packet I'd brought the week before.

'Yes,' he said.

'I'm calling to see if the paper is going to run an editorial,' I told him.

'It's in the pipeline,' he answered.

I had no idea what he was talking about. 'Does that mean you're going to write it?' I asked.

'I've already written it,' he said, 'but I don't know when it's going to run.'

'Could I call you later to find out?' I asked.

'Yes,' he answered. 'If it hasn't run in a few days, call me.'

"Every morning I grabbed the newspaper. I couldn't turn to the editorial page fast enough. When it wasn't there my stomach tightened. The day it was finally in, I was stuttering with excitement. I called my sister, I called Kathy, I called the RESULTS office. I kept reading the editorial over and over. I got three phone calls that night from others in Columbia who were watching the paper for me."

The State editorial asserted, "AID administrator Alan Woods, an appointee of outgoing President Reagan, says the legislation should not be treated in an atmosphere of haste...Haste indeed! What about the [40,000] Third World children who, according to UNICEF, die every day because of starvation and hunger-related diseases?"

With AID opposed to the measure, Vice President Bush wasn't likely to endorse the bill unless we were able to make it a national issue. But Willie Horton and the Pledge of Allegiance were the national news during the 1988 elections, and we had our work cut out for us. On our September 17 conference call, volunteers targeted newspaper and television editorials, radio interviews, and letters to the editor.

"If a growing number of senators and representatives prevail," wrote the *Milwaukee Journal*, "the next President of the United States will be compelled to draft a plan for reducing poverty around the globe. Democratic nominee Michael Dukakis has endorsed the concept. Will Vice President George Bush do the same?...He should, for the commitment to diminishing human misery knows no partisan bounds...."

On October 11, a letter was delivered to the White House, signed by 36 Republican members of Congress, urging Vice President Bush to endorse the legislation. By then there were 191 House cosponsors, 26 Senate cosponsors and 46 supporters from private voluntary organizations.

But with Congress adjourned, *The State* in South Carolina summed up the 1988 outcome best. "Michael Dukakis has endorsed the Global Poverty Reduction Act. At last count, 26 senators and [191] House members, including South Carolina's John Spratt, Liz Patterson, and Floyd Spence, had signed on as cosponsors. Regrettably, they must now serve as pallbearers."

With Congress adjourned and returning home for the election, RESULTS actively worked for the bill's reintroduction in the next Congress. Barbara Charbonnet's interaction with Rep. Marge Roukema (R-NJ) at a campaign stop told part of the story.

"For some reason," recalled Barbara, a mom and part-time staff member of RESULTS in 1988, "I've never felt quite good enough. I grew up in an upper-middle-class family of five in New Orleans in the '50s and '60s. I went to a private Catholic girls' convent school for 14 years—14 years with the same 34 girls and a rotation of nuns that hadn't varied in generations.

"My images of God were not complicated," Barbara continued. "I was to love and serve God, as catechism taught, which meant, 'Be good, pray, and you'll get what you deserve.' I took this very seriously. I was at the top of my class, I took care of my little brothers, and worked at the Crippled Children's Hospital on Sundays, teaching catechism to retarded and disabled kids.

"When I was 16, my mother had a stroke from which she never fully recovered. This was the beginning of the end for me. I went to church every day for months, but God did not answer my prayers to heal her. I had been betrayed big-time. My departure for college the summer after Kent State saw a young woman with a lot of questions about right and wrong, about morality and immorality.

"Within four years, the disappointment was complete. I was a hippie resigned to living within a system that didn't work, a God that didn't care, and a life that had no meaning. I started on a spiritual journey through a community called Pathwork. It put me on the road to forgiveness and self-love.

"Enter Ken, whom I had known for years in Pathwork, and enter RESULTS. I was disdainful of RESULTS for a while. Waitressing three to four nights a week, acting classes, auditions, and a budding romance left little time for social activism. I thought Ken was a 'very good person' for doing this hunger work.

"One night, while Ken was at one of his RESULTS meetings, I was home alone watching TV. It was during the height of the Ethiopian famine in 1984-85. I watched a BBC documentary about what was going on there. I was very upset by what I saw. All my outrage about life's injustices rushed to the surface. When Ken came home, I asked him to tell me about RESULTS. I knew I was a partner from that moment on. RESULTS allowed me to express everything I had to give. I am a junkie for feeling effective, for feeling that I make a difference."

One of Barbara's clearest experiences of making a difference was an unexpected encounter on a train platform. By this time, she and Ken were married and had a little girl. "It was the day before the 1988 election," Barbara recalled, "at 7:30 in the morning. Our daughter Whitney was 16 months old, and I had to drive Ken to the train station every morning for his commute to work in New York City. After the train pulled out, I noticed my congresswoman, Marge Roukema, campaigning on the platform. I had just had a letter published in *The Record* about the Global Poverty Reduction Act. Despite our efforts to meet with Marge about the bill and conversations with her aides, she had not yet, many months after its introduction, signed on as one of the 191 cosponsors of the bill. Now was my chance to talk to her about it. Not even taking a moment to consider whether or not I had brushed my hair that morning, I jumped out of the car, leaving Whitney in the car seat, and rushed over to her before she departed. 'Marge,' I said, introducing myself, 'I want to ask you about a bill in Congress that you haven't cosponsored and that I've been writing you about. It's a very important bill and one that is relevant to the work you are committed to doing on the Select Committee on Hunger.' "

Roukema was the senior Republican on the hunger committee.

" 'It's about the Global Poverty Reduction Act,' I explained. 'Did you see the letter to the editor I wrote that was published a few weeks ago?' "

" 'Oh,' Rep. Roukema responded, 'I haven't had time to read your letter yet, I've been so busy campaigning, but one of my aides did put it on my desk and I will read it when I get back to Washington.' "

" 'Can I tell you a little about the legislation?' I asked.

"After a quickie Laser Talk on the subject the congresswoman responded, 'Well, I think the bill must be asking for a lot of money, otherwise I would have signed on by now. It sounds too good.'

" 'No,' I said, 'The bill is not an appropriations bill, it only asks that we hold ourselves accountable for the foreign aid money that we do spend by setting up goals by which we could measure whether it's working or not.'

" 'Well,' she said, 'it must be a partisan issue. Only Democrats are signing on to the bill.'

" 'No,' I countered, 'it has support from both sides of the aisle,' and I named a few of the lead Republicans on the bill. 'Marge,' I said, 'I would like you to cosponsor the bill when it is reintroduced next year. I am *sure* you will be reelected tomorrow, and I want you to know that there are people like me out here who want foreign aid to work and want to save children's lives.'

" 'Oh you dear,' she said, leaning into my car to see the baby. 'Let me give your daughter one of my campaign pins,' she said, pinning a 'Reelect Roukema' button on her lapel this frosty November morning.

" 'Thank you,' I said, getting back into my car, still unsure that she would respond positively to my request. Nonetheless, it was a great way to have started the day. I had practiced my speaking enough that I could do just what

I had done. I was really proud of myself. And two months later, when the bill was reintroduced in the new Congress, Congresswoman Roukema was the fourteenth cosponsor on the list. I *had* done a good job!"

That train platform was an important part of Barbara's journey to reclaim her democracy—and an important part of the journey of the Global Poverty Reduction Act.

CHAPTER 18

The Global Poverty Reduction Act: Part II

If there is a mystical chord in democracy, it probably revolves around the notion that unexpected music can resonate from politics when people are pursuing questions larger than self... I have seen that ennobling effect in people many, many times—expressed by those who found themselves engaged in genuine acts of democratic expression, who claimed their right to define the larger destiny of their community, their nations.

William Greider, Who Will Tell the People?

A review of the U.S. foreign aid program had been called for by House Foreign Affairs Committee Chairman Dante Fascell in 1988 and was being carried out by Reps. Lee Hamilton and Ben Gilman. This Congressional review prompted similar efforts from Michigan State University and other groups of development experts who wanted to have input on new directions for our foreign assistance program. The Global Poverty Reduction Act was RESULTS' entry into the mix of proposals.

The *State of the World's Children 1989* report, released at the end of 1988, spoke about the Global Poverty Reduction Act and the support that had built up over the preceding year. "In other words," the section from the UNICEF report concluded, "the Global Poverty Reduction Act (GPRA) is an example of the public interest in seeing real aid used for real development."

At the time of the UNICEF report's release there was intense pressure to modify the legislation. Various forces were at work. One was a sincere desire to improve the bill, but another was the pressure from AID, from certain Hill staffers and from some within the private voluntary organizations to kill or at least weaken the measure. This was out of a concern that the bill was too ambitious and a concern that other legislative proposals could easily be smothered by the support we were building. RESULTS performed a high-wire act in the development community. On the one hand, we played the role of pusher and prodder—always trying to break new ground. But on the other hand, we had to find ways to be part of a consensus. The difficult part was knowing when we should continue to push and when it was time to accept the current reality.

Michael Rigby and I agreed that we had to see what modifications were being called for, but we promised the RESULTS groups we would never cut the heart out of the measure. RESULTS sent a letter to 160 people from the private voluntary organizations, international agencies, academia, AID, and the Hill, asking for written comments on the GPRA by January 3. We scheduled a consultation for January 6.

After the consultation, Reps. Levine and Miller weren't convinced that a compelling case had been made for any modifications, and they decided to reintroduce the Global Poverty Reduction Act without any changes. They believed that it was important to have their bill introduced before the Hamilton/Gilman working group on foreign assistance released its report because once the Hamilton/Gilman report was out, committee members would be expected to support its findings. We were thrilled with their decision.

George Bush was inaugurated President of the United States on January 20, 1989, and on that same day, the Global Poverty Reduction Act was reintroduced in the House of Representatives. Three weeks later, the first packet for editorial writers was mailed to RESULTS groups. We hit hard at what we saw as the deficiencies in the Hamilton/Gilman report and other reports released around the same time. Although each of the reports had its own special contribution to make, all of them seemed to be devoid of one key element—a compelling vision. None of them called for eliminating the worst aspects of poverty by the turn of the century as the Global Poverty Reduction Act did. The omission was understandable. Avoiding a major offensive against poverty was the result of a deep resignation—a sense that we didn't know what worked. Ultimately it was a deficiency of vision.

RESULTS volunteers constantly struggled with this issue of vision.

"Sen. Proxmire, our liberal Democratic senator, had never accepted any of the requests we made of him over the last two years," recalled Jack Waters of Milwaukee, Wisconsin. "During our meeting with him in a hotel lobby in Waukesha, Wisconsin, we were talking about immunizing children and increasing food production. At one point, Sen. Proxmire said he felt our cause was noble, but he didn't think it was possible to end hunger within one generation, possibly it would take two or three. At that point I said, 'Senator, you probably know better than I, but how many people in 1961 thought we could put a man on the moon by the end of the decade? It probably wasn't many, but it was the vision of achieving this goal that drove us as a government and as a people to persevere and achieve that goal.'

" 'At some point,' I continued, 'you had seen that the best way you could make a difference in the world was to become a senator. And from the time you set that goal for yourself until it was achieved, you had to overcome many obstacles. You didn't allow the roadblocks to stop you, but you kept your vision in front of you and broke through the barriers. After much persistence you finally achieved your goal and become a United States Senator...that is all we're talking about. We have a vision of a world free from hunger and disease. The goal of immunizing the world's children by 1990 and increasing food production in the poorest food-deficit countries are rungs on a ladder—obstacles to overcome on the way toward our vision.'

"Shortly after that the meeting ended. As we were walking to our car, Wendy Sexton turned to me and said, 'You know, Jack, when you began talking about vision I thought for sure you were going to lose him. But it was as if for a second he looked away and remembered why he had become a senator.'

I would like to say that from that point forward Sen. Proxmire did everything we requested," Jack continued. "He did not. But I do know that the following May, when 12 citizens from Wisconsin met with him in Washington, he did accept all of our requests, and I know that at least for a brief period of time during our meeting in that hotel lobby he remembered why he became a senator. For me, that is one of the greatest gifts of RESULTS; that a 28-year-old insurance salesman from Milwaukee, Wisconsin could remind a U.S. senator what he was committed to."

RESULTS volunteers around the country set out to communicate their vision to members of Congress, especially their senators. One of the Indiana partners who met with Sen. Richard Lugar was Nick Arena. "As a child, my experience of hunger and poverty was limited," recalled Nick, an investment banker from Dayton, Ohio, who started in Steve Arnold's RESULTS group in Bloomington, Indiana. "My father's parents were immigrants from Italy. My grandmother would tell me stories of how little there was to eat 'back in the old country.' She was the oldest of eight children. Her brother, my great uncle, is retarded due to a vicious bout with scarlet fever on the steerage class boat they took from Italy to Ellis Island. There was no medicine to deal with scarlet fever or any other illnesses on the boat. My grandmother also showed me pictures of a brother of hers who had died of measles when he was four. She considered herself fortunate just to have lost one brother when other families she knew had lost several children due to diseases. At the time, I could not imagine other children dying from diseases my brothers and I had easily overcome."

Nick's story mirrors one from my own family. The first thing my maternal grandparents, Joseph and Sophie Rosenthal, had to do when they arrived in the United States from Romania in about 1910 was to arrange for the burial of their first child. One of my aunts told me later that my grandparents were lucky the child had died only 48 hours from shore or they would have had to have her buried at sea. The preventable childhood diseases and malnutrition that take so many lives in the Third World are not as distant as they seem. They're in our own families, only one or two generations removed.

"One of my scariest experiences happened in 1989," Nick Arena continued. "My son had been born the previous May and my participation with RESULTS was minimal. The RESULTS group leader Steve Arnold called one morning to say that Sen. Lugar would be in town, autographing his new book at a local bookstore. Steve asked if I would come to speak to the senator about the Global Poverty Reduction Act. I agreed. I arrived at the store near closing time, but it was still fairly crowded. The RESULTS partners were huddled in one corner, planning for their meeting. Steve asked me again if I would speak with Lugar on the GPRA. Steve gave me some coaching on how the bill called for U.S. foreign aid to get to the poorest of the poor and called for the U.S. to play a leadership role in ending the worst aspects of poverty by the end of the century. I learned that Lugar was on the fence and that hearing from constituents could make a difference. I got in line with my fussing six-month-old son. It was his first meeting with Sen. Lugar, too. I became scared about having to make the difference with Lugar. Who was I? Someone else should be doing this—surely someone who didn't have a crying baby in their arms. My turn came and I gave it all I had. I said that it was awfully lucky for my son to have been born in the U.S. and that my concern was with the fathers and mothers whose children were dying at epidemic rates. I couldn't imagine losing my son, knowing that his death could have been easily prevented. I asked the senator to cosponsor the bill, and he said that he would consider it seriously. He said he shared my vision for parents everywhere to be able to take care of their children. I really felt he meant it and would do something.

"I guess he did," Nick concluded. "Lugar became a cosponsor several weeks later."

By April 14, the cosponsor list had grown to 195 in the House and 34 in the Senate. The next day, the Atlanta RESULTS group produced an important constituent letter to President Bush. "I write to encourage your support of the Global Poverty Reduction Act (HR 594 and S 369)," wrote Jimmy Carter in a letter generated by Steve Valk and his Atlanta RESULTS partners. "The United States cannot afford to remain idle in a world where more than 40,000 people (many of them children) die each day of hunger and related illness," Carter continued in his letter to Bush. "I hope you will take this opportunity to make our country an example to the rest of the developed world by crafting a foreign policy targeted at eliminating the worst aspects of absolute poverty by the year 2000."

The time approached when Chairman Dante Fascell would mark up his foreign aid authorization bill. Reps. Levine and Miller committed to introducing a Global Poverty Reduction Amendment if, as expected, Chairman

Fascell omitted it from his bill. In fact, we expected Fascell not only to omit the language, but to fight the GPRA amendment. Given the level of AID's opposition to the measure, he had little choice. We met with Rep. Levine on April 20.

"If it comes up for a vote, and Rep. Fascell asks for support," Levine told us, "a number of the cosponsors will go with Chairman Fascell, not with us. See what you can do about getting a few more cosponsors on the Foreign Affairs Committee."

Twenty-seven of the 46 Foreign Affairs Committee members were already cosponsors, nearly 60 percent of the committee. We pushed for additional support.

The GPRA amendment was returned from legislative counsel[22] on Monday, May 22. Rep. Levine's aide called that same day. She was under great pressure from Chairman Fascell's staff to weaken the measure by taking out the specific mortality, literacy, and reduction of poverty goals. This was where the real horse-trading began. "Would you be willing to accept a weaker version of the amendment?" she asked, attempting to head off a committee fight with the chairman. "Would you accept an amendment that said goals are to be set in the area of child mortality, literacy, and poverty, but that AID will determine what they should be?"

It was one of those moments of truth. The heart of what we'd been working on for 14 months could be thrown out the window in one phone conversation. AID had said repeatedly that the goals in our bill were too ambitious. We believed that the agency was unwilling to be pushed because it didn't see its mandate as reaching the poorest of the poor.

We had delivered nearly two-thirds of the committee as cosponsors, 205 cosponsors in the full House, and support in more than 80 editorials. I thought we deserved the chance to have a full hearing. "If RESULTS volunteers who are on their jobs right now as teachers, insurance salespersons, and computer technicians got home and found out that I'd accepted this weakening," I said, "they'd throw me out!"

The amendment was not weakened, but the attempts continued when the committee actually met for markup.

Two days later, on Wednesday, May 24, markup began in the House Foreign Affairs Committee with 12 GPRA cosponsors present, 11 non-sponsors present, and 17 GPRA cosponsors absent. By now there was no question that Chairman Fascell planned to oppose the amendment. Things didn't look good. "Is *this* how it ends?" I thought to myself. "We lose because more than half of our cosponsors aren't even in the room." I dashed out, called Michael

[22]Legislative counsel is a body of the House and Senate which takes draft legislation and puts it in proper legal language prior to its being introduced as a bill or offered as an amendment.

Rigby and my executive assistant, David Schnetzer, and asked them to phone each of the committee cosponsors who were absent. When I returned, Rep. Bereuter (R-NE) was offering an amendment on poverty alleviation. Good intentions, but it had no teeth. It was accepted. Then the committee left the room for a vote on the floor of the House.

When the committee returned, more of the cosponsors were there and Reps. Levine and Miller offered their amendment. "Why do we need this?" Chairman Fascell asked with an air of irritation. "We just agreed to an amendment by Rep. Bereuter on poverty alleviation."

Reps. Levine and Miller responded, but Fascell didn't back off. He called on Bereuter. "I know there's been a major grassroots effort by RESULTS, and I respect their work," said Rep. Bereuter, "but I've not become a cosponsor because I have some questions about the bill."

Bereuter asked if the bill was too paternalistic in telling other countries what to do, and he wanted to know if the goals were too ambitious. But Levine and Miller had done their homework.

"The World Health Organization (WHO) and UNICEF's Joint Committee on Health Policy had agreed to goals for the year 2000 including two which are almost identical to the first two in this amendment, the goals on child mortality and female literacy," Levine answered. "These goals," Levine said, quoting the joint committee, "are scientifically and technically sound and socially acceptable and goals which the international community finds are of the highest priority among those which could be accomplished."

"If I understand my colleagues correctly," Bereuter concluded, "I plan to vote for this amendment."

Chairman Fascell called for the vote.

"All in favor say aye," Fascell bellowed.

The support was strong.

"All opposed, nay," Fascell called out.

There was silence—a very beautiful silence.

"The ayes have it. The amendment is adopted," Fascell announced, slamming his gavel and calling for the next amendment.

The person next to me leaned over and whispered, "Fascell voted for it."

"Did he really?" I asked. "I wasn't watching his mouth."

"Yes," he answered, "Fascell voted for it." Other folks in the room from the private groups smiled, offered a thumbs-up, and whispered congratulations. Pizzas and flowers were sent to Reps. Levine, Miller, Fascell, Bereuter, and their staffs.

"Celebrate with your groups, inform your editorial writers, and keep going," I urged in a letter to RESULTS groups several days later. "Continue to get more House cosponsors in case the Administration tries to weaken or kill this section when the foreign aid bill goes to the floor of the House."

But the real fight came later, in the Senate.

On June 29, the foreign aid authorization bill passed in the House of Representatives and included the Global Poverty Reduction Act. Although we didn't support a number of the provisions contained in the foreign aid authorization bill, such as billions of dollars for military foreign aid, we had reason to celebrate the inclusion of the Global Poverty Reduction Act section. A news release was sent by RESULTS, rebutting AID's continued opposition. "Despite solid Congressional backing," the release stated, "the Agency for International Development (AID) expressed its opposition to the measure in a May letter to House Republican lead sponsor John Miller (WA), saying, 'the bill as currently written is unrealistic—an exercise in programmed failure whose targets would not be met.' However, the first two goals are identical to two goals endorsed in a May 22 vote of the Executive Board of the World Health Organization (WHO)....The agency further criticized the bill, saying, 'Only one of the three performance measures offered focuses directly on the reduction of poverty. The others focus directly on the severity of narrow symptoms of poverty.' "Lead Senate sponsor Rudy Boschwitz (R-MN) responded by saying, 'Of course we want to see a real decline in poverty. But a development strategy which fails to also significantly reduce child deaths and increase literacy is not a strategy which is relevant to the problem of poverty.'

"Responding to further complaints about the reliability of data collected on these indicators," the news release concluded, "lead Democratic sponsor Tom Harkin (D-IA) emphasized that 'we must not allow technique to drive policy. In 1960 we didn't have the metals or propulsion to get a man on the moon, but that was not what set the policy. We set the priority and then developed what was needed to achieve it. That's what we must do here.' "

Eight days before the Global Poverty Reduction Act amendment passed in the Foreign Affairs Committee, Michael Rigby, our first legislative director, submitted a letter of resignation. "The last few years working with you, Dorsey, and the rest of the staff and volunteers of RESULTS and the Educational Fund in the United States and overseas have been the most rewarding and satisfying of my life," Michael began. "It has been a great privilege to play a part in the development of this organization, and I am unreservedly proud of what we have accomplished together."

Despite the pride of accomplishment, the unchecked frenzy of activity and the political hardball we'd been playing had taken their toll on Michael.

"The rapid growth of RESULTS," Michael continued, "with the attendant burgeoning responsibilities have exhausted my resources, and I find myself no longer able to balance my responsibility to myself and to my family with the demands of the job." The pace in the office was unrelenting and my management style was worse. During Michael's 2 1/2-year tenure I made eight trips to Britain, three trips to West Germany, two trips to Japan, and one trip around the world which included Australia. Between 1985 and 1989, the U.S. RESULTS budget expanded tenfold and the staff eightfold. Initially, my management style was fine, because there was no one to manage. Later I was gracious with volunteers but abrasive and impatient with staff. In my Executive Director's report, given four days after Michael's letter of resignation, I focused on the need for "staff sustainability." What I began to confront was the gap between an organization committed to the well-being of people everywhere and the lack of the same within the office. It wasn't until 12 months later, when Shirley Tainton, Director of RESULTS Australia, came to Washington and became project manager of the World Summit for Children Candlelight Vigils, that we understood what good management was.

Michael agreed to shorten his hours and stay another two months.

The Global Poverty Reduction Act stumbled toward the finish line in the Senate when Sen. Rudy Boschwitz, who had not yet returned from his home state of Minnesota, missed a hurriedly called Foreign Relations Committee markup of the foreign aid authorization bill. Other cosponsors were present, but none was prepared to offer the GPRA amendment. Years later RESULTS began to focus on having each of our members of Congress do more than just cosponsor the bills we were pushing—we wanted as many of them as possible to speak for these issues.

We began plans to have the amendment offered on the Senate floor. Editorial writer packets were mailed to group leaders from Washington, D.C. on Thursday, July 13. At the bottom of the cover letter I scrawled the postscript "Do your magic." Four days later, on Monday, July 17, an editorial published in the *Anchorage Daily News* was faxed to our office—more of the magic that kept me going during the most difficult times.

"Among the motherhood, flag and apple pie ideas in politics," wrote the *Daily News*, "here's a notion that should go on the list. Let's make sure U.S. foreign aid helps eliminate global poverty and save young children's lives. How could anyone object to so noble a goal? But in Washington, D.C., never underestimate the potential for petty disagreement....The House agreed to back those standards. But in working on the foreign aid bill, the Senate Foreign Relations Committee declined to write those goals into law....The standards proposed in the foreign aid bill may be ambitious, but they reflect exactly what we should be trying to accomplish."

"The good news," wrote *The Olympian* of Washington state two days later, "is the House has completed work on both measures and passed them on to the Senate. The bad news is that due to a scheduling mix-up, the Global Poverty Reduction Act has been allowed to fall through the cracks in the Senate committee system. This must be rectified."

"Though the Senate Foreign Relations Committee omitted the global poverty act in the version of the bill it sent to the floor," wrote the *Milwaukee Journal* two days later, "the full Senate can and should remedy the deficiency. Wisconsin's Bob Kasten, as ranking Republican on a Senate subcommittee that can influence the bill, could play a key role if he decides to get behind the global poverty act. So far, though, he has failed to sign on. How about it, Senator?"

Letters went to Sens. Leahy and Kasten, signed by more than 25 private groups urging inclusion of the GPRA in their subcommittee's bill. The foreign operations subcommittee of appropriations did include a section on the global reduction of poverty which called on the administrator of AID to consult with Congress as well as governmental and nongovernmental organizations to "establish a system of quantitative and qualitative indicators of poverty reduction...on a country-by-country basis. These indicators shall include the percentage of persons living below the absolute poverty level, rates of infant and child mortality, rates of literacy for men and women, per capita income and purchasing power, rate of employment, and other factors measuring poverty reduction and economic growth...."

Leahy's provision also required AID to spell out its poverty reduction objectives for each country, the progress being made on these objectives, and steps it will take to achieve them when the agency makes its annual presentation to Congress. While this last section offered some hope, we still were concerned that AID would select goals which presented little vision or challenge.

RESULTS, ironically, seemed to be going in 20 directions at once. With the end of the fiscal year upon us, we pushed on the GPRA, microenterprise lending, UNICEF, and the child survival activities which would grow to $200 million that year. But there were a host of other activities, as well. RESULTS Educational Fund, relatively inactive for a number of years, released its first video, "Overcoming Global Poverty," narrated by Raul Julia and beautifully produced, on a shoestring budget, by RESULTS volunteer Jeffrey Golden.

We faced the tragic deaths of Rep. Mickey Leland, House Select Committee on Hunger staff members Hugh Johnson and Patrice Johnson, and the others who died in a plane crash in Ethiopia. RESULTS and the World Development Movement helped draft identical letters which were sent by members of Congress to U.S. Treasury Secretary Nicholas Brady and by members of Parliament to Brady's counterparts in Britain, Australia, and Canada in preparation for the World Bank and International Monetary Fund meetings to be attended by the world's finance ministers in September 1989. We drafted an op-ed piece with the same messages as the letters being circulated: (1) all World Bank-supported adjustment programs should include specific targets for improvements in child mortality rates, female literacy rates, etc.; (2) structural adjustment policies should include measures that bring positive benefit to those most vulnerable; (3) the World Bank should give greater priority to projects that enhance the economic productivity of the poorest 20 percent (e.g., access to land, irrigation, credit, etc.); and (4) a borrowing country's efforts to reduce poverty should be a major and separate criterion for the allocation of assistance.

Parliamentary leaders from Australia, Britain, Japan, the United States, and West Germany agreed to sign the op-ed piece which we'd titled, "Children aren't the debtors." It was first offered to the *New York Times*. They rejected it. I then offered it to the *Washington Post*. Another rejection. I went next to the *Wall Street Journal* and got our third rejection. It was sent next to the *Christian Science Monitor* for our fourth rejection.

There was little time left, so I asked Jennifer Robey, who'd taken on the additional role of legislative associate with Michael Rigby's departure, to fax it to the *Los Angeles Times*. She talked with them, they changed the title to "Stop Starving the World's Poor to Pay Debts," and published it on September 25. It was reprinted in the *International Herald Tribune*, 10 additional newspapers in the U.S., the *Daily Yomiuri* in Japan, the *Süddeutsche Zeitung* in Germany, the *Financial Review* in Australia, and other papers around the world.

At the beginning of August, I announced that Alex Counts had agreed to become RESULTS Legislative Director upon his return from Bangladesh in October. One of his last achievements as a Fulbright Fellow at Grameen Bank was launching *Grameen Dialogue*, a quarterly newsletter updating the progress of Grameen and its replications around the world.

"I can see an emerging movement of which Grameen is a part, that recognizes poverty to be lack of socio-economic empowerment rather than lack of 'economic growth' or insufficient 'charity,' " Alex Counts wrote in the first issue. "The emergence of this alternative development movement, in its many forms, is one of the most promising things in the world today."

Movement is a word that was in the air at RESULTS. Discussions at our international conference on how to energize a movement were a result of our building frustration with the pace of change. We continued to push for stronger global poverty reduction language in the foreign aid appropriations bill, the only foreign assistance bill that would pass in 1989. But during a late-night Senate vote on the bill, lead sponsor Sen. Rudy Boschwitz, under intense pressure from the Bush Administration, offered the GPRA as a "sense of Congress resolution," which meant that the Senate considered it a good idea, but AID wasn't required to implement it.

"The night of the vote," Boschwitz's former legislative aide Brad Gordon recalled, "there was a lot of intense heat from [acting AID administrator Mark] Edelman. Alan Woods, who was deceased at that point, had been a tremendous friend of Sen. Kit Bond (R-MO). I remember that when it came down to even offering the sense of Congress language on it, Bond got up and made a speech against it. We had been told that if in fact we pushed for the original language in the original bill, Bond was prepared to get up and talk all night about it. So you had a lot of heat coming out of the Administration and the threat of a late-night filibuster, which eventually led Boschwitz to get what we could get in 1989."

At 10:45 p.m. I watched the vote on C-Span on the TV in Boschwitz's outer office and saw this weak version pass. After the vote Boschwitz returned to his office, and I accompanied him down the elevator to the parking garage. I expressed my disappointment and he blasted me for being too pushy.

"I remember you meeting Sen. Boschwitz in the elevator," Gordon continued, "and he was really angry at that point. I think he was angry because of what happened on the floor of the Senate and you were just being a target."

It was painfully clear that we'd pushed to the outer edges of the envelope and that the envelope was too small. The outer edges didn't include room for eliminating the worst aspects of poverty by the year 2000 with specific, measurable goals.

The language in Sen. Leahy's foreign aid appropriations bill was not as specific as we wanted, but it had teeth. Leahy called for AID to set measurable goals in areas such as infant mortality and literacy but didn't mandate specific targets. He left that to AID. Boschwitz's amendment outlined the specific goals, but didn't require AID to use them. Our only hope was the Senate foreign aid appropriations bill which included Sen. Leahy's language. We needed the House and Senate conferees to adopt the Senate language in conference where the differences between the two bills would be worked out.

Reps. Levine and Miller and Sens. Boschwitz and Harkin sent letters to the chairs and ranking Republicans on the foreign aid subcommittees of appropriations, asking them to accept the Senate language.

By November 3, the House/Senate conference was complete. We got the binding language calling on AID to set goals, not the sense of Congress resolution. It was the end of a lobbying campaign that had lasted nearly two years.

When we confronted resistance to the GPRA and its call for structural change in our foreign aid program, we shouldn't have been surprised. But we were. Our citizen advocacy wasn't enjoying clear wins anymore. We were getting closer to systemic issues. This time the system wasn't working as well for the poor and thwarted anyone who wanted it to.

The difficulty we had on the Global Poverty Reduction Act primarily boiled down to the fact that it was seen as too ambitious—too utopian. The Hunger Project's Africa Prize laureate Dr. Bernard Ouedraogo, leader of the grassroots group Six-S, was asked if ending hunger by the turn of the century was utopian.

"I have already had the occasion to see that when one has no utopia," Bernard Ouedraogo responded, "one is dead for the first time—his second death being the biological one. To be afraid of the word utopia is to be afraid of one's self, because man lives by utopias...."

In the end, perhaps this was the greatest gift of RESULTS. The quest for utopias was allowed, even encouraged. We didn't have to be part of the walking dead.

CHAPTER 19

RESULTS Conferences

More Time for Healing

Power, properly understood, is the ability to achieve purpose. It is the strength required to bring about social, political or economic changes. In this sense power is not only desirable but necessary in order to implement the demands of love and justice. One of the greatest problems of history is that the concepts of love and power are usually contrasted as polar opposites. Love is identified as a resignation of power and power with a denial of love....What is needed is a realization that power without love is reckless and abusive and that love without power is sentimental and anemic. Power at its best is love implementing the demands of justice. Justice at its best is love correcting everything that stands against love.

Martin Luther King

David Korten, a leading development thinker and activist, came to Washington from his home in the Philippines and spoke at the 1989 RESULTS International Conference. He was dazzled by the RESULTS volunteers. He went on to a meeting of InterAction, the association of U.S.-based private groups working in the Third World. Upon his return to the Philippines, Korten wrote of his surprise at "the reserve and sometimes hostility with which some people spoke of RESULTS, even while acknowledging your effectiveness in political mobilization. As best I could determine, the negative feelings came from a feeling by some people that their advice to RESULTS had not been heard and that RESULTS sometimes reduced its effectiveness by a lack of willingness to engage in necessary political compromise."

Former Boschwitz aide Brad Gordon distinguished between the civic healing that was going on in RESULTS around the country and the hardball we had to play in Washington, D.C.

"There is a real dichotomy between your grassroots people who are...very earnest and sincere and dedicated folks," Gordon recalled, "and you, who are also very earnest, dedicated and sincere, but who knows how to play hardball. I didn't have the perception that the grassroots people were hardball players. Once you're at the table, it's you that makes it happen. You're the one that's persistent, you're the one on the phone everyday, you're the one who refuses to take what others push on you, and frankly I think RESULTS would be just like any other do-good, quiet organization out there, were it not for your persistence and dedication and the fact that you piss people off. That is your strength."

I knew that I could take certain stands only because of the work of the RESULTS volunteers. Without their prowess with their members of Congress, the local media, and their communities, I would merely be perceived as a wacko. If you have no power, people don't have to deal with you. If you have no power, you can't piss people off. People who have no power are irrelevant politically. My power was from the RESULTS volunteers, and whatever we amassed was amassed in an effort to speak on behalf of the poor.

By the end of 1989, RESULTS finally moved to become a member of InterAction, but I still perceived the charge that we lacked a "willingness to engage in necessary compromise" as a compliment. Excluding tiny loans for destitute women was unacceptable to us. A foreign assistance program devoid of an ambitious and measurable vision was unacceptable to us. We weren't as interested in achieving political compromise as we were in altering the political climate. *My* greatest challenge was to maintain our vision, to be willing to do battle, but not to make disagreements personal.

The RESULTS grassroots network allowed us to take tougher stands, but we realized that that was not enough—something more was needed. At the RESULTS International Conference, we engaged in an open discussion of movements. People lined up at microphones set at the front of the room and had a minute each to offer their suggestions on what was next for RESULTS, especially in the area of movement building.

"It was a great experience," Korten wrote of the conference in his letter. "I was highly impressed by your members. They are among the best informed and committed people I have met anywhere. They are also a joy to be with. The sense of mutual support and appreciation is exhilarating. I have never attended a better organized or conducted meeting that so involved people in a highly participatory way, yet kept right to the point and the schedule. The effectiveness of your leadership was much in evidence. For me, nothing more effectively captured the essence of RESULTS than the statement of Carla Cole: 'Before I met Sam Harris I didn't know who my congressman was. Now he knows who I am!' "

David Cohen, co-director of the Advocacy Institute and former president of Common Cause, once asked me what it was about the culture of RESULTS that allowed us to be so effective with so little time spent haggling among ourselves. I told him that I thought it might be because it's so difficult to get into the RESULTS culture. First you have to hear about a RESULTS presentation, then you have to go to it, then you have to agree to three meetings a month, then you have to take a test. If you make it that far, you're probably ready for action.

At RESULTS conferences, my background as a music teacher was very much in evidence. Part of each conference was taken up with singing. We were one part Mormon Tabernacle Choir, one part Nader's Raiders—perhaps the best singing lobbyists since the civil rights movement. There are some things that just can't be communicated by words alone. Music has the ability to transport, to inspire, to unify. It's been an important element of many movements. Perhaps my greatest joy is standing awash in the glorious sound of 300 RESULTS volunteers singing "The Rose" in three-part harmony.

Our inquiry into movements was part of an organizational introspection coming out of our Global Poverty Reduction Act defeat in 1988, the first year it was introduced. Inspired by excerpts from a 1959 speech by Dr. E.H. Land to the employees of the Polaroid Corporation, I wrote the groups about the extent to which failure, and especially our ability to support each other through our failures, had contributed to making RESULTS what it was. "When I say that RESULTS volunteers had about 600 letters to the editor printed last year," I reminded them, "I'm also saying that 4,000 of us mailed letters that *weren't* published (3,400 failures). When I say that RESULTS volunteers initiated 100 editorials last year, I'm also saying that we requested editorials more than 1,000 times (900 failures)...When I say that attendance at recent education and action meetings nationwide was 1,500, I'm also saying that another 1,000 said they would come but didn't (1,000 failures)....

"I've often referred to RESULTS as an experiment. I've never fully realized until now that experimenters in the physical sciences know their successes come from their failures, but that we experimenters in the *social* sciences often get knocked out of the ring by our failures."

I included the excerpt from Land:

> In the physical sciences, in chemistry and physics and in mathematics, when you work in the lab, you fail, fail, fail, fail. When you've failed enough times, you have 3000-speed film. If you want color film, you have to fail 10 times as many times. Failure here is the very essence of progress.
>
> The secret of science is that it has learned to fail without emotion and embarrassment. A scientist is a person who is a continuous failure....

> But in the social sciences, we start an experiment on how do I make you twice the guy you are, and we fail the first week and everybody laughs. They say, 'Well, he should have known better' or 'He didn't have the background' or 'You can't change human nature' or some such nonsense.
>
> The trouble with experimentation in the social sciences is that we are always guilty about failure....
>
> I want to end up with a company which, socially, is nothing but failure. I want failure all over the place, people failing all day long in some social experiment so that when we look back five years from now and say, 'We have 700 people who never dreamed they could handle languages; another 500 who can handle mathematics; we have made inventors out of people who thought they could never do anything; and we are still failing.'

It was in 1989 that we saw the Chinese student stand in front of the column of tanks in quest of democracy. We only have to stand in front of a pen to write our first letter, in front of a telephone to call our editorial writer, or in front of our member of Congress or Parliament to share our vision for the end of hunger and poverty. Yet it's still something most people are unwilling to do. We came to RESULTS conferences to gather the courage to do these things—to gather the courage to act—which was also the courage to fail.

CHAPTER 20

Getting Coverage on RESULTS

I Love a Parade

In our time, what is at issue is the very nature of humankind, the image we have of our limits and possibilities. History is not yet done with its exploration...of what it means to be human.

C. Wright Mills

We decided to do something about the anonymity we experienced during the 1988 elections, with aides to the presidential candidates asking over and over again, "What is RESULTS?" At the beginning of 1989, we hired Suzy Shure for a three-month consultancy to promote the organization. Suzy, an American who lived in Britain for 11 years, had helped bring RESULTS there and was back in the United States. She is a human dynamo who believes fervently in the promise of RESULTS. One week after starting, she was sitting across from Walter Anderson, editor of *Parade* magazine. Suzy's commitment and enthusiasm and Anderson's hunger for things that work created a powerful synergy.

Within minutes of talking with Suzy, Anderson was on the phone with Edward Klein, who had been editor of the *New York Times Sunday Magazine* for 11 years and now was among *Parade's* contributing writers. "Do you remember the story we talked about—the individual makes a difference?" Anderson asked Klein over the phone. "These people are doing it!" Anderson handed the phone to Suzy, who talked with Klein. While still sitting in Anderson's office, Suzy called me in Washington and set up my first meeting with Ed Klein. By January 27, I was sitting in Klein's New York City apartment, telling the story of RESULTS, a story that would reach *Parade's* 33 million readers.

Klein attended a speech I gave that evening at The Open Center in New York City and a meeting of the local RESULTS group several weeks later. We continued to talk over the phone.

During my first interview with Klein, I spoke of my initial hopelessness and my early involvement in The Hunger Project. Some six weeks later, Klein called to say a line editor wanted to know my connection to est, whose founder, Werner Erhard, had been one of the principal founders of The Hunger Project. In the article Klein would describe est as "a self-empowerment group popular in the 1970s." But that was later. Right now, senior people at *Parade* were furious and questioned my honesty and credibility.

"Had I been hiding my involvement in est?" they wanted to know. "How many people in RESULTS had done est? Did I agree that est was a kind of brainwashing? Would I be willing to disavow my involvement in it?"

It was a harrowing experience. I had gotten a great deal from the est training and related workshops, including an even deeper sense of my own commitment to service. When the value I was getting diminished, my participation stopped. But I wasn't willing to trash it or the experience for anything, not even an article in *Parade.*

I wasn't hiding anything, and the attack was very painful—this guilt by association. Though many of the initial participants in RESULTS had first gotten involved through The Hunger Project or est, they were moved into action by RESULTS' unique model that was created for healing the break between people and government.

RESULTS work had us constantly face the hopelessness felt by so many people, but later I would reflect on the cynicism in the media. It seemed that the media's attitude was: "Since everything is a sham—since life doesn't work and it's not about to—it's the media's job to protect the public from the charlatans." We become much better at the witch hunt for failures and frauds than we are at finding successes.

For now, I asked Art Simon, President of Bread for the World; Paul McCleary, Executive Director of the Christian Children's Fund; Mildred Leet, Co-Director of the Trickle-up Program and other friends and leaders in the anti-hunger community if they would be willing to vouch for my integrity. They said yes and their names were forwarded to *Parade*, but they were never contacted.

The *Parade* article was published on July 23, 1989 with the one-inch headline, "THEY DEFY THE ODDS." The subtitle read, "Washington politicians are besieged daily by lobbyists for every cause. Here's how one group—tackling the enormous problem of world hunger—got results."

Besides more than 700 responses from strangers, letters poured in from former high school students and other friends with whom I'd lost touch.

Perhaps the most moving came from Ken Jenkins, the former principal at North Miami Beach Senior High School in Florida, the high school at which I had taught music almost two decades earlier. "From a beginning guitar class to Capitol Hill in less than 18 years is quite a leap of accomplishment," Jenkins wrote from Appalachian State University in North Carolina. "I remember and retell the story of a young music teacher who, in a flash of impishness, suggested to his principal that one day they switch uniforms. The music teacher was to trade his jeans and guru shirt for coat and tie, while the principal would wear jeans, sandals, beads, and a hippie shirt. They did, and the students in the school had a wonderful day talking about the role reversal. Frankly, the suit the teacher wore that day didn't come close to looking like the suit pictured in *Parade* (7-23-89). The event would have been an unqualified success had the superintendent not chosen that day for a drop-in visit to his maverick principal.

"That same music teacher," Jenkins continued, "had the audacity to propose a mini-course designed to build political awareness in the students at North Miami Beach High School. The same principal had no earthly idea what that course had to do with music instruction, but, somehow, the course got offered. Even then, the music teacher had a vision of his cause, and an unswerving commitment to make a difference in the world. He chose as his vehicle the issue of hunger. The music teacher, two decades later, leads an international organization whose goal is to eradicate world hunger by 2000. The principal now teaches college students, prospective teachers, and principals about the necessity of vision as a vehicle for accomplishing anything beyond the ordinary and routine. What a wonderful example you have provided the man who was once your leader.

"I am pleased at your accomplishments. I am even prouder of the courage you have maintained throughout your career. I coordinate a special scholarship program for prospective teachers in North Carolina here at Appalachian. I try to instill in them a belief in the vitality of vision, and that they will make a difference. Wouldn't it be great if you were to speak to these students, not only about your project, but of the demands of keeping your own dreams alive? Could you see a way to visit the mountains of North Carolina and share a bit of you with them?

"Meanwhile, please accept my deepest respect for what you have done and for what you will do. What an amazing story."

Before the *Parade* article was published, I expressed my excitement about it. I let the groups know that purchasing a full-page ad, the equivalent of the article, would have cost $307,000, nearly three-quarters of our annual budget at the time. I also let them know that *Parade's* 33 million circulation is seven times greater than that of *Time* magazine.

To capitalize on the *Parade* article, we organized trips to start new groups in cities where *Parade* was distributed. We expected hundreds of responses from people who didn't live anywhere near an existing group. For these people, we launched *Entry Point*, our quarterly newsletter. While each issue had two action pages with instructions on writing letters to members of Congress on domestic and global hunger, the title attempted to remind people that writing a letter to a member of Congress was an "entry point," *not* an "ending point," in creating the political will to end hunger.

I had a continuous commitment to inspire myself and the groups, something that I often fulfilled by quoting others. On a train to New York City, I read a column in which A.M. Rosenthal described the *New York Times'* preparations 20 years earlier for the first landing on the moon. The paper ordered one-inch type; "Shouting is one way to express joy," recounted Rosenthal. They commissioned a poem for the front page; "What the poet wrote would count most, but we also wanted to say to our readers, look, this paper does not know how to express how it feels this day," Rosenthal continued. "But like every person who watched, we felt we personally were part of the beauty and achievement, the great soaring. We loved those three men because we knew their adventure was born of the elegance of the human mind and desire. They allowed us to feel part of that elegance. Humanity was loving itself, which does not happen often."

Wasn't that what I saw in the work of RESULTS—the elegance of the human mind and desire—the call for humanity to love itself?

As it turned out, 1989 was the most remarkable year for RESULTS volunteers in the number of pieces they got published. Six-month-old RESULTS Japan generated 15 published pieces; West Germany, 63; Canada, 90; Australia, 172; the U.K., 206; and the U.S., 1,027. That totaled 1,573 pieces globally, or 4.3 published pieces a day generated by RESULTS volunteers—nearly double any previous year.

Each piece was a call for humanity to love itself.

CHAPTER 21

Checking Implementation

Is the Microenterprise Poverty Lending Program Working?

Bill Clinton: *...the South Shore Bank's Good Faith Fund loans to real low-income people, mostly for self-employment ventures—[and it] was based on the work of Muhammad Yunus at the Grameen Bank, in Bangladesh.*

William Greider: *I'm intrigued because with a few eccentric exceptions, I think you're the only politician I've ever encountered who has heard of the Grameen Bank....*

Bill Clinton: *I think Muhammad Yunus should be given a Nobel Prize....Several years ago, this friend of Hillary's arranged for me to meet with Yunus in Washington, and I spent an hour and a half with him. I was just blown away. It was obvious what the parallels were. He made enterprise work. He promoted independence, not dependence...I just loved it. I loved it.*

Interview in Rolling Stone *magazine,*
September 1992

In 1989, RESULTS volunteers vicariously experienced life in a Bangladeshi village through letters from Alex Counts, a RESULTS volunteer who was spending 10 months with Grameen Bank on a Fulbright Scholarship and who would go from Grameen to RESULTS as our legislative director. While a student at Cornell University, Alex had started RESULTS groups on eight college campuses. His long, handwritten letters from a Bangladeshi village were typed and mailed to RESULTS groups around the world. "I now think of development in terms of 'restoration of dignity,' " Alex wrote in his first letter to RESULTS volunteers. "Other indices like increased income, better infrastructure, better services, more immunization, more credit—*may be* correlated to restored dignity. But not always. If incomes rise, but dignity is still suppressed (as with income supplementation, e.g., welfare), I am not impressed. If dignity *is* restored, *real* development occurs, and the appropriate correlates (income, immunization, etc.) do appropriate things. But they play off restored dignity, confidence, and self-esteem.

"Let me give you an example of a different kind of development," Alex continued. "The other day I was walking with a branch manager to Dampara village, where Grameen was doing superb work. We passed a food-for-work road-building project run by a U.S. private voluntary organization under PL 480 [a U.S. food aid program]. The project *was* building a road, and *was* feeding people. But...the dour faces of those working contrasted sharply with the beaming faces of Grameen Bank (GB) borrowers [who] were soon excitedly and proudly bringing me to see their cows bought with GB loans, their new houses built with GB house loans, their children learning at the GB center school. Now, building a road *is* better than just giving out food. But it is nowhere near the *process* going on with GB borrowers."

Alex's letters renewed our resolve to fight for the needs and dignity of people who are poor. But there was another, perhaps deeper, payoff for me and for many others. We had seen the videos and read the reports, but none of us had touched the project—felt the project. Grameen had a "too good to be true" quality about it, especially in a world where nothing seemed to work. Alex was our representative—our eyes and ears. What he reported back to us was inspirational—Grameen was more important than we imagined.

On a separate track, Danielle Yariv was hired by RESULTS Educational Fund to begin a study of how the microenterprise monies appropriated for fiscal year 1988 were being spent. The contrast between what Danielle found in studying AID's implementation of the microenterprise program and the inspiration we found in Alex's letters describing Grameen Bank's version of microenterprise was dramatic.

The RESULTS Educational Fund report "Where Credit is Due" investigated implementation of the microenterprise legislation. During the legislative battle in 1987, the Agency for International Development had fought the concept of providing very small loans to the poorest of the poor. In the end Congress earmarked $50 million for microenterprise lending. Using non-binding report language, Congress targeted businesses owned by women and the poorest 20 percent of the population and recommended that loans not exceed $300. This, of course, meant AID didn't have to comply.

It was a letter from the head of AID stating that the agency had "complied with, and indeed exceeded, both the letter and the spirit of the microenterprise legislation," that gave us the foundation we needed to justify looking into implementation. Danielle studied 10 countries that accounted for 50 percent of the global program. There were visits to three of the countries and a desk study of the other seven. Given AID's resistance to directing tiny loans to the poorest of the poor, we wanted to know if the program was being implemented properly.

Three weeks before the official release date, Reps. Feighan and Gilman and Sen. DeConcini, alarmed by early word of the report's findings, called for a General Accounting Office (GAO) investigation of the program. In their letter to the head of the GAO, the members of Congress cited an AID cable stating that a project in Jordan expected "that the average loan will be in the neighborhood of $15,000 to $20,000."

"[J]ust a tad over $300," said the *Orange County Register.*

"Clearly, changes must be made in the way AID operates and monitors the microenterprise loan program," wrote the *Salt Lake Tribune.* "Congress should insist that AID clean up its act or transfer control of the program to a separate entity truly committed to its principles of helping the poorest of the poor."

Danielle's report was an important ingredient in creating the political will to end hunger. GAO investigators spent their first two weeks at AID, and by the time they arrived at the RESULTS office, they were singing AID's tune: Aren't the poor hard to reach? Doesn't this require too much paperwork? Isn't a great deal of technical assistance required, and isn't that inefficient with such small loans?

We were grateful to have done our own independent assessment and to be able to hand them "Where Credit is Due." Indeed, GAO's findings, released at the beginning of 1991, corroborated our own. "The missions we visited," GAO reported, "did not specifically target their microenterprise projects to the poorest 50 percent of the population or emphasize credit assistance to women or the poorest 20 percent of the population. Also, loans frequently exceeded $300...."

Five months after the GAO study was released, FINCA director John Hatch oversaw the first loan in El Salvador from a large AID contract. Seventeen months later Hatch reported the creation of 707 village banks, loans averaging $52 to more than 18,000 borrowers—95 percent of whom were women—and a repayment rate of 99.7 percent. The stories of transformation would mirror those from Grameen and other similar banks around the world.

"I went to my first meeting and was afraid I could not [take and repay a loan]," said Francisca Rojas, one of the borrowers in El Salvador. "But the bank promoter who was there believed I could do it, and I was so desperate that I tried it."

Francisca had been orphaned at the age of nine and lived by herself in a ditch beside the road. A woman found her, took her home, and put her to work washing and ironing. Francisca ran away when she was 17 and had her first child when she was 18.

With her first loan, Francisca bought spices, noodles, and little ceramic pieces on a tray which she sold at the market. After three loans of $50 each, she had saved $45. "I never saved before," Francisca continued. "I used to earn $17.50 a week. Now I earn from $35 to $53 each week. I can spend almost twice as much for food, live in a much nicer home, buy medicines, and save money. I feel safer now. I sleep calmly at night because I am not so worried about how to pay back a money lender. I don't have to prostrate myself to anyone. I have confidence. When you have been as poor as I have been, there is a lot of shame. Even when I was a child, people wouldn't look at me. I guess they were afraid I would ask them for something. I never had any friends. Now each week I come to our bank meeting. They are glad to see me. Now I have friends. This is the most important thing," she concluded.

Finally, our lobbying and oversight work were beginning to pay off. Fighting for the rights of people like Francisca was the most important thing.

CHAPTER 22

Shining a Light on the Needs of Children

The 1990 World Summit for Children Candlelight Vigils

This is the true joy in life, being used for a purpose recognized by yourself as a mighty one; being a force of nature instead of a feverish selfish little clod of ailments and grievances complaining that the world will not devote itself to making you happy.

I am of the opinion that my life belongs to the whole community, and as long as I live, it is my privilege to do for it whatever I can.

I want to be thoroughly used up when I die, for the harder I work the more I live. I rejoice in life for its own sake. Life is no brief candle to me. It is a sort of splendid torch which I have got hold of for the moment, and I want to make it burn as brightly as possible before handing it on to future generations.

George Bernard Shaw, Man and Superman

Clearly, 1990 was a year of dramatic change in RESULTS—a year in which we literally recreated ourselves in an attempt to realize our vision of eliminating the worst aspects of poverty. The first to seize the initiative was our neighbor to the north, RESULTS Canada.

"I was on the beach in Dakar, Senegal, with my father," recalled Jean

François Tardif, a RESULTS leader from Canada. "At the age of 12, I had already started to think about what I would like to do in life, about how I, a child with some ideas of my own...would make a tangible difference in society. That afternoon, for the first time, I was communicating aloud my desire to be able one day to serve some social justice purpose. My father, a career diplomat with foreign policy experience, had just been explaining that those who truly influence society are the ones who go beyond the theory and are willing to become conversant with the less inspiring details of how things work in practice. I would recall that calm tropical afternoon 20 years later with an amused albeit nostalgic smile. Perhaps the kind of smile one reserves for the naive, 20th-century Don Quixotes.

"Not surprisingly, when I heard about RESULTS for the first time, my interest was automatically triggered," Jean François continued. "I had attended several universities, honing my skills in the area of public policy and public administration. But despite the now-extensive knowledge of the practical details of government programs that three master's degrees could provide and despite some experience in student activism, I still felt helpless. RESULTS seemed to offer something beyond the two avenues I had been familiar with up to that point: the mere academic identification of ideal solutions and the standard social activist's expression of outrage.

"The guests at the introductory RESULTS evening had had the opportunity to experience a real meeting with a real action. The messages had been communicated clearly, and like everyone else in the room, I knew this was not academic, this was not a rally, this was simply citizens exercising, somewhat awkwardly perhaps, their power to make a difference with government. At the end of the evening, one more partner was still needed to start a group. I distinctly saw that if I kept on holding out just because participating might be inconvenient, the idea of a RESULTS group in Ottawa would be shelved. Grudgingly, I consented to become a partner.

"The first month was not easy, especially because I had taken some liberty with the RESULTS format at the introductory evening: given no one had the address of the local French-language newspaper, I had a wonderful excuse not to draft my letter that evening. The following month I, as one of the four partners, would have to face the participants. I could not do that without having sent my letter. So the first month had been one of guilt, consisting of resolve early in the day, something urgent inevitably creeping up, which would precipitate postponing the letter-writing to the following day. The weekend before the education and action meeting, I finally sat down and wrote a very long letter to the editor, as if the length would somehow compensate for the delay in sending it. For the longest time, nothing happened and then one day, a colleague came to ask if I was the one who had written an opinion piece opposite the editorial page.

"With astonishment, I grabbed the paper, only to notice indeed the half-page article with two photographs, captions, and at the bottom, this authoritative opinion leader's signature: mine. If obscure allies on the editorial board could transform long-winded letters into op-eds which students and activists could clip for future reference, then indeed, resignation about world hunger was definitely a difficult position to defend, and surely there were good reasons to now play full out.

"The opportunity to play full out would not take long to show up," Jean François continued. "It came in the form of a very short human powerhouse passionately devoted to justice and dignity, Inez Coles. In November 1988, Inez had become National Coordinator of RESULTS Canada. Before taking the volunteer job, she had been very clear: what she was going to provide to groups across Canada was nurturing, support, and energy. She needed an associate who would identify the most critical actions for RESULTS Canada to undertake, the ones behind which she could throw all her support, the actions which would truly make a tangible difference in the world. This associate would be a person knowledgeable in public policies and conversant with technical details of government. This time, I was willing to step forward without knowing what it would take.

"One month later, in December 1988, I had to identify my first monthly action for RESULTS Canada. Fortunately, December is the month in which UNICEF launches its *State of the World's Children* report. In that year's report, there was the recommendation for a Summit of Heads of State and Government to address the scandal of 40,000 children dying each day from preventable causes. Given that this was precisely what RESULTS was all about, why not request that Canada host that meeting? The idea was accepted by RESULTS leaders across Canada, and James Grant personally threw his weight behind the proposal."

Jean François and his Canadian colleagues went to the media immediately and called UNICEF Executive Director Jim Grant to see if he would join them on their conference call. One year later, Grant introduced me to his wife at a reception in Washington, D.C. "This is Sam Harris, director of RESULTS," he said with a twinkle in his eye. "You remember that group in Canada that woke us up with their phone call on Christmas morning last year." The twinkle was for the work that had been done. The first salvo came from one of Canada's national newspapers.

"UNICEF suggests the time may have come for a summit of world leaders to apply more urgent remedies," wrote the *Globe and Mail* of Canada. "Would anyone argue that it was overstating the case?"

On January 8, 1989, Grant was RESULTS Canada's conference call guest. David Crane, a reporter for the *Toronto Star*, another of Canada's national newspapers, covered the call. "Canada could help save millions of young lives by helping organize a world summit for children this year, says the head of the United Nations Children's Fund," Crane wrote the next day in the *Star*.

"Last night's conference call was organized by RESULTS Canada, a volunteer group linked with similar groups in the United States, Australia, Britain, and West Germany. It is campaigning not only to have Prime Minister Brian Mulroney support such a children's summit but also to host it." Ten months later, Mulroney was one of the six heads of state who initiated the summit and would later serve as its co-chair, but only after a major push from many in Canada, instigated by the RESULTS groups there.

"While Inez and some of the other RESULTS leaders were making things happen with the media," Jean François explained, "I knew it was my job to get a public declaration of support signed by as many parliamentarians as possible. Members of the opposition were the most likely to sign. To get their signature, the endorsement of the Foreign Policy Committee of the leading opposition party was key.

"The Honorable André Ouellet was chair of the Liberal Party's Foreign Policy Comnittee," Jean François continued. "He was the most senior French-speaking Liberal parliamentarian. When his party was in power, he was a minister and one of the most prominent politicians in the country. He worked in Ottawa and was francophone and that, in itself, pointed to me, as the only Ottawa-based French-speaking volunteer at the time, to be the one to meet with him.

"How does one request the endorsement of the Liberal Party's Foreign Policy Committee? A quick call to Mr. Ouellet's secretary indicated that the committee was meeting in just a few days. After a short conversation, the secretary agreed that our parliamentary declaration on the World Summit for Children would be put on the agenda. I would meet with Ouellet a few minutes before the committee meeting.

"Mr. Ouellet was not known for being soft-spoken, but that day he appeared almost shy. I was nervous," Jean François confided, "because I was painfully aware that I could make a difference. RESULTS had as one of its purposes to break through the thought that individuals don't make a difference. During the few seconds I had to explain our declaration, I shared with Mr. Ouellet the Action Sheet of the month which provided a good overview of the issue, but I didn't really know whether what I was saying was communicating, whether the opportunity of the World Summit for Children was properly being explained, whether the vision I wanted to share was coming across.

"The committee's meeting was about to begin. Mr. Ouellet would speak to the item, and I would remain available outside the room to be called in if needed. Mr. Ouellet's suite was very small...an office, a meeting room, and a secretarial space in between. But the walls were filled with photographs of Mr. Ouellet and foreign dignitaries. There was nothing to do but wait and sip coffee which was being graciously refilled on a regular basis. Time was slipping, and it was likely that they would not call me in. Once again, I felt alone and resolute. Perhaps more alone than that day on the beach because I had now relinquished control of the issue I cared about the most into the hands of a politician for whose party I had never even voted.

"And then a miracle happened," Jean François continued. "An apologetic Mr. Ouellet left the meeting room. He had forgotten about me. The committee was not sure how to give a formal endorsement to the declaration as a body, so all the committee members just signed the declaration individually. I was jubilant; what I had bargained for was an obscure letter of support from the bureaucracy of the party, and what I was getting instead were the actual signatures of the party's key opinion leaders!

"The following day, the Liberal Party Policy Committee issued a totally unexpected press release: it demanded that the government of Canada take a leadership role in making the Summit for Children happen. The press release had an appendix: the Action Sheet of RESULTS for that month! Much to our surprise, we had now been put on the map as the official lobbyists for the World Summit for Children."

RESULTS Canada was not the only country at work. In early 1989, RESULTS in the United Kingdom, Australia, and West Germany followed Canada in pushing their own governments to host a World Summit for Children. But in Canada, that was their exclusive focus.

"We got the feeling that this glorious achievement might not be enough," Jean François continued. "The declaration was being signed by a steady number of members of Parliament (MPs), but it was obvious that we were talking of several months to reach a majority of the ridings.[23] From the media's perspective, the issue appeared to be running out of steam, and from the government's point of view, the momentum seemed to be disappearing. We needed to impress upon the highest levels of government that the signing of the Parliamentary declaration was far from dying off and, to the contrary, they could count on us to rally over one third of the House of Commons to our cause.

"Joe Clark was the undisputed master of Canada's foreign policy," Jean François explained. "A former prime minister, he had extensive experience in the international arena, and ultimately, he would make the decision as to Canada's involvement in the Summit for Children. Our chances of meeting with him were non-existent. He barely had time for official visits, signing treaties, meetings with ambassadors, and the like. I chose to request, as a fall-back, to meet with Mr. Clark's chief of staff, Mr. Leo Duguay, the person Mr. Clark was the most likely to listen to in forming his position—and Canada's policy—on the World Summit for Children.

---

[23]A riding in Canada is basically the same as a Congressional District in the United States. The primary difference is that a member of the Canadian Parliament has a much smaller number of constituents.

"This time, I couldn't make the visit by myself....The Ottawa partners would accompany me. We requested a meeting at lunch time so we could get away from work. I forced myself to prepare notes for the meeting. The idea was to appear credible. I made them illegible enough so Mr. Duguay didn't see that we had a script. My partners agreed to rehearse the meeting. We also made plans to arrive together so we didn't have to wait or look for one another. RESULTS, through the Laser Talks and the rigorous planning and conduct of meetings, had taught us the discipline required to be as effective as can be at this one. The security guard already had our names, and we were escorted up to the minister's office, where Mr. Duguay met us....Now I was resolute, but not alone anymore. Aside from my Ottawa partners, I was backed by hundreds of letters written by citizens and, as such, I belonged in this immense deluxe suite. In fact, there would probably be room in Mr. Duguay's office for the signatories of all the letters sent in the previous months. The mahogany furniture was far from filling the space, and the pale beige carpet not only widened the room but seemed to absorb our words and create a strange sense of remoteness. Mr. Duguay, it was true, did not look overly happy to meet with us. He was a former member of Parliament, defeated in the previous elections, whose number one task was to keep Mr. Clark out of difficult situations. He was accompanied by Mr. Grauer, the Director of Economic Relations with Developing Countries. We were told the department had no other directorate which could deal appropriately with the issue of the summit. Needless to say, both were by their very positions not very hot to see Canada host this summit: a lot of potential trouble for Mr. Clark and certainly not much to gain in terms of economic benefits.

"My partners and I shared our commitment to bringing the summit into existence," Jean François explained. "Our strategy in requesting that Canada host the summit was to make sure some country got the ball rolling. Our hosts raised objection after objection: Canada didn't have the appropriate security or the appropriate translation services; did we really need one more seminar ending in hollow words; should we not provide much-needed relief to Third World children instead of wasting our funds on gigantic photo opportunities?"

"I had had quite an extensive experience in dealing with foreign service types and the diplomatic corps. Generally, even in cases of disagreement, the conversation evolved to an open exchange of views. This afternoon, there was no openness at all, no concessions, no willingness to seek common ground. Obviously, this was not social chatter, it was lobbying, and it was not comfortable. We were clearly not going to win any arguments. So the only option left for us was to reiterate our point of view and to let them know that we would continue to lobby our members of Parliament. This was not an ultimatum or blackmail, but just explaining over and over that we believed enough in the potential of the Summit for Children that our participants would continue to ask their MPs to throw their support behind this initiative.

"We parted without much apparent progress. My partners and I met downstairs in the cafeteria. All the diplomats were back at work. We discussed the meeting. The spirit was high because we clearly did not make fools of ourselves. But I personally was uneasy at how little we had managed to enlist them in the vision.

"A few weeks later, we learned that Canada had decided not to host the summit, but, instead, had become the first country to pledge the seed money required to set up a secretariat for the summit at the United Nations. Prime Minister Mulroney would eventually serve as its co-chair, but this would not be a direct result of RESULTS action. By then, other senior officials had taken up the lobbying."

Five months after the Canadians began lobbying for the summit, RESULTS in the U.S. pushed for passage of House Resolution 120, which endorsed the call for a World Summit for Children. And 1989 was also the year we had begun to study movements. At the RESULTS International Conference in June 1989, we asked: "What is a movement and how can we energize a movement?" We envisioned some dramatic action that would galvanize millions of people and raise our issue to a new level of priority.

There were other questions posed. In 1988, British Prime Minister Margaret Thatcher said, "I'm a Green." Within the context of European politics, Mrs. Thatcher's Conservative Party was on the right, Labor was on the left, and the Greens were even farther to the left. So this was a pretty radical statement. What role did movements play in her change of thinking, or at least in her change of speaking?

Toward the end of his second term, President Reagan walked in Red Square with Mr. Gorbachev and said, "The Russians are just like us." It wasn't many years before that Mr. Reagan had called the Soviet Union the "evil empire." Did it mean that now *we too* were the "evil empire," or had the president changed his thinking? What role did movements play in *this* change?

The *State of the World's Children 1990* report from UNICEF announced the summit. We believed the summit offered an opportunity to energize a movement for children. We began to ask ourselves, "How can we make sure the summit doesn't come and go without anyone noticing?" Old responses surfaced first. Maybe we should host 50 news conferences, double our usual number. Maybe we should launch a massive postcard campaign to President Bush. But the recognition of our need to energize a movement pushed us to more dramatic *action*.

"I can envision 50 mini-summits and news conferences in the U.S. around the Summit for Children," I wrote RESULTS Monthly Sponsors on January 24, 1990. "I can envision a candlelight vigil with 40,000 people at the UN on the evening of the summit...."

I'm not sure where the candlelight vigil idea came from. Perhaps it was an image from the democracy movements which swept across Eastern Europe at the end of 1989. Perhaps it was the search for a gentle protest—a witness. But the vigil idea took hold and we were off and running. When the vigils finally got underway, our legislative activities continued, but the major focus of RESULTS turned to the vigils. We felt that we'd lobbied successfully to the edges of the space available, and something massive was needed to expand that space. We were out to see if empowering the World Summit for Children with a tremendous mobilization, not our usual lobbying work, could provide that new opening.

The idea for international involvement came out of a phone conversation with John Coonrod at The Hunger Project in New York City. "Why don't you have candlelight vigils start in West Germany, which is six hours ahead of us?" John asked. "That way it could be on the evening news in this country."

I shared this German vigil idea on my weekly call with Shirley Tainton, National Manager of RESULTS Australia.

"We want the vigils to start in Australia and have them sweep around the world," she insisted.

The vigils eventually started in New Zealand and Antarctica and included 75 countries. It was a grassroots movement-building campaign unlike anything we had ever taken on.

One of our more politically savvy board members made it clear that convening a Summit for Children didn't guarantee that leaders of the major industrialized countries would attend. Most heads of state would take their cue from President Bush. If the president attended, participation would be very good; if he didn't, it could be disastrous.

We took on the challenge. In February, groups wrote the president, urging him to attend. Of course, having the president attend was only the starting point. I reminded people of the Cancun Summit on North/South Development attended by President Reagan and 21 other heads of state in 1981. The gathering, which was proposed by the Commission on North/South Development, headed by Chancellor Willy Brandt of West Germany, was largely forgettable.

At the time of the 1981 Cancun Summit, RESULTS had fewer than 10 groups, mostly in Southern California. We had done everything possible to promote the Cancun Summit. Now we had 150 groups in seven countries, and we began discussions with other organizations on how to use the summit to launch a decade of progress for children. RESULTS had been an expert on citizen lobbying, but not on movement building. We believed we had to develop both skills.

At the end of February, 10 days before departing on an around-the-world trip, I sent letters to non-profit groups, inviting them to serve on the U.S.

Advisory Committee of the Candlelight Vigils. The U.S. Committee for UNICEF was the first to join RESULTS and RESULTS Educational Fund, followed soon thereafter by the National Council for International Health.

I talked to many people, but by far the most memorable conversation was with the next advisory committee member, the Child Welfare League of America (CWLA). Joyce Strom, Assistant Director of CWLA at the time, is a cross between Mother Teresa and Roseanne Arnold. Joyce is a feisty, funny, and caring woman. We'd known each other for four years, and I'd discussed the vigil idea with her before. An activist at heart, she, probably more than most, knew what we were getting ourselves into, and whatever it was, we were in over our heads. When I called to see if CWLA would come on the advisory committee, she said, "Wait, let me ask David." David Liederman, a former Massachusetts state legislator, was director of CWLA. Joyce put her hand over the phone, only partially muffling her conversation.

"David!" she shouted to Liederman in the next room, "Remember the Candlelight Vigils I told you about for the World Summit for Children? Can I put us on the Advisory Committee?"

"Yes, it's a good thing," I heard her respond to a question from Liederman.

A moment later Joyce spoke back into the phone, "You can put us on," she said. "Now cover my ass."

Her last statement, one of humor and love, was a reminder that we were about to succeed or fail in a public way. We were Babe Ruth at home plate, we'd pointed over the center field bleachers, and the first pitch was coming. As it did, I left town. Well, actually, I left the country on a trip that took me to Britain, Germany, Bangladesh, Japan, and Australia. It was a trip that would plant the seeds for the vigils' success.

I spent one day each in Britain and Germany, speaking with RESULTS partners about the World Summit for Children Candlelight Vigils. Then it was on to Bangladesh to join 28 others from four RESULTS countries on a five-day visit to the Grameen Bank.

Then I traveled on to Japan for a week of RESULTS presentations and workdays. A meeting with Shingo Nomura on the final day brought the Candlelight Vigils its first contribution, nearly a tenth of its budget. Nomura-san, a Japanese businessman, had grown up "on UNICEF milk" after World War II and was committed to giving something back in appreciation for what he'd received. His gifts included several million dollars to The Hunger Project. His office building, a jewel of understated elegance in the back alleys of the Hanzomon district of Tokyo, had won awards for its design. Nomura-san had a vast collection of Shona sculpture, a rich indigenous art form from Zimbabwe.

We had met once before in Tokyo. At that meeting he agreed to provide nearly $7,000 for six fax machines and one photocopy machine. The fax machines were to help the all-volunteer RESULTS groups in Japan exchange translation drafts of materials originally in English.

As at the previous meeting, we spoke through his translator. Nomura-san and I were the same age. His commitment was very deep and I felt very much his partner. I told him about my visit to Bangladesh, about RESULTS in Japan, and eventually about the World Summit for Children and Candlelight Vigils.

Before the meeting began I'd decided to ask for $40,000 to pay for the first two Candlelight Vigils staff members. But each time I waited for the translator to finish, I held an internal debate. "Is $40,000 the right amount to ask for?" I wondered under my breath. "What if he's very moved by the project and would be willing to give much more? But what if he's already over-committed?" I countered to myself. "Am I being disrespectful?"

It was a busy meeting with three conversations going on at once—one in English, one in Japanese, and one going on in my head. At the appropriate time, I asked, "Would you be willing to make a gift of $40,000 to the World Summit for Children Candlelight Vigils?"

He listened to the translation, thought for a moment, and said, "So you would like me to make a contribution of $40,000?" "Yes, it would get us off to a very good start," I replied.

He listened to the translation, thought for a while—a silence I will long remember—and then said, "I will contribute $40,000 to the project and I will do so by April 15."

April 15 was less than a month away. I thanked him for his generosity and for his leadership. When I look in my diary for that day, two items stand out. One was my meeting with Nomura-san and the other, the reminder to take my malaria pills. For me they represent the disparity between rich and poor and the question about how the Nomura-san in each of us can be called forth—that part of each of us actively looking for ways to give something back. That was one of the reasons for the Candlelight Vigils.

The final five days were spent in Australia. There were three RESULTS fundraising dinners, radio and television interviews, and a conversation with RESULTS Australia National Manager Shirley Tainton at the Sydney airport, which was as pivotal as the meeting with Nomura-san.

Shirley, raised in South Africa, moved with her family to Australia after graduating from high school. A caring wildwoman, Shirley was able to empower people miraculously. She had talked about leaving the RESULTS staff to focus more on her personal life. My own drive toward constant work left little room for personal life, but I understood the concept. I was seldom responsible for my own well-being, but when people felt they needed to make a change, I always encouraged it. Shirley's departure would be a great loss.

At the airport Shirley told me she was interested in coming to Washington for six months to work on the Candlelight Vigils, as the coordinator of all non-U.S. vigils. Coming to Washington to work on the vigils didn't seem like an exercise in focusing on one's personal life. But the vision for the summit was stronger than the need to pull back, and she wanted to be part of it. Heads of state were coming together for a meeting which could alter the course of history. We agreed to the arrangement, and Shirley arrived in D.C. four weeks later. Not long after that she recognized the need for someone to manage the overall project as I struggled with fundraising. Shirley became project manager one month after her arrival. Her skills at both energizing and nurturing the staff were two levers that I had trouble getting a hold of at the same time.

The Bangladesh delegation returned home before I did. As the rest of the staff charged ahead on the Candlelight Vigils, Alex Counts, our legislative director, and Sharon Mason, our financial manager and *Entry Point* editor, held down the RESULTS fort and our ongoing lobbying efforts.

A number of times during our Candlelight Vigil campaign, a cartoon of Bob Geldof came to mind. While the Candlelight Vigils were never as big as Geldof's Band Aid or Live Aid, coordinating them was far beyond what I saw as my capability. The cartoon had God knocking on Geldof's door during the Ethiopian famine of 1984. When the disheveled rock star answered, God responded, "He'll do." I always imagined God looking at me in 1990 and responding, "He'll do, but he's going to need a lot of help!"

A call I made the day after I returned from Australia was part of an avalanche of help, unexpected rivers of energy which fed the Candlelight Vigils. It was after midnight east coast time when I called Valerie Harper, a RESULTS board member, at her home in California. Valerie, best known for her television role as Rhoda, has a heart as big as the world which she follows more faithfully than most. I don't know what I expected from the conversation, maybe just an exploration of possibilities, certainly not an explosion of commitment. From my perspective, my description of the project was not as powerful as Valerie's response to it. Within minutes, we had a celebrity briefing scheduled in Los Angeles for May 6, just four weeks away. This would be followed three weeks later by a full-page ad in the *New York Times* signed by 146 celebrities urging Bush and Gorbachev to attend the summit, by a second celebrity briefing seven days after that, and by our first national television appearance eight days later.

The first celebrity briefing pressed me up against an existential question which had haunted me six years before during one of my 21-city trips. I spoke in a beautiful home in New Orleans and needed to change into my clothes for the RESULTS presentation. As I put on one of my pant legs the question struck me: "Who gave me permission to be leading like this?" "I did," came my quick answer. "And besides, if I didn't do it, nobody else would."

Valerie Harper and Raul Julia, both members of the RESULTS board, arrived at the first celebrity briefing early, as did Harvey Korman, another friend from early RESULTS days in Los Angeles. But as the other celebrities began to arrive, it was as if I were putting on that pant leg again in New Orleans. The same question sounded anew, "Who gave me permission to be leading?" This time, the reassuring *answer* didn't come as quickly as did the celebrity guests: Levar Burton from *Roots*; Susan Dey from *LA Law*; Carol Kane from *Taxi*; Stepfanie Kramer from *Hunter*; Paul Mazursky, the director; Edward James Olmos from *Miami Vice* and *Stand and Deliver*; Katey Sagal from *Married with Children*; Vidal Sassoon; and child stars Mayim Bialik from *Blossom*, Soleil Moon Frye from *Punky Brewster*, and Jeremy Miller from *Growing Pains*. All showed up. I welcomed everyone and made some opening remarks, still wondering who chose me. I introduced a video, and again, just as with the *20/20* video that came to our rescue in 1984, this powerful video segment from *60 Minutes* titled "40,000 a Day" brought me back to my answer. For this room, the video asked and answered several pivotal questions. The first two were: How big is the problem facing children, and if it is big, why haven't I heard much about it?

Mike Wallace began the program by asking the viewers what their reaction would be if they heard that 40,000 children had died that day in a natural disaster. "How do you think that television and the newspapers and wire services would react to such stunning news?" he asked. "Well, that does in fact happen every day, and the news media simply do not cover the story....Every single day in the Third World, 40,000 children under the age of five die—not from famine—most of them die of preventable diseases....The same news media that mobilized camera crews and reporters and news teams and sent them to Alaska to cover those three whales trapped in the ice there [in 1988]."

The video went on to address a second important question: Is there anything that can be done? Wallace answered by describing a project in the Oringa region of Tanzania which had saved the lives of over 5,000 children and improved the lives of tens of thousands more, and "the cost to keep this program going," Wallace continued, "is about $5 per child per year."

Wallace pressed his guest, UNICEF Deputy Executive Director Richard Jolly, about the cost of saving the lives of children from malnutrition and preventable diseases such as measles and dehydration. "Wait, wait," Wallace asked excitedly, "you're saying that $5 could save one of these 40,000 kids who die?"

"Yes," responded Jolly so fast as if to be interrupting.

"The cost [of saving one of these 40,000 children who die] every day?" asked Wallace incredulously.

"Yes," responded Jolly

"Five dollars a year?" repeated Wallace.

"Yes," Jolly responded, again at the pace of certainty.

It was like the joyous interplay of voices in a fugue by Bach, but these voices called out to save lives.

The video concluded with an exchange between Wallace and UNICEF Goodwill Ambassador Audrey Hepburn that addressed a topic especially made for this room. Wallace talked about how hard it was to get these issues covered, and that often celebrities must be used to get the interest of the media.

"You don't mind being used?" Wallace asked Hepburn provocatively.

"Not in this way," Hepburn responded. "You call it using. I don't think it's the right term. To me it's a marvelous opportunity that *I* am using, I hope, to help *a* child—maybe more—and certainly to keep my sanity." For a moment Hepburn was the school teacher chastising Wallace, her star pupil, and we all came away the better for it.

A discussion period followed the video, and the celebrities filled out commitment forms we provided. It seemed that everyone committed to everything: speaking for the vigils on radio and television, speaking at the vigils at the end of September, putting their names on an ad in the *New York Times*, and even allowing a fundraising letter to be sent to a list of their friends. This final item was the one piece we never used.

However, the ad in the *Times* moved into high gear. We wanted it to appear in three weeks when Bush and Gorbachev were at their summit in Washington. Six celebrities signed a letter urging hundreds of their colleagues to join them in signing the ad. A celebrity list, and a wave of support, came from Jerry Michaud, Director of the End Hunger Network. Jerry, a former priest and graphic designer, began to prepare the ad. He has the dedication of a priest and the audacity of an ex-priest—like one of the Berrigan brothers, but without the jail terms.

The real energy behind the name-gathering was a phoning blitz by Valerie Harper. She talked to celebrities, she talked with their assistants, and she took on raising the $13,000 to place the ad. Valerie was on the phone day and night. More than 50 had agreed to sign. She called Steve Allen and Jane Meadows, and Jane agreed to make calls as did others. The peak of calling was over Memorial Day weekend, the last days we had to gather names. No pool-side barbecues this year. We entered the weekend with 100 signers. Some had the message read to them over the phone. Others asked for a fax. Valerie called our office and we sent the faxes from there.

We learned that a full-page ad was $35,000 the day we wanted it to run. There was a reduced price, $13,000, but that would run any day the *New York Times* had space for it over a two-week period. Valerie talked with Jim Stergiou, who placed the ads at the *Times*. Jim saw the importance of the World Summit for Children and vowed to do everything he could to get the $13,000 ad in on a day Bush and Gorbachev were in Washington, D.C. When the fundraising wasn't moving, Valerie and her husband, Tony Cacciotti, decided to pay for the ad and for reprints in *Daily Variety* and *The Hollywood Reporter*.

"I can get you page 13 of the first section, Friday, June 1," Stergiou told Valerie on the phone, "or the Week In Review on Sunday, June 3."

Valerie called me with the message. It was all perfect, either of the days worked.

"I can get you on page 11 on June 1, but I have to know in a few hours," Stergiou called back.

And so, on June 1, a full-page ad appeared in the front section of the *New York Times*. Bush and Gorbachev were at their superpower summit and neither had agreed to attend the World Summit for Children.

"Mankind can no longer put up with the fact that millions of children die each year," read a statement by President Mikhail Gorbachev in the upper right-hand corner of the ad.

"Our national character can be measured by how we care for our children," read a statement by President George Bush in the upper left-hand corner of the ad.

"Leaders of the world's two most powerful nations have let themselves be counted," the statement signed by more than 140 celebrities began. "It is now time for real action. Like so many of us, our national leaders are numbed by the enormity of the problem—40,000 children dying each day from malnutrition and disease.

"In the new climate of openness and disarmament the time is certainly ripe for such a summit. But the truth is that, unless the most influential countries participate fully, the potential of the summit to achieve real positive change will be lost. It's time to back words with action," the statement concluded seven paragraphs later. The signers ranged from Harry Belafonte to Jackson Browne, from Frank Sinatra to Sting and from Randy Travis to Elizabeth Taylor, who was the last to sign, giving her OK from a hospital bed.

"I returned last night from an encouraging audience with His Holiness the Pope on the future of the world's children and our joint efforts to make a difference," wrote Jim Grant of UNICEF in a letter to me the next day. "I returned to discover the *New York Times* advertisement. Clearly, you and your colleagues have already made a dramatic difference for the World Summit for Children and for children the world over." A similar letter went to Valerie, Tony, and their daughter Christina.

Seven days after the ad appeared, Valerie hosted a second briefing. Melissa Gilbert of *Little House on the Prairie*, Sara Gilbert of *Roseanne*, and Jimmy Smits of *LA Law* were among those attending. At the briefing, songwriters David Pomeranz and David Shire premiered "In Our Hands," a song I'd asked them to write for the Candlelight Vigils. Pomeranz had written the Barry Manilow hits "Tryin' to Get That Feelin' Again" and "The Old Songs." Shire had written the film scores to *Saturday Night Fever*, *All the President's Men*, and *Norma Rae*. He performed the vigil song several months later with Kathie Lee Gifford on her show with Regis Philbin, and Kathie Lee sang it again, one year later, at the Miss America Pageant.

Just before the second celebrity briefing, *CBS This Morning* expressed interest in doing a segment and asked what celebrity we could get. Jimmy Smits agreed to appear, and we had our first national television coverage eight days later.

More than any project, the Candlelight Vigils validated for me the words of W.H. Murray from *The Scottish Himalayan Expedition*:

> Until one is committed, there is hesitancy, the chance to draw back, always ineffectiveness. Concerning all acts of initiative (and creation), there is one elementary truth, the ignorance of which kills countless ideas and splendid plans: that the moment one commits oneself then Providence moves too. All sorts of things occur to help one that would never otherwise have occurred. A whole stream of events issues from the decision, raising in one's favor all manner of unforeseen incidents and meetings and material assistance, which no man could have dreamt would have come his way.
>
> I have learned a deep respect for one of Goethe's couplets:
>
> Whatever you can do or dream you can, begin it.
> Boldness has genius, power and magic in it.

The stream of events, the unforeseen incidents, and the material assistance were everywhere.

The RESULTS International Conference began two days before the *CBS This Morning* appearance. One of the homework assignments was to prepare answers to interview questions such as: Why is the World Summit for Children being held? Why are you putting your energy into this Candlelight Vigil when we need to be concerned about the planet being destroyed? Throughout the conference, time was taken to pair up and practice asking and answering the questions, a key to becoming better spokespersons. As the RESULTS conference and my first appearance on network television approached, I looked forward to another benefit from the assignment. Over the years, I listened to the silence in a room as people wrote their first letter to a member of Congress and then heard the passion and poetry in people as some of the letters were read aloud. This time I was looking for a gem that I could take with me to the TV appearance. After the paired exercise, someone stood in the far corner of the room and answered the need to be concerned about the environment. "Children are like the environment," I heard him say, "without either we have no future."

I took it with me when I flew to New York that night. The *CBS This Morning* segment was at 7:40 a.m. on Monday morning, June 18, which meant Jimmy Smits was on at 4:40 a.m. Los Angeles time. One of the objectives of the Candlelight Vigils was to get our issue into the national media where there seemed to be a reality warp. The letters and editorials we generated locally spoke of eliminating the needless deaths of 40,000 children each day. But we seldom saw this message in the national media. It was as if it didn't exist in the national consciousness, because it wasn't covered by the national media.

The morning after the appearance on *CBS This Morning* we kicked-off the vigils with a news conference at the conclusion of the RESULTS International Conference. Camera crews were there from national television in West Germany, Japan, the Soviet Union, and from Spanish television, but none from the U.S.

By July 2, we announced in our second issue of the Candlelight Vigil newsletter, *Vigil Voice,* a total of 195 vigils scheduled in 17 countries. Five days later, I was shaken by the eloquence of one of the celebrities who was new to the campaign. While I was on a flight from Seattle back to D.C., Carol Kane appeared on the *Arsenio Hall Show*. Dorsey Lawson spent hours working with Carol, and the end result was startling. Carol spoke out of a deep commitment that people really grapple with the problem and what they could do about it. Her words revealed an armor I'd been wearing to protect myself from rejection. It was as if, with all my work, I still held something back—didn't push all the way, so I could save face.

After talking about her film career, Arsenio said, "I know you're into something that's very important to you, and I want you to be able to tell people about it, because it's important to us, whether we know it or not."

"I'm here to talk about the children of the world," Carol responded as the audience applauded. "And, unfortunately, I'd like to start by asking you, 'What would be your reaction if I told you that 40,000 children died today of a natural disaster? What would be your reaction to that?'"

"Out of ignorance," Arsenio replied, "I'd probably tell you that I wasn't aware."

Carol was brilliant. After talking about her career and putting Arsenio and the audience at ease, she started by asking Arsenio a question. It was what we had taught RESULTS volunteers for years when calling an editorial writer. What initially was her issue started to become his.

"That's not ignorance," Carol assured Arsenio. "The fact is 40,000 children did die today and [40,000 more] died yesterday, and 40,000 more will die tomorrow. But you're not ignorant that you don't know about it. The fact is the media is not covering this. This is not good news. I mean...it's not good copy...like who's Madonna dating. So what does this mean?" Carol continued. "Does this mean that we don't care? Are we endorsing the fact that the media and the world leaders are not addressing this?" She was beginning to challenge the audience to not just take what they were fed by the media.

"How are these kids dying though?" Arsenio interrupted.

"This is the thing that's got me," said Carol, "[they're dying from] almost entirely preventable diseases such as measles which a six-cent vaccination [will prevent]."

"This sounds like a simple solution," said Arsenio, "but why not the...curing of measles instead of the Hubble [space telescope] if it's only [six] cents?"

"Because, I guess," said Carol innocently, "the world leaders feel that it's been more important to spend this money on the military. But we have an opportunity right now. This is why I'm on, and I'm taking your time—it's very critical. On September 23, all over the world, our country very much included, there will be something called the Candlelight Vigil for children...you know kids cannot speak for themselves—little children—so you can speak for them just by lighting a candle and shedding some light on the fact that you care if they live or die. And then six days later, there will be the largest summit in history, called the World Summit for Children, at the UN. So far, 45 world leaders and heads of state are coming to this summit. More than any other in history. And, who's not coming so far, is your president and mine, Mr. Bush....Let's get him to commit now. You can light a candle and shed some light on the needs of these kids.

"Now, I just want to say," Carol continued, "that for $2.5 billion we can save 20,000 of these kids. Now $2.5 billion is what the world spends every day in military spending. It's what Russia spends on vodka in one month...So it's just a question of asking them to do something very daring, very brave, and rerouting this funding to the children. Without the children, you know, there's no future...they need you to show up, and if you agree that they should be our main priority, call 1-800-WE-AGREE. They will tell you where the vigil is close to your home."

"Wait a minute," Arsenio interrupted. "What's that date again?"

"September 23," Carol answered. "Thank you, you're so sweet."

"No [I'm not]," Arsenio responded, embarrassed by the compliment.

"Really," Carol insisted, "because a lot of people don't let you talk about anything that doesn't get a big yuck on a talk show."

Arsenio began to blush.

"That's true. You know that. It's true," said Carol, gently chastising Arsenio for his modesty.

"1-800-WE-AGREE," Carol continued. "And when they said this to me this morning, I said, 'how do you spell agree?' Arsenio, do you know how to spell agree?"

"Uh, Arachnophobia," responded Arsenio, using the title of a film that had just been released.

Carol pretended to smack Arsenio and repeated, "1-800-WE-AGREE. If there is not a vigil in your neighborhood, they will tell you everything you need to do to organize one. We're not asking for anything but your body and your voice and holding a candle to help the children of the world."

It was another brilliant moment. As Carol asked Arsenio to spell 'agree,' I imagined one million viewers spelling it in their heads. It turned out that

10,000 people called the 800 number. We were overwhelmed in more ways than one. First of all, 10,000 names were more than three times as many as any list RESULTS had had up to this point. But we were also overwhelmed because the calls cost us about $1.25 each. That was more than $12,000 for this success.

The most painful part of the campaign for me was fundraising. I'd never been so up against a wall. I seemed to spend nearly every waking hour working on or worrying about fundraising. There was a constant juggling to make payroll. Eventually, providence would move on fundraising also, but not for several months.

Carol's appearance with Arsenio was amazingly powerful. One example was the story of Karen Morris, a young mother of two from Del Rio, Texas.

"When I heard Carol Kane say on the *Arsenio Hall Show* that 40,000 children die every day of hunger and hunger-related diseases," Karen remembered, "I could not believe it! When she said almost all of them could be saved, I thought, 'Why aren't they?' "

Karen called the Candlelight Vigils office and was asked if she'd like to host a vigil. "I loved the idea," she said, "but I have a husband, a five-year-old daughter, and a two-year-old son. We had just moved to Del Rio, so I knew virtually no one. The biggest thing I had ever tried before was organizing birthday parties for my kids. I was looking over the materials the vigil office sent me," Karen continued, "when the Nike commercial came on TV—'Just Do It!' So I made a couple of calls to people who were already planning vigils...a man in Memphis told me: 'Go to work—you can do it.' So...I went to work. I called a girlfriend, Lisa Adanto, and begged her to help."

And as Karen went to work, so did thousands of others. By August 16, we announced 550 vigils scheduled in 55 countries. Two weeks later, there were more than 1,470 vigils in 75 countries, and amazing things were happening.

The vigil in London would be at St. Paul's Cathedral. A picture of three little girls at that vigil was on the front page of *The Times* of London the next morning. Australia's First Lady, Hazel Hawke, agreed to be the patron of the Australian vigils. Jimmy Carter and Gerald Ford signed on to be Honorary Co-Chairs in the U.S. The Olympic torch in Calgary was to be re-lit for the vigil there; and in Rapid City, South Dakota, the vigil was to be held at Mt. Rushmore. All around the world people were making plans.

"I called the mayor's office and got a great location for the vigil," continued Karen Morris in Del Rio. "We called the radio stations and newspapers and told them what we were doing. They thought it was great. They both set up interviews. The newspaper didn't worry me, but the radio scared me to death! However, everyone was so nice that even the radio interview was pretty easy. And I must say, it helped to know what I was talking about. I had studied everything the Candlelight Vigils sent me and could answer the questions....

"Summer Stokes, a nine-year-old friend of ours, found out what we were doing and wanted to help. So she wrote a story about children in need to read at the vigil. Our local paper printed her story, with her byline, along with a front-page article about her. Radio station KDLK recorded Summer reading her story and ran it several times a day for the week before the vigils. So we were getting new kinds of publicity."

And the national vigils began to get the publicity of our dreams, including an hour on the *Oprah Winfrey Show*. The show Oprah and her producers prepared for the World Summit for Children Candlelight Vigil was moving beyond words. As the show opened, a children's choir of more than 60 sang an African song, "Oh freedom, oh freedom, oh freedom." The lights in the studio were low and actors Louis Gossett Jr., Valerie Harper, Raul Julia, and Oprah each stood next to a child wearing our Candlelight Vigil T-shirt. The celebrities held unlit candles, the children held lit candles.

"Every single day around the world 40,000 children under the age of five die of malnutrition and preventable diseases," declared Oprah, with the children singing in the background. "At this alarming rate, by the end of the decade, 150 million lives will be lost—150 million children's lives, each one a child who had dreams, a child who had potential, a child who had a family and what should have been a future. And in our ninth part of our year-long series dedicated to children, we are calling on you for their freedom. Freedom from hunger, freedom from disease, and freedom from war."

The children continued singing in the background. After each of the Candlelight Vigils celebrities spoke, they leaned over and lit their candle from the candle of the child standing next to them. The combination of the spoken words, the candle-lighting, and the singing reached deep inside.

"In our country, the United States," boomed Raul Julia, "millions of people are homeless. One out of every four is a child. We're asking world leaders to put our children first and end child poverty by the year 2000."

"In our world," pronounced Valerie Harper, "7,000 young children die every day from dehydration caused by diarrhea. If parents knew how to prepare a 10-cent solution of sugar, salt, and water, they could save their children's lives. World leaders, please, put our children first."

"In our world," intoned Louis Gossett Jr. after Valerie lit her candle, "7,000 children die every day from pneumonia and bronchial infection. Yet just one dollar's worth of antibiotics could save their lives. World leaders, put our children first."

"In our world, 1,000 children went blind today," declared Oprah. "Yet just a few greens in their evening meal or a two-cent capsule of vitamin A twice a year could save their sight. The candles we're lighting today represent the lives of children we hope to save. But without the commitment of our world leaders," Oprah continued, her voice pleading, "our fight is futile. In just one week, 71 world leaders will convene at the United Nations in New York City for one reason—that is to address the daily global crisis, the deaths of our children, 40,000 children a day. And we are asking you not to ignore this tragedy. We're asking you to help the children...."

Oprah gave an 800 number for people to call and contribute $10. Half would go to UNICEF for children in the Third World, and the other half would go to Save the Children for children in this country. Oprah gave the number over and over. So many people called, the phone lines shut down. It took four days for some to get through. The 800 number was called by 46,000 and another 9,000 called RESULTS Educational Fund's 900 number to find out where the candlelight vigil nearest them would be. Oprah's show aired in the U.S. on Friday, September 21, two days before the vigils, and was beamed to 10 other countries.

At 6:30 a.m., the morning of the vigils, I was on the phone with Joan Russell at Casey Base in Antarctica where 26 scientists held a vigil at the Australian base. I asked what the weather was like in Antarctica that day. "Today has been the most beautiful day on earth," said Russell. "And in fact, it's a very fitting day to celebrate. We've had about 14 hours of daylight, brilliant sunshine, a full hemisphere of cloudless blue sky." I knew she was talking not only about the beauty of the day, but about the beauty of people coming together around the world to address the unfinished business of caring for children.

Holly Garrard, the RESULTS group leader from Rapid City, South Dakota, was another of the thousands of vigil organizers around the world. "When I first read about the Candlelight Vigils in the letters to RESULTS groups leaders, I wasn't exactly sure what they were talking about," said Holly, echoing the sentiments of most RESULTS volunteers. "I'd never participated in a candlelight vigil, and I couldn't even envision what it would be like.

"Before the RESULTS International Conference," Holly continued, "I could imagine something simple, at our church or maybe on the steps of city hall. But the synergy in the room at the international conference moved me. People's awareness of the possibility convinced me to do something wonderful. Before I left Washington, D.C., I called my local newspaper and did an interview over the phone. Before I picked up the phone, I was fully committed to doing whatever it took. On the flight home, I could imagine something bigger than the church or the city hall. I began to think about the football field. A day or so after I got back home, the article was in the paper titled, 'Local Woman Plans Vigil.' Everyone who read it knew what I was up to.

"The next morning, I went to work and shared my enthusiasm about it. I walked with a friend from work to lunch downtown. I was bubbling over, telling her all the things that I learned and giving my picture of what the vigil could be and what we'd need, and she said, 'Why don't we have it at Mt. Rushmore?' I was silent at first, being a bit intimidated by hosting a vigil at the foot of Mt. Rushmore. But obviously Mt. Rushmore was the right place. It would be not just a Rapid City vigil but a Black Hills vigil for all of western South Dakota.

"The first thing I did was go to the director of the Rapid City children's chorus and ask if she'd be a part of it. When she said yes, I knew it was going to work, I knew things were going to fall into place. That same week, I got in touch with the Little Wound School Indian Dancers. One of their leaders said yes immediately. The third thing I did that week was to start raising money for the event. I spoke to the Rotary Club, my church, and my company, College Survival. College Survival established the Brande Foundation and decided to make the vigil one of its projects.

"My biggest stumbling block was that I felt I didn't get enough people involved in the planning process. I wasn't able to enroll people as well as I would like, and I often felt alone.

"We worked hard to get the word out. I met the person in charge of distributing information in the schools. As long as I provided the brochures, they would distribute them to the 10,000 students. The Candlelight Vigil TV spots with Valerie Harper and Louis Gossett Jr. sent to us by the main office were aired on the ABC and NBC affiliates more than 75 times.

"I invited the local ABC affiliate's news director, whose family owns the station, to be the moderator. I called her, and she said yes by just hearing about it on the phone. I hadn't even mailed her anything. She was eight months pregnant when she moderated. When I called to have her MC, I also asked if they'd co-sponsor. The TV station covered the children practicing their song ahead of time and ran it on the news. We had six ads run in the newspaper. The morning of the vigil, I got a call from a woman who had been recently widowed. She had planned a trip to the Black Hills with her husband before he died, and she came along anyway. She read about the vigil in the paper and called me because my name was listed as the contact. She was nervous about going out alone at night, so I invited her to come along with me. She was a retired school teacher. I picked her up at her motel. She helped pass out programs and candles.

"Once it all started I was in the audience like everyone else. I didn't want to be on the stage myself. The moment I remember most about the vigil was when we sang 'In Our Hands.' The candles were lit and the stage lights were turned out. I remember it was very still, and all of a sudden the lights of Mt. Rushmore came on. It was so moving.

"After completing the vigil at Mt. Rushmore, I knew I was capable of more than I had thought I was. My appreciation of my talents grew, and it strengthened my resolve to be involved in this worldwide issue and organization."

On that day, Holly had many partners. Starting in Antarctica and New Zealand, the vigils swept around the world: 250,000 people attended vigils in Togo; 65,000 attended one in Kharkov, in the Ukraine; Grameen Bank borrowers in Bangladesh held vigils at more than 12,000 sites; *Time* magazine ran a 1 1/2-page color picture of the New York City vigil; four heads of state (Argentina, Australia, Denmark, and the Philippines) participated in the vigils in their countries. The special observances and ceremonies that took place around the world were testimony to the universality of the events: from the ringing of 108 Buddhist temple bells in South Korea to the vigil on the side of Mt. Fuji in Japan. But perhaps the most compelling of all were the five vigils that took place in the searing heat of Ethiopian refugee camps.

One week later I attended the summit itself. My arrival at the UN for the summit said it all. Because 71 heads of state were attending, traffic was cut off for blocks. My cab got me as close as possible, and I walked the rest of the way. When I got to the front of the UN, there was a line of black limousines delivering heads of state to my right. As I looked to my left, the direction from which they were coming, there were black limousines interspersed with vehicles with flashing red lights as far as the eye could see. My first thought was "a funeral—the largest funeral I've ever seen—a funeral for the children." A moment later the thought shifted to "coming to the rescue—the leaders are coming to the rescue." Tears began to well up, and I hadn't even entered the building yet.

Early in the summit program the video "341" was shown to the heads of state. It was estimated that 341 children would die during the 12 minutes it took to view the specially made tape. UNICEF Executive Director Jim Grant, speaking just after the video, pointed to the screen and said, "This is why we are here." After a short pause he continued, "One week ago, over a million candles were lit by ordinary people around the world for the success of this summit. Each of those candles represented the inextinguishable hope in the hearts of people everywhere that, amid all the problems and the dangers of the years ahead, the world can still be made a better place."

In October 1990 the *New York Times* said, "The largest global summit meeting in history pledged to do better by the world's children. Their promises were eloquent, their goals ambitious. But children cannot survive or thrive on promises. The world's leaders now have an obligation to find the resources and the political will necessary to translate hope into reality."

The World Summit for Children was a beacon in a world of nations groping in the darkness. The leaders agreed to cutting child deaths by at least one-third, halving child malnutrition and maternal mortality, and providing universal access to basic education, clean water, safe sanitation, and family planning information and services.

The World Summit for Children Keeping the Promise campaign is a decade-long effort to mobilize the world's children and adults to see to it that the promises of the World Summit for Children are fulfilled. Materials have been prepared for schools and places of worship and will be developed for organizations and the work-place. They will give everyone an opportunity to play a part in fulfilling the summit's goals.

CHAPTER 23

Starting RESULTS in the USSR

Today may represent the beginning of a change in the lives of the world's children. Today, in this hall, they may finally have found the voices and the friends they have long been seeking. With all the demands on governments to fund worthwhile activities, there will never be enough money to do everything and priorities will have to be established and difficult choices made. Funding is important but it is not, in the end, the decisive factor in the war on child suffering. Political will is.

Canadian Prime Minister Brian Mulroney
at the World Summit for Children

One Candlelight Vigil participant was a country I didn't think we should expand to, but it produced the largest single vigil in the world. Dixine Hardesty, a California RESULTS leader with a love for whitewater rafting, followed her passion to what was then the Soviet Union and took RESULTS along. "In the spring of 1989," Dixine recalled, "I had a rare opportunity to participate in a joint Soviet-American whitewater rafting expedition in Siberia. A few weeks before the expedition, I found myself sitting in a group of eight partners in a workshop at the RESULTS International Conference in Washington, D.C. The workshop question for group discussion was, 'What are you grappling with?' My usual answer would have been 'nothing,' because I considered myself a weak partner. But this time, I *was* grappling with something. I knew I would be creating life-long friendships with Soviet people during my expedition and realized I was probably going to do nothing about bringing RESULTS there, an opportunity any other RESULTS partner would seize in a heartbeat. The Cold War was still going on, but Gorbachev was allowing our American rafting team to receive special diplomatic visas to conduct this expedition. I told this to my little group, and at the break, my buddy David Firshein came up to me and said, 'We need to get you the RESULTS brochure translated into Russian so you can get this thing DONE!...I have some connections...don't worry, I will handle it.' And he did. The next thing I knew, I was on a plane to Moscow with a stack of Russian RESULTS brochures and a SECAM format video The Hunger Project had just reproduced with Russian narration. "After my arrival in the USSR," Dixine continued, "I discovered that 99.9 percent of the people I encountered spoke no English at all. The only way I could communicate about RESULTS was to hand someone a brochure, smile, and nod my head. Guessing from the people's reactions to the brochure, I was starting to believe that there was a good chance this thing could actually catch on. I started having visions of Sam's nightmares about Action Sheets in Russian and decided that I needed to find someone who would be responsible for finding a RESULTS USSR national leader who could speak English."

Dixine set her sights on Pony, the interpreter of the expedition. Pony was a 21-year-old English major at Moscow University.

"Near the last days of the expedition," Dixine continued, "after everyone had exhausted themselves of the gift-giving orgy that Americans and Soviets always have together, I took Pony aside and explained to her that I wanted to give her the greatest gift I was bringing from America. I told her about RESULTS and asked if she thought the Soviet people were ready for such a concept as lobbying their government. 'Of course we are,' she retorted, 'we now have Perestroika!' She told me she had friends that would get involved in RESULTS. She became very excited when I gave her the stack of brochures and the video, in a water-proof ziplock bag, no less.

"Back in California, I soon began to receive letters from Pony's friend, Olga, wanting more information about RESULTS. Olga, a journalism student at Moscow University, was a leading editor for the *Student Meridian* magazine (circulation 1.1 million). I wrote her explaining everything I could think of, from how we serve snacks at our education and action meetings to why we create positive relationships with our representatives. At the same time, because the brochure had the RESULTS address on it, Sam was receiving letters in Russian from other Soviets asking for more RESULTS information. He decided to pass along the letters and his dilemma to Karen Cloud, a brilliant Santa Barbara partner who had started RESULTS from scratch in Australia."

RESULTS leaders from Canada visited Moscow and led the first RESULTS presentation that officially started the group and identified the new partners.

"Numerous letters and phone conversations between Olga, Karen, and myself resulted in slow, but steady progress," Dixine continued. "Thanks to Karen, who strategically mastered the secrets of the Soviet visa structure, the next international conference included our first partners from the Soviet

Union: Olga; her boss, Yuri; and Andrei, an associate *Student Meridian* editor. At the beginning of the conference, each group in the U.S. and each of the other countries came to the stage and introduced themselves to the 300 participants. As the finale in the introductory 'parade of groups,' the three Soviets stood on the conference stage holding their big red USSR flag and received a roaring standing ovation that lasted more than 10 minutes. They were astounded by the emotion and energy in the room! They held up several RESULTS editorials and news articles they had generated, along with a picture on the front page of *Pravda* of Olga handing President Gorbachev a copy of the *Student Meridian* magazine containing an article about RESULTS, with his reply that she and her RESULTS partners were 'the new generation of Perestroika.' Through all the commotion and excitement, Andrei smiled at me from the stage. All I could do was cry."

As senior editors of *Student Meridian*, all were members of the Communist Party and had impressive access to senior Soviet government officials. "In the summer of 1990," Dixine continued, "I had yet another opportunity to return to the Soviet Union to co-lead another rafting expedition. I decided that I would take an extra few weeks to stay with Olga and Andrei and work with them on RESULTS matters. When I arrived in Moscow, Olga told me that she had arranged for us to meet with the Soviet Minister of Education. Never in my wildest dreams did I ever believe that a minister in the USSR would meet with me for *any* reason. Indeed, the meeting transpired, and we told him about RESULTS and the candlelight vigils that RESULTS was initiating to bring worldwide attention to the upcoming World Summit for Children. The minister said that he was glad to see an organization like RESULTS come to the Soviet Union. He also told us it would be very difficult to get official permission to have such a vigil event in Moscow, but that he would use his influence to help Olga arrange for a location for the Moscow vigil."

With the unraveling of Eastern bloc Communism at the end of 1989, there was little enthusiasm from Soviet authorities for mass rallies and demonstrations.

"Upon returning to Moscow after my expedition," Dixine recalled, "Andrei informed me that he had arranged for the two of us to take the train down to the city of Kharkov in the Ukraine (population 2 million), where his brother Igor was the leading editor of the *Evening Kharkov* newspaper. He told me his brother wanted to start a RESULTS group there. That's all he needed to say, and I was packed and ready to go. Keeping my English-speaking, non-visa-holding mouth shut, we took the 10-hour train ride south. Upon arrival, we met Igor, who had prearranged meetings for us with various groups, individuals, and officials in the city to discuss RESULTS, the World Summit for Children, and the Candlelight Vigils. Igor knew everyone in town. We met with the head of the Children's Fund, the priest of the most predominant church in the city, the director of the orphanage, and other people involved with children. We also had a meeting with six individuals Igor had enrolled in launching the Kharkov RESULTS group.

"Andrei was my interpreter through all of the meetings," Dixine continued. "As I spoke about RESULTS and the vigils, and waited for Andrei's translation, I was amazed at the emotional reactions on their faces, and I could see that the words I was saying were having more of an impact than I ever would have imagined. They had tears of joy in their eyes, with replies like, 'This is the most important gift anyone has ever brought for us!' and, 'We can't believe that Americans, who have everything, care about poor people in other countries so much as to get this involved in such a difficult cause.' They repeatedly asked me if I was the leader of the RESULTS organization. I had a difficult time convincing them I was only a volunteer. I actually couldn't believe it was me doing this, as if it should have been someone more qualified, with a bigger history of RESULTS accomplishments. They kissed and hugged me, gave me flowers, and started making plans.

"Igor arranged to have stories of all the meetings printed on the front page of the *Evening Kharkov* for three consecutive days. In Kharkov, folks actually wait in the city square for the newspaper to come out. A few hours before mass printing of the entire paper is complete, copies of the first few pages are displayed in a glass case in the square. Each day, a crowd of people gathers around the glass case to be the first ones to preview the news. It was very exciting for me to see those front-page articles in Kharkov, especially since I had never been successful in generating an editorial back home. When Igor saw my excitement over the articles, he asked, 'Then you are pleased?' At the end of my four days in Kharkov, Igor escorted Andrei and me back to the train station. As we were boarding, Igor announced to me, 'I think after having these meetings with the various officials and newly formed RESULTS group, we will have a candlelight vigil event of at least 5,000 people.' I patted him on the shoulder and cynically replied, 'Yeah, yeah, just do your best.' Igor smiled, and then Andrei and I left for Moscow and my flight home. Six weeks later, back in my engineering office in California, I received a fax from Andrei in Moscow, informing me that Kharkov just had a candlelight vigil of 65,000 people! It was the largest candlelight vigil in the world. Moscow had several events of their own throughout the city.

"With the help of Karen's proven expertise in Soviet paper-chasing, Igor was able to attend the next RESULTS International Conference," Dixine concluded. "In addition to several news articles, he brought with him a video of the Kharkov vigils that someone in his city was able to produce, yet no one there was able to view because no one had a video player! Someone on the RESULTS staff had it converted from SECAM to the U.S. format so that a segment of the video could be played at the conference. Everyone in the room had heard of the Kharkov vigil's success, but when Igor stood on the stage, modestly told his story, and showed his video, he received the same kind of roaring ovation that his brother had received at the previous year's conference. During all the commotion and excitement, he looked at me from the stage and smiled. All I could do was cry."

CHAPTER 24

How to Heal the Break Between People and Government

The Presentation Is the First Step

I have received occasional visits from Shirley Williams and other RESULTS representatives for several years now. My first impulse was to dismiss them as starry-eyed dreamers, but instead of misty idealism, they always came with a concrete plan with a track record of success in helping the poorest of the world's poor.

Alan W. Bock, Senior Columnist
The Orange County Register, *September 27, 1987*

A question I'm often asked, in one form or another, is, "Where do you find these people? Aren't the RESULTS volunteers born leaders?"

Obviously, some people *are* much more ready to act than others. But ready or not, we all face barriers to action: discouragement, cynicism, alienation, and frustration. It's what I call the break between people and government. This break comes from the hopelessness we feel about issues, in RESULTS' case hunger, but it could be *any* issue. It comes from our sense that political will has nothing to do with us. The break between people and government comes from our sense of ineffectiveness and our belief that political priorities are in the hands of special interests. But there's more. These barriers to action also include our lack of timely information on legislation, our inexperience with things such as writing to a member of Congress, and our sense that there is no ongoing structure of support that would work—a structure that would continue to train and encourage us.

These are all components of the break between people and government. The presentation to start a RESULTS group is designed to set the healing process in motion and awaken the commitment to service that is deep within each of us. It is a call to democracy. The purpose of a RESULTS presentation is to inspire people with the difference they can make, working with others, to create the political will to end hunger. The intent is to start a RESULTS group with a core of four partners. Each presentation is different, but they share common threads.

The presentation that follows took place in the meeting room of a local community center. Metal folding chairs were set in a circle on a well-worn carpet. The florescent lighting was a little bright, but workable. This was the first time any of the participants had been to a RESULTS presentation.

The invitation process had been exacting. As leader of the meeting, it was my job to find a local host. Identifying a local host is an arduous process that starts with seeking leads and continues with phone conversations to introduce myself, describe RESULTS, and determine if there is interest in hosting a meeting. It's best when the local host is committed to starting a group and being one of the four partners. When I find a host, I ask him or her to find four others to be part of an inviting team. Within two weeks, the five of them gather around a speaker phone, and I introduce them to RESULTS and launch the inviting process. The five inviters agreed to invite a total of 60 persons over the phone with a follow-up by mail. After four weeks of inviting, a total of 15 was expected.

As always, I wore a coat and tie for the presentation. Most of the others were dressed more casually. There was a mix of excitement and apprehension in the air—excitement that this meeting might make a difference and apprehension that it wouldn't.

There were 12 seated in the circle—the host, the four other inviters, six of the invited guests and I. We expected several more. I noticed that the inviting team seemed discouraged. I told them that the others would be arriving soon and that it was always like this.

Low attendance and the difficulty of leading exciting education and action meetings month after month are what usually kill RESULTS groups. It's a kind of "catch 22." You invite your friends, and they don't come, so you're discouraged. Or, you invite your friends, they *do* come, and it's a boring meeting, and you're discouraged again. Either way, you lose. This is why we include so much support and training, with special attention on powerful speaking.

I thanked everyone for coming and took a moment to acknowledge the work done by the host and team of inviters. The meeting continued with a section we call the "focusing activity." At this meeting, it would be a piece read aloud, with each person in the group taking a turn.

"You've come from home, from work, or from school," I told them, "and your attention is likely to be focused anywhere but on tonight's meeting. This reading will give you a sense of the problem of world hunger and some of the solutions. You'll see that people like you and me are the ones who can do something about it."

The focusing activity was an eight-page, 8 1/2 by 11-inch sized newspaper called *A Shift In The Wind*. It came from The Hunger Project. Most of the type was headline-sized and there were only a few words on each page. I asked the host of the evening to read first.

"If you really knew," the host began, "the ability you have to make a difference in the world. It will take you about five minutes to read this entire newspaper word for word. In those five minutes, a transformation can take place that will not only affect the quality of your own life, but also the quality of life for all humanity...."

We turned to the second page and I asked the next person to read.

"Eighteen children die every minute," he began. "More people have died as a consequence of hunger in the past six years than have been killed in all the wars, revolutions and murders in the past 150 years....The devastation is equivalent to a Hiroshima every three days."

The numbers are startling, and it was the first time that most of the newly invited people had had to grapple with them.

"No one dies of hunger because there is not enough [food] to go around," the third reader continued.

The newspaper asserts that eliminating hunger would contribute to defusing the population bomb because when parents know that their children will live, they're more likely to practice family planning. It also says that there are no technological barriers to ending hunger.

The fifth reader continued at the top of page five:

"Hunger is not inevitable," she began. "Everyone knows that people will always starve the way everyone knew that man would never fly.

> At one time in human history, everyone knew that...
> the world was flat, the sun revolved around the earth,
> slavery was an economic necessity,
> a four-minute mile was impossible,
> polio and smallpox would always be with us,
> and no one would ever set foot on the moon...
> until courageous people challenged old beliefs and a new idea's time had come.

"What's missing?" the next page asked.

> If there is enough to go around,

> If there are solutions we can afford,
> If hunger is not inevitable,
> Why do millions of us continue to starve?
> In 1977, the National Academy of Sciences published the results of a two-year study on world hunger conducted with the assistance of more than 1,500 experts from around the world.

"The quote you're about to read," I interrupted, "points directly to why we are here tonight. It points directly to the purpose of this evening and of RESULTS. It calls for the *political will* to end hunger."

The reader continued:

> [The National Academy of Sciences] report concludes that, 'If there is the political will in this country and abroad...it should be possible to overcome the worst aspects of widespread hunger and malnutrition within one generation.'

It was quotes like this one that prompted me to ask thousands of high school students the name of their member of Congress. It was their responses that led to the creation of RESULTS.

The final page concluded: "You make the difference. The ability to create a worldwide commitment to end hunger in this century resides *only* within individuals...Hunger persists in a condition in which we believe we are powerless—that there is nothing we can do to make a difference. It is a condition characterized either by conflict, arguments, and opinions or hopeless, helpless frustration. When we recognize the truth—*that hunger can be ended*—that condition is transformed, and our natural desire to make a difference in the world can be expressed. Commitment generates action. Action transforms an idea into reality. The worldwide commitment to end hunger begins within you...."

As usual, a feeling of unity began to emerge in the room, but it was very fragile at this point.

"Is there anyone who'd like to say something?" I asked.

"I walked in here and wasn't sure why I came," a woman volunteered. "I wasn't sure if I was in the right place. Now I'm sure I am."

A man raised his hand. "This is all well and good," he said, "but it's a lot more complicated than this!"

I agreed and asked him to bear with us. Throughout the evening, I gave people an opportunity to express their feelings, not with an eye to changing anything, but just to offer a chance to get whatever was on their minds out into the open.

After welcoming the three latecomers who had arrived during the focusing activity, I continued with a quote by Sen. Mark Hatfield (R-OR). It was my way of thanking everyone for being there.

"We stand by as children starve by the millions," Hatfield said, "because we lack the will to eliminate hunger. Yet we have found the will to develop missiles capable of flying over the polar cap and landing within a few hundred feet of their target. This is not innovation. It is a profound distortion of humanity's purpose on earth."

"I say that you are here tonight because of your commitment to correcting the distortion of humanity's purpose on earth," I told them.

There are two reasons I use the Hatfield quote. One is that the quote is so moving to me and it allows me to say to people, "this is not going to be an ordinary meeting." I also use it to acknowledge people's commitment to seeing justice done. You don't have to be Martin Luther King Jr. before you deserve acknowledgment for your commitment. For me, it is something that is always there, and pointing to it can help bring it out.

"In a moment," I continued, "I'm going to ask you to tell us your name, your occupation, what you're committed to in life, and what you'd like to get out of this meeting."

We aren't often asked what we're committed to in life, but it's important to consider because that's where participation in a group like RESULTS comes from. I asked the evening's host to go first.

"My name is Sally Moody, and I'm a high school teacher," she began. "What am I committed to in life?" Sally asked aloud. "I'm committed to my family. I have two little girls, a four year old and a six year old, and I want to do whatever I can to improve the world they grow up in. Doing something about hunger is a step in that direction. I'd like to come away feeling I can make a difference with my government. I don't feel that way now. Oh yeah," she added, "I'd like us to start a RESULTS group tonight."

The next person turned her gaze away from Sally and began.

"My name is Ellen Steele," said the woman sitting next to Sally. "I'm working in a homeless shelter here in town. Things keep getting worse instead of better. I have no idea how I can change that, but I know I have to try. I saw a flier about tonight, so I came."

Several other people introduced themselves. Some noticed that their vision seemed to be larger than the lives they were living. They seemed to be open to letting more of the world in. Others seemed more protective.

After everyone had spoken, I introduced myself. I shared my initial hopelessness, my route into the issue of hunger, and I talked about statements calling for the political will to end hunger. I told them I asked 7,000 high school students the name of their member of Congress and that only 200 knew the answer.

"There are 140 RESULTS groups in nine countries (Australia, Canada, El Salvador, Germany, Great Britain, Japan, Russia, the Ukraine, and the United States)," I said in describing RESULTS and how it works. "Each group has a minimum of four key volunteers we call 'partners' who attend three meetings a month for a four-month period."

I know it's important to be unapologetic about the three meetings a month. In our microwave, instant-coffee, sound-bite world, three meetings a month is asking a lot. But I know this kind of commitment is important if we are to develop community leaders.

"The first of the three meetings," I continued, "is a nationwide telephone conference call each month with a guest speaker and 200 to 300 RESULTS partners on the phone together. Some of the guests have included the head of UNICEF and other UN agencies, members of the House and Senate, hunger experts, and presidential candidates. It's a bit like an extension course once a month by telephone."

Most people had never heard of a conference call linking 200 to 300 people. I knew they were intrigued.

"The second meeting is the delivery meeting where we learn to speak the issues," I explained. "One of the things that's missing is spokespersons—people who can *speak* clearly on the issues and the opportunities for action. You see, if I went over a basic piece of information and asked if you understood and you nodded your heads yes, that would be good, but you aren't dangerous to the conditions of ignorance and apathy until you can speak powerfully. The delivery meeting focuses on that.

"The third meeting is the education and action meeting," I continued, "where the four or five partners invite their friends so that 10, 15, or 20 gather to study an issue and write letters to an elected official or the newspaper. What does all this activity add up to?" I asked rhetorically. "Let me go over one of our victories and show what this kind of effort and training can accomplish."

I described a victory in tripling the Child Survival Fund from $25 million to $75 million. It's an exciting story to tell, and it lets people know that things can work—that there are ways to make their voice heard.

At each presentation, I observe an interesting phenomenon. When things get exciting, people begin to consider becoming a partner in a local RESULTS group. But when things get boring the feeling changes to, "No way, I'm not going to be a part of this." It's my job to ask the right questions so people see the opportunity they have to make a difference in the world.

I asked everyone to reach under their chairs for the RESULTS brochure and to read silently from a quote at the top of the second panel. It reads, "If there is the political will in this country and abroad...it should be possible to overcome the worst aspects of widespread hunger and malnutrition within one generation."

"Raise your hand if you've never seen this quote from the National Academy of Sciences Food and Nutrition Report," I said.

Ten people raised their hands, everyone but the inviting team. The team of inviters had seen it when we met on our first speaker-box call. "I'm going to have the quote read aloud twice," I continued, "and then ask you to answer two questions. I only want to hear from the 10 of you who've never seen the quote before." Other than during introductions, many of the people hadn't spoken yet. I was very intent on hearing from everyone.

"The first question I'll ask is, 'What is political will?' Just respond, 'Political will is'—and then give your answer.

"The second question," I continued, "is, 'How would you respond if this quote had been directed to you personally?' For example, let's say a news commentator walked up to you on the street, read this quote to you, and asked for your reaction. What would you *say*?"

"We'll start with the first question," I told them, " 'What is political will?' "

I asked for someone to read the quote aloud the first time. One of the latecomers volunteered: "If there is the political will in this country and abroad...it should be possible to overcome the worst aspects of widespread hunger and malnutrition within one generation."

I thanked the first reader and asked for someone to read it a second time. The quote was read aloud a second time and I repeated my question, " 'What is political will?' " There was a long silence. The tendency is to avoid silences, but I usually bask in them. It gives people more time to think and eliminates the illusion that they are off the hook because someone else has answered.

"What is political will?" I asked again, and then a hand went up.

"I'd say political will is when people in power decide to do something," responded a high school student who'd come with her mom. "That's political will."

"Political will is when people in power decide to do something," I repeated. "That's political will." Throughout this part of the meeting I never try to discuss or change people's responses, I just repeat them. I want people to feel comfortable speaking their mind and not feel they are being judged. This section is important to healing the break between people and government. People can begin to see the role they play in creating political will.

"OK," I asked, "Who else? What is political will?" I wasn't going to stop until I heard from all of them on either the first or the second question. Some members of the group buried their heads in the brochure, searching, I think, for anonymity.

An elderly gentleman spoke up. "I'd say political will is when the people want something done and those in power respond because they want to stay there."

"Political will," I repeated, "is when the people want something done and those in power respond because they want to stay there."

This process of question, answer, and repetition continued until five or six had responded.

"Read the quote again if you need to," I told the group, "and then I want one of the 10 who hadn't seen this quote before tonight to answer the second question, 'What would you say if a reporter asked for your response?' "

This was tougher, but someone took on the spirit of the evening and replied. "I'd say, 'Yes, we can do it if we all get involved.' "

"Yes, we can do it if we all get involved," I repeated. "Who's next?" I asked. "How would you respond if this quote had been said to you personally?"

"I'd say there must be some mistake," joked a man wearing a bow tie. "I'd say, you've come to the wrong house."

"There must be some mistake," I repeated, "you've come to the wrong house. So, you're basically saying 'I'm not the one,' " I continued, the only time I commented on a reply.

"I'm so resigned about politics," responded a woman who hadn't spoken yet. "It keeps me from saying any government program can work. But it's hard for me to say that because I'm afraid others are likely to shoot me down and I'll feel foolish."

I repeated her comment and thanked her for her honesty.

"Now I'd like you to read the quote on the first panel of the brochure," I said to the woman who had just spoken. "It's by the late Bartlett Giamatti. Giamatti was baseball commissioner but made this statement when he was president of Yale. I'd like each of you to tell me if you think it's true."

"What concerns me most today," the woman began, "is the way we have disconnected ideas from power in America, and created for ourselves thoughtful citizens who disdain politics and politicians, when more than ever we need to value politics and what politicians do...."

I repeated the quote because I believe it begins to express the depth of our cynicism and discouragement. The entire quote was read a second time.

I waited for the group to respond, but there was more silence. This is a strange moment, a little like someone in a dysfunctional family blurting out a family secret and then explicating it. In this case it was more like a secret in a politically dysfunctional society. It is both horrifying and refreshing.

"What do you think?" I asked. "Is this quote true?"

The evening's host raised her hand. "I want to say that I think the quote *is* true and it makes me want to do something to change it." Several people in the room nodded their heads in agreement.

"I've used Giamatti's statement in more than 100 presentations," I told them, "and each time people agreed that it's true. Every once in a while someone questions the 'thoughtful citizens' part, but they always agree with the rest. Turn to the back panel," I continued, "to the quote by James Grant, executive director of UNICEF. This would be *my* answer to the question, 'What is political will?' " I told them.

The man in the bow tie read the quote, "Each of the great social achievements of recent decades has come about not because of government proclamations, but because people organized, made demands, and made it good politics for governments to respond. It is the political will of the people that makes and sustains the political will of governments."

"This is the good news and the bad news," I told them. "If the political will of the people is asleep at the wheel, then the political will of government is likely to be asleep at the wheel. RESULTS is here to bring a wake-up call to citizens and to government.

"I want you to look at one more quote that's a favorite of mine," I continued. "It's one that helped keep me going when things got tough. It's by R. Buckminster Fuller, the futurist and inventor of things such as the geodesic dome. The quote is on the bottom of the third panel of the brochure. Fuller said, 'The things to do are—the things that need doing; that *you* see need to be done, and that *no one else* seems to see need to be done.'

"When 6,800 out of 7,000 high school students didn't know the names of their members of Congress, I knew there was something that needed doing," I told the group, "and I knew it was going to be hard. The quote really says something about looking for yourself at what needs doing and not just going along with the crowd. Participating in RESULTS is an act of not going along with the crowd."

Before we moved to the next section of the meeting, I again went over what we look for to start a RESULTS group. Participation in RESULTS involves a sincere desire to make a difference in the world. Partners commit to attending three meetings each month, and I reviewed the three meetings again. I pointed to the brochure panel that the group would fill out at the end of the evening to participate in the local group. It's crucial to keep the question before the group: Are you willing to be a partner in this group? I do this by reminding them at the beginning, in the middle, and at the end of the meeting what it takes to be a partner.

The next section of the meeting is the education and action section where the participants learn about an issue and have an opportunity to take action. The first part of the meeting helps to melt some of the cynicism, but people aren't prepared to take action yet.

"Here's what will happen next," I told the group. "I'm going to make a presentation on this evening's issue, show a short video, take you through a quick learning exercise, guide you through writing a letter to your representative, have a few letters read out loud, and then see who would like to participate in a local RESULTS group.

"The issue for this evening," I continued, "is the World Summit for Children Implementation Act, a bill that would provide the U.S. share of the funds needed to fulfill the promises made at the World Summit for Children."

I described the gathering of heads of state and government in September 1990 where 71 leaders and high-level delegations from 88 other countries agreed to goals for the year 2000: cut child deaths by at least one-third; cut child malnutrition and maternal mortality by one-half; and provide universal access to basic education, clean water and safe sanitation, and family planning education and services. I reminded them that 40,000 children died *each day* from largely preventable causes. I told them that 100 million children of primary school age are not enrolled in any form of schooling and that half a million women die each year from complications in pregnancy and childbirth.

The briefing outlined the problems and how the legislation would fund cost-effective programs to address them. Millions of children could be saved by vaccination programs costing $15 per child.[24] Millions more could be saved if parents knew how to prepare 10 cents worth of sugar, salt, and water to prevent death from dehydration. Millions could be saved by a dollar's worth of antibiotics. Inexpensive systems for clean water and safe sanitation could be provided which would help fight unnecessary disease. In some countries, a year's worth of primary school could be provided for $30 per child. Most of the group were shocked by the information and by the notion that people like them could do anything about it.

After the briefing I showed the video "341." The title referred to the number of children who would die during the 12 minutes it took to view the program. The video had been shown to the world leaders at the Children's Summit.

"We were all children once," the video begins, as children's faces fade and then become the faces of the world leaders attending the summit. "But some children never grow up to their potential, and some never grow up at all. Every day in our world 40,000 children die. Each death, the death of a child who had a personality and a potential, a family and a future. Forty thousand a day. A quarter of a million a week—a child every two seconds."

As the program continued, a child's face was shown every two seconds. Each face went from color to black and white. There was a number with each child. The number climbed every two seconds—15—16—17—18...all the way to 341.

"And behind every child who dies," the program declared, "10 more live on with malnutrition—unable to grow normally in body or in mind. By any measure, this is the greatest tragedy of our times. But because it happens every day, it simply isn't news."

The silence in the room at the end of the video was broken by my call for comments.

"I didn't know how bad it was," one of the participants said, his voice quivering with emotion. "I think of my own son and can only imagine the pain the parents feel. I'd like to come away with a team to work with so I don't spend my whole life turning away from these problems."

"What about children in this country?" someone else asked. "Was there a summit for them?"

I described 1990 as the year of the promises to children. In addition to

---

[24]In the 1980s it was estimated that a child in the Third World could be immunized for $5. Escalating costs and reaching those hardest to reach increased the cost to $15 per child in the early 1990s.

the World Summit for Children at the United Nations, there was a U.S. Education Summit attended by the president and the nation's 50 governors, and there were health goals set for the year 2000 by the U.S. Public Health Service. One of its goals matched the UN Summit's goal of cutting infant deaths by one-third by the year 2000. One of the Education Summit's six goals was that every American child should start school ready to learn.

The briefing and the video offered the kind of training the group might have expected from an evening like this. The next section went far beyond that.

"There are two things I want to say about what we are going to do next," I announced. "First, if you are from another organization and you're looking for something potent to take with you, something worth stealing—this next section, the Laser Talk, is what you're looking for. Second, I want to warn everyone that learning the Laser Talk is a little like being back in school, but it's among the most powerful activities in RESULTS.

"Here's how it works," I explained. "I'm going to deliver a two-minute talk. After the talk, I'll ask questions to see what you remember. I only want those who are new this evening to call out the answers. After we've done that, I'll go back to the beginning, ask the questions again, but this time I want you to just think the answers—don't shout them out loud. Let me show you what I mean.

"The talk begins like this: In 1990, 71 heads of state and government met in New York City at the World Summit for Children. Around the world 35,000 children die each day from largely preventable malnutrition and disease.[25] After I finish, I'll ask those who are new to shout out answers to questions like this, 'In 1990 how many heads of state and government met?' Don't be shy, just shout it out," I told them.

"Seventy-one," said the man in the bow tie. "That's right," I said, "but everyone should call out the answer. 'In 1990, 71 heads of state and government met.'

"At what event?" I asked.

"The World Summit for Children," everyone responded.

"Good," I replied.

"Now," I continued, "How many children die each day?"

"Thirty-five thousand" was the reply.

"Good," I told them. "Thirty-five thousand children die each day. From what?" I asked.

"Preventable malnutrition and disease," answered the new people in the room.

---

[25]UNICEF's *State of the World's Children 1993* report estimated, for the first time, that 35,000 children die each day, which is 5,000 fewer deaths than we'd been citing for many years.

"Very good," I responded.

"This time, I'll ask the same questions," I said, "but I want you to just think the answers—don't call them out. For example, in 1990 how many heads of state and government met? Remember, don't call out the answer, just think it to yourself."

After a brief silence, I said, "In 1990, 71 heads of state and government met. Now, what was the name of the event?" I asked. "Again, don't call out the answers, just think it to yourself."

After another silence I said, "They met at the World Summit for Children."

After the demonstration, we were ready to go through the whole process. There was an air of anticipation in the room. People wondered if they could remember more than the one or two sentences we'd practiced.

"Put your pens away," I told them. "I don't want anyone to take notes during this exercise." Everyone took a deep breath, and I started the talk. The group listened intently. I'm sure they retained more of the information than they imagined they would. After the two question periods—shouting out the answers and just thinking them—they each took a partner and practiced presenting the talk. Then I asked for a volunteer to come to the front of the room to deliver the talk—someone who'd never heard this information before tonight. Most of the group checked to make sure their hands were *not* raised—in fact some were sliding their hands off their laps and moving them closer to the floor.

They were all relieved when a woman volunteered. When she finished, everyone applauded. After all, she had gotten them off the hook, and she had done a great job.

Again, the room felt different. They not only understood the information and had seen a video about it, but now they could speak about it. We were ready for action.

I passed out the RESULTS Action Sheet, which reviewed what the group had already learned (including the needed action), and envelopes that the group addressed to their members of Congress.

"Who is writing their first letter to a member of Congress?" I asked. Most of the hands went up.

"OK," I continued. "Who hasn't written a letter to their member of Congress in the last three years?" Everyone's hand went up.

Their letters asked their members of Congress to cosponsor the World Summit for Children Implementation Act, which called for funding programs that represented the U.S. share of keeping the summit's promises. They shared their commitment to the well-being of children, explained the bill in brief, urged cosponsorship, and asked for a reply.

The letter-writing section is always a powerful part of the meeting. Surely the silence during this section is one of the sounds of democracy.

"I know some of you haven't finished your letter," I interrupted 10 minutes later, "but I'd like a few who have finished to read their letters aloud as the rest of us continue writing. Who's finished and would like to start?"

A tentative hand went up, and I encouraged the volunteer.

"I'm a grandmother who has lived in this community for more than 60 years," her letter began. "I'm ashamed to say that this is my first letter to you, but I'm sure it will not be my last." As she continued to read, her letter seemed to enhance the importance of all the others. Ours would not be lone voices in the wilderness. There was a feeling of great power.

I asked for someone else to read their letter aloud. "My name is Sally Moody, and I'm a high school teacher," began the evening's host. "I have two little girls, a four year old and a six year old. I can't imagine having to watch one of them die, and yet that is what the parents of 35,000 children must do each day." As Sally finished, I wondered how many times the representative got letters like *these.*

"What do we do if the representative doesn't answer our letter?" asked the man with the bow tie.

"Give your representative four to six weeks," I responded, "and if you don't get a reply, call the office in Washington. Ask for the aide who handles this issue, tell him or her about your letter and your concern that it might have gotten lost in the mail. This letter is just the starting point for RESULTS," I continued. "If we start a group here tonight, we'll go on to meet with the representatives and with their aides." I could feel hope building in the room, hope that enough people would agree to become partners.

"What was it like to write this letter tonight?" I asked after a third letter had been read aloud.

The participant who complained at the beginning that things were more complicated raised his hand. "Well, I still know things are more complicated," he said, "but this is a good start, and I want to thank you. And, by the way, it felt great to write the letter. With my attitude, sometimes the only thing I do is point out that things aren't working. It was great to take action for once."

"Anyone else?" I asked. "What was it like to write this letter?"

"I didn't want to do it when I came this evening," a woman responded. "But once I started, I loved it. Oh yes, I want you all to know that I went to high school with our representative, and this isn't the last time he'll be hearing from me."

I thanked everyone and announced that this was the time to see if there would be a RESULTS group started in their community. I went over the required three meetings a month for four months. After explaining each briefly, I asked if anyone had a question.

"OK," I asked after receiving no questions, "who's totally excited about becoming a partner and checking that box right now? If you're totally excited and checking the partner box, raise your hand." My hand shot up to show people what I meant, and two of the participants put their hands up. That was two, and we needed two more.

"OK," I continued, "who is not totally excited but still checking the box and becoming a partner tonight?"

Another hand went up. That was three, and we needed one more.

"Who's depressed and checking the box?" I joked.

There were a few chuckles, but no hands.

"Who's thinking about checking the box or has a question?" I asked.

"What if I have to be out of town two weeks next month?" someone asked.

"That's fine," I told him, "just let your group know about it."

"What if you go into a city and only get one or two partners?" someone else asked.

"Here's how I look at it," I replied, "I'll either start a group or I'll plant a time bomb—and I'll take either."

After that, a hand went up, and someone said, "I want to be the fourth partner." A moment later, there were five partners, and the rest of the group said they'd come to the monthly education and action meetings. Several became monthly sponsors pledging financial support.

The last few minutes were a celebration. These people had participated in the birth of a RESULTS group and the rebirth of their democracy.

CHAPTER 25

How to Do It!

RESULTS Innovations

Rehabilitating American democracy...requires much more than reforming the government. It means that citizens at large must also reinvent themselves.

William Greider, Who Will Tell the People?

Everything in this section presupposes access to accurate information and opportunities for legislative action, which are often available from a local or national organization. When a national organization is considering incorporating RESULTS' techniques, I always encourage a pilot project first—take a few innovations and test them in a small number of cities.

Learning to be an articulate spokesperson is central. Initially it's hopelessness that keeps us from effective action. When the hopelessness is replaced by a positive vision, the next barrier to reclaiming our democracy is our inability to speak briefly and powerfully about the issues that concern us. The need for powerful speaking can't be overemphasized. In the Introduction to this book, I said, "Members of Congress know everything we've ever asked them to know—which isn't very much." The same is true of editorial writers and other people of influence. It's almost as if there were a conspiracy "not to know." The only antidote is to educate ourselves to speak the unspoken. Understanding is OK, but insufficient to bring about change. We aren't "dangerous" until we can speak to the issue. We must train ourselves to be dangerous to the conditions of ignorance and apathy.

One of the crucial missing ingredients in bringing about needed policy changes is spokespersons—people who can speak of the opportunities before us. The Bones Exercise shows how to take an article and synthesize it into a two-minute talk. When that two-minute talk is honed further, you have the Laser Talk. We also have a special process for teaching the Laser Talk to a group of people. The Bones Exercise, honing it to the Laser Talk, and teaching the Laser Talk are among RESULTS' secret weapons. If we are to reclaim our democracy, first we must reclaim our sense of what is possible and then we must reclaim our voices.

The Bones Exercise

Rationale: The Bones Exercise allows an individual or group to take an article and Action Sheet and prepare a two-minute talk. The talk can be used when writing a member of Congress or a letter to the editor, when making calls to an editorial writer or a legislative aide, when training other citizens, or when speaking with friends.

Needs: An article or Action Sheet which outlines a particular problem, workable solutions to it, and a *specific action* Congress or the Executive branch can take.

What makes it work: Group support and potent information. Specific action—e.g., cosponsor a bill, sign a letter to some other decisionmaker, vote for or against an amendment, etc.

Pitfalls: The biggest pitfalls are lethargy and the unspoken conspiracy "not to know." If we know, there is a pull to act responsibly. Learning to speak new information powerfully is at the center of RESULTS' work, and yet some of our groups still avoid this action. Another pitfall is writing a talk from materials that present no clear sense of a problem, the solutions, or possible actions—materials that are boring. Learning to speak is key, but it's hard to do without being linked to an organization that provides potent information.

For the Bones Exercise, you need to do the following:

Secure materials: Get exciting materials on an issue you care about.

Read: Read the background material aloud with each person taking a turn. When it's appropriate, pause and discuss what you are reading and how it relates to the action being taken.

Have each person write the following on a sheet of paper, leaving space between each section:

Title: Title of talk or report

Problem: What is the problem being addressed?

Solutions: What can be done about this problem? Are there programs that have proved to be effective?

Examples: In your presentation of the problem and solution, be specific. Use examples, statistics, facts, and success stories to create an accurate and vivid picture.

Opportunity: What is the bill or other initiative that would help implement the solutions? What is your specific request for action?

Write and share sections of your talk

Decide together what your title will be. Then take a few minutes for the group to write the problem in their own words. Pause and share this with each other. If you like what someone else has said, add it to your own report. Then go through the same process with solution, examples, and opportunity.

There are no right or wrong answers. The group interaction becomes a way in which each person can put together a unique presentation. For some, just speaking may be a big step. Correct only misinformation, not the quality of the presentation.

Deliver the talk

After you have completed the exercise, pair up and deliver the entire talk to your partner. After each person has spoken, the other should offer feedback, both factual and stylistic. Start with something positive, then suggest improvements, then reiterate the positive. Remember, the purpose of this exercise is to support each other in becoming effective advocates. Encourage each other!

It is inspiring to complete the exercise by having everyone in the room take a turn delivering their talk. But if you have a large group, or if you're running short on time, have just one or two people give the talk to the group. Acknowledge yourselves for the work you are doing.

Creating the Laser Talk

When the two-minute talk developed during the Bones Exercise is honed further, you have the Laser Talk. With the Bones Exercise, you are limited by the material found in the article or Action Sheet you've chosen. But by adding additional bits of information from other materials in order to improve the talk, you hone the two-minute talk into what we call the Laser Talk.

The Laser Talk

The Laser Talk follows the same basic format as the Bones Exercise (i.e., problem, solution, examples, opportunity for action) and summarizes points made earlier in the RESULTS education and action meeting. It doesn't introduce new information.

Rationale: Learning to be a spokesperson is at the center of RESULTS' work. Teaching the Laser Talk allows a group to quickly learn a two-minute talk and use what they've learned to take action.

Needs: A leader who has prepared a brief, inspiring talk which covers a problem, solutions, and actions individuals can urge the Congress or Executive branch to take.

What makes it work: Group support, potent information, and commitment to empowering others.

Pitfalls: The biggest pitfall is again the unspoken conspiracy "not to know." Another pitfall is a poorly written talk (e.g., no clear sense of the problem, the solutions, or needed action). The final pitfall is not setting up the exercise properly. Learning a Laser Talk is like being back in school. That must be acknowledged.

The purpose of the exercise is to give people an opportunity to experience the difference they can make by learning to speak the issues.

The presenter might take the talk developed during the Bones Exercise and enhance it with information from the video that will be shown at the education and action meeting. In any event, the person teaching the Laser Talk should check with other RESULTS partners to be sure that the talk has been prepared in an inspiring way. Over time, partners build up a repertoire of Laser Talks that are available to them at a moment's notice. They might range in subject from "What is RESULTS?" to "Banking on the Poor." You never know when you'll end up meeting your member of Congress unexpectedly. You'll be glad if you're ready to "Seize the Day!"

Teaching the Laser Talk

1. Introduce the exercise and its purpose. Only those who are new to this information should participate in the parts that call for group response.
2. The presenter delivers the two-minute talk. For example, a talk might begin, "UNICEF estimates that 35,000 children die each day from malnutrition and preventable disease...."
3. The presenter delivers the talk again, leaving out key facts and figures, and asking the listeners who are new to fill in the blanks by shouting out the answers. For example:

   Q: According to UNICEF, the number of children who die each day is _______?
   The new people respond: 35,000.
   Q: These deaths are from _______?
   The new people respond: Malnutrition and preventable disease.

4. See if there are any quick questions from the people who are learning the

talk. Defer more time-consuming questions until later in order to keep the exercise moving.

5. The presenter delivers the whole talk again, using the same question format. But this time people think the answers rather than calling them out. After leaving time for participants to think the answer, the presenter gives it. For example:

   Q: According to UNICEF, how many children die each day?
   (Silence as participants think the answer. The leader then gives the answer: 35,000.)
   Q: These deaths are from ______?
   (Silence as participants think the answer. The leader then gives the answer: Malnutrition and preventable disease.)

6. The presenter should give a very brief outline of the talk.
7. The listeners pair up and take turns delivering the entire talk to each other.
8. The presenter asks for a volunteer to deliver the talk in front of the room. If no one volunteers, the presenter asks someone to volunteer their partner.
9. The volunteer delivers the talk in front of the room.
10. Everyone acknowledges the brave volunteer.

This is often the most fun part of the meeting and works best if done in that spirit. However, some may find the experience uncomfortable. People don't have to participate. The Laser Talk is a powerful first step toward speaking out on an important issue.

Complete this part of your meeting by asking people if they can see the value in training themselves to speak in such a concise way. Would it be of value if they could do so at a meeting with their member of Congress or an editorial writer?

RESULTS' Three Meetings a Month

The National Conference Call

Each group in RESULTS has an average of partners, key volunteers who agree to participate in three meetings a month. The meetings are (1) the national conference call, (2) the delivery meeting, and (3) the education and action meeting where the partners invite their friends to write letters to the president, members of Congress, or newspapers.

The first of RESULTS' monthly meetings is the national conference call, which is like an extension course once a month by telephone. It is a powerful organizing tool that brings 200 to 300 people together each month. On the call, partners are briefed by a guest speaker, are coached on specific actions for the month, role-play phone calls to editorial writers and members of

Congress, and commit to specific actions on the roll call taken before hanging up. What follows are the logistics of the national conference call.

Rationale: People from around the nation (and sometimes from around the world) are brought together on a conference call for information, empowerment, inspiration, training, and also support.

Needs: People committed to the task at hand. Money to pay for the call. A conference call agenda, focus, and guest.[26] In RESULTS, the groups need a speaker-box so partners can gather at one site.

What makes it work: A well-prepared call and people committed to using the time together to move a specific campaign and vision forward.

Pitfalls: The pitfalls include a call with no clear purpose, people who are unavailable when the call begins, and distractions such as room noise during the call.

Cost: There are several ways to arrange a conference call. For years, we've used AT&T. RESULTS volunteers sit around a speaker phone, usually in someone's home, and the AT&T operators link them together. The call has traditionally cost us $10 per site to hook up through AT&T and, because our call is on a Saturday, the cost per minute is only an additional 11 cents per site. Eighty-five sites with an average of three people in each room will connect 255 people. The cost would be as follows:

85 sites @ $10	850.00
85 x 11¢ min. x 90 min.	841.50
Total	$1,691.50

With this call, we are investing $6.63 in each person.
A call connecting 12 sites for one hour on a weekend would cost $199.20:

12 sites @ $10	120.00
12 x 11¢ min. x 60 min.	79.20
Total	$199.20

[26] The conference call guest is an expert on the action being taken by the groups. A short biography is needed to introduce the guest. Several questions are prepared in advance and asked before opening it up for spontaneous questions from around the country.

RESULTS' earliest calls connected three cities without the help of an operator. Using three-way calling, an hour might cost a total of $20.

3 sites (no operator)	
3 x 11¢ min. x 60 min.	19.80
Total	$19.80

Most organizations experience renewed commitment when people gather at a regular conference. The conference call is like a mini-mini conference each month and allows a similar level of renewal.

The following are excerpts from the RESULTS Group Manual:

The RESULTS national conference call is held on the second Saturday of each month from 2:00 to 3:30 p.m. Eastern Time. We urge groups to tape the call for future reference and for use by partners who cannot attend.

Given the condition of apathy and resignation within which we often work, the conference call is a place where we can recharge our batteries and find support. The national staff updates partners on current legislative issues and provides coaching.

The conference call is one of our most effective empowerment tools. However, just showing up for the call doesn't guarantee success. Here are some important points to ensure the success of the call:

1. **The Speaker Box:** Make sure the speaker box is in good condition and that you know how to use it, especially the privacy button.[27]
2. **The Guest:** Getting information from the guest on the call is only part of what you are there for. Empowering the guest is often as important as having her on the call. You can contribute to that by the way you listen and by the questions you ask.[28]
3. **Preparation**: All partners have the responsibility to make the conference call work and to use the time before, during, and after the call effectively. Don't expect the call to entertain you. You must stay current with RESULTS' work and with the mailings and background information so that you can listen, ask questions, and share on the call in such a way that you forward the action.

---

[27]The privacy button, when activated, allows people to speak in the room without being heard by others on the call.

[28]On RESULTS conference calls, two or three questions are prepared and given to the guest in advance. Volunteers from around the country are selected to ask these questions one or two days ahead of time. After these questions are asked, we open it up to spontaneous questions from around the country. To avoid confusion, the leader will say, "Now we'll take some questions from around the country. Give your name and city—go ahead." As someone gives his name and city, the leader acknowledges that person by saying, "OK, that's Scott in Salt Lake City. Go ahead, Scott." If the leader hears two people, the response would be, "Let's go to Scott in Salt Lake City first and Keith in Seattle second."

Remember, the call is an opportunity for you to gain insight and inspiration and get what you need in order to take effective action with your legislators, the media, and the people around you. The call is a tool you can use to empower yourself, but remember, in the end you are the source of your own empowerment.

What follows is a sample conference call agenda:

2:00-2:05	Welcome, special welcome to new groups, instructions for those who might be disconnected (5 min.—Sam)
2:05-2:25	Guest (20 min.—Joanne)
2:25-2:35	Legislative update. Roll-play call to editorial writer on latest action (10 min.—Joanne)
2:35-2:45	Information for education and action meetings and relating two successes from last month's meetings (10 min.—Nick)
2:45-2:50	Report on upcoming trip to start new RESULTS groups (5 min.—Keith)
2:50-2:55	Report on upcoming regional conferences (5 min.—Lynn)
2:55-3:07	Launch fundraising campaign (12 min.—Sam and Lynn)
3:07-3:27	Roll call (20 min.—Sam) 1. How many in your room? 2. How many going to regional conference? 3. How many new monthly sponsors will be generated from the people in your group? 4. How many editorial writers will be called by Wednesday?
3:27-3:30	Conclusion: inspiring quote and reminder to practice calls to editorial writer when we hang up (3 min.—Sam)

Post-Conference Call Meeting

It is very useful for partners to meet together for 30 to 45 minutes after the conference call to work with the material presented on the call. If phone calls to your member of Congress or editorial writers have been recommended, this is the time to practice those calls by doing some role-playing or "mocks." You can also use this meeting to make specific action plans for the month. Set up schedules and a support structure for yourselves. This is the time to set goals for those you're inviting to your next education and action meeting. If no mocks have been recommended on the call, you can use the time to practice your inviting skills.

A Reminder

If a national group wants to incorporate the conference call with their volunteers, I recommend a pilot project first. Just take a small number of cities, let them know it's an experiment, and use the pilot project to work out the kinks.

The Delivery Meeting

The delivery meeting is the second of RESULTS' three monthly meetings. It's about two hours long and is usually held the week following the national conference call. The purpose of the delivery meeting is to learn to speak powerfully about RESULTS' issues, to forward group projects, and to prepare for the third meeting of the month, the education and action meeting.

The largest portion of the delivery meeting is spent on the Bones Exercise. Group leaders should have copies of the Action Sheets and background material for each partner at the delivery meeting. These materials are mailed to each group leader from the national office.

This is a sample of the delivery meeting agenda:

Sharing	It is important that your group have time to connect with each other. If necessary, appoint a timekeeper to keep you on schedule.
10 min.	Go over updates from RESULTS mailings and weekly communicator calls.[29]
10 min.	Read the month's Action Sheet. State in your own words the action and its purpose.
60 min.	Read the background material and proceed to the Bones Exercise.
15 min.	Align on the agenda for your education and action (E&A) meeting (see E&A agenda that follows). Assign parts and practice them as needed.
10 min.	Discuss inviting for the E&A meeting: How's it going? Is everyone getting the support they need? How many guests are you targeting?
10 min.	Make commitments on actions for the following week. Are there any updates on projects (e.g., meetings with a member of Congress, etc.)?
OR	
	Take time to practice other skills that relate to our work.
5 min.	Completion.

The Education and Action Meeting

This is the third of RESULTS' monthly meetings. Here's how it works.

Rationale: The education and action meeting gives people the information, support, and time they need to learn about an issue and write a powerful letter to an elected official or the media.

[29]Each week the group leaders receive a support call from their regional coordinators.

Needs: An Action Sheet, paper, pens, envelopes, Congressional District maps, a well-planned meeting, and a willingness to address both the hopelessness in people and the desire to make a difference.

What makes it work: A timely and well-written Action Sheet, good inviting, powerful speaking, and people committed to moving a campaign or vision forward.

Pitfalls: Weak inviting, poor speaking, poor planning, weak action, weak vision.

The following are excerpts from the RESULTS Group Manual:

The education and action meeting is a two-hour meeting held the last week of the month. Since this is the meeting to which you invite guests on a regular basis, it's helpful to set up a consistent schedule that's easy to remember (e.g., the last Tuesday of every month).

The education and action meeting is the major source of outreach for most groups. It's where many people get their first glimpse of participatory democracy and where some are inspired to join the group as a partner. A well-run meeting will give people the opportunity to experience, first-hand, the difference they make, and it will expand the constituency calling for the political will to end hunger.

Finding innovative ways to involve participants in learning the issues can become a fun and inspiring way to educate guests: make up a game to illustrate the effects of Third World debt, invite a speaker to your meeting who is an expert on the subject of the month, or invite someone who has traveled to the developing world and has hands-on experience with people who are poor.

The education and action meeting should allow each person to discover that he or she is the one to create the political will to end hunger. Your job is to create relationship, inspiration, and enrollment as the essential components of your meeting.

The following sample agenda is designed around those components. It provides an outline of a basic education and action meeting. Remember, you can provide your guests with flawless education, but if you don't inspire them about the difference they can make, you won't have accomplished your goal.

Sample Education and Action Meeting Agenda

First there is the relationship and inspiration section.

1-2 min. Welcome: Make sure people feel welcomed.

5-10 min. Focusing activity: People have come from work, school, or home. The focusing activity should bring them together in a way that touches their hearts and connects them with the problem of hunger and poverty. You can show a video or read aloud from an inspiring article about hunger and poverty. You might also share your own vision for the end of hunger.

5 min. Purpose and agenda of the meeting: Let people know the goal and the program for the evening.

5-10 min. What is RESULTS? Introduce newcomers to RESULTS so they are clear about its purpose and the need for creating the political will to end hunger. Let them know how they can participate (e.g., as partners, monthly sponsors, etc.).

10 min. Introductions: Give people a chance to learn who else is in the room and to inspire each other. Participants should introduce themselves and share what brought them to the meeting. They might state their name, occupation, and either what they want to get out of the meeting or what they're committed to in life.

Then there is the education and action section:

5-10 min. Background report: Introduce the issue. This is a talk built out of the Action Sheet, background material, and any other information on the evening's topic.

10 min. Video: Introduce the video by pointing out key sections at which you'd like participants to look.

25 min. Teaching the Laser Talk: Give guests the opportunity to experience the difference they can make when empowered to speak the issue—active rather than passive learning.

5 min. Review: Pass out the Action Sheets and review the evening's action. Are there any questions? Does everyone know the name of their member of Congress? The Action Sheet is a useful reference when writing the letters.

20 min. Write letters: Address envelopes together. Maintain quiet in the room during the first 10 to 15 minutes of the letter-writing period. If guests need extra help, have them step outside with one of the partners to get their questions answered.

5 min. Share letters: As people are putting the finishing touches on their letters, have one or two persons who have already finished read their letters aloud.

Next comes the relationship and enrollment section of the meeting.

15 min. Participation: Give people the opportunity to participate with the local RESULTS group on an ongoing basis.

1. Describe the partner agreements (three meetings a month, etc.). Speak about how being a partner in RESULTS

affects your life. Ask if anyone in the room has any questions. Ask if anyone wants to become a partner. Is anyone thinking about making this commitment?

2. Tell your guests about monthly sponsorship. Explain that as a lobby, contributions to RESULTS are not tax-deductible. Make sure to emphasize the importance of contributing via electronic funds transfer.[30] Tell what inspires you most about contributing to RESULTS. Ask if anyone wishes to make this commitment.
3. Announce the date of your next education and action meeting. Who would like to be reminded about attending that meeting?

5 min. Completion: Thank everyone for coming. You may want to invite people to stay for refreshments and some informal time together. Make sure that newcomers are attended to by the person who invited them. Remember, RESULTS does not reimburse you for any of your education and action meeting expenses other than photocopying. Postage and any other costs should be covered by the participants.

Other groups looking to incorporate aspects of the education and action meeting should remember that, in addition to inspiration, the most important areas are having people learn to speak the issue and take the action by writing their letter at the meeting.

---

[30]Electronic funds transfer is a way people can contribute financially to RESULTS. Individuals authorize their bank to transfer a set amount to RESULTS on the 20th of each month. It's our most dependable source of funding.

CHAPTER 26

Working with a Member of Congress

I see that the efforts of people as citizens are more effective than their efforts as individuals. This is an idea that we in the twentieth century have not yet come to terms with: What any of us can do, good or bad, as individuals, is dramatically enhanced when we are acting collectively as citizens.

Obviously we can do things as individuals—if you see somebody hungry, you can feed him—but the problem would not have happened in the first place if we had done our jobs as citizens.

Dr. Jean Mayer, Former President, Tufts University

Rationale: The best way to empower a member of Congress is to work with him or her in as many ways as possible—especially face-to-face.

Needs: A clear commitment to making a difference, whatever the circumstances.

What makes it work: The ingredients are: (1) a strong presence in the community; (2) people writing, meeting, and phoning the elected official; (3) having your issues and views expressed in the media; and (4) growing support from other community groups. Perhaps the most important ingredients are a positive vision and persistence.

Pitfalls: An agenda other than empowerment, poor planning, timidity, a lack of persistence, unspecific requests, thinking your member of Congress is either too difficult to convince or "too good" to bother working with.

The following are excerpts from the RESULTS Group Manual.

Being able to express your convictions about ending hunger and poverty with passion, accuracy, and inspiration—whether in a meeting, in a letter, or over the phone—is one of your most powerful tools in working with your member of Congress (MC).

- **Writing Letters:** The best letters are brief and legible. They contain a few noteworthy facts and a specific request. Your heartfelt message—whether handwritten or typed—carries more weight than a preprinted postcard or petition campaign.
- **Face-to-Face Meetings:** Personal meetings with members of Congress are even more effective than letters. There is a lot of pressure on members of Congress to respond favorably to a request that comes from a constituent who has taken the time to schedule and prepare for a meeting. Members of Congress rightly fear that if too many constituents come away from face-to-face meetings feeling unhappy, resentment will build in the Congressional District.

When meeting a member of Congress, keep these points in mind. They have been key to success in the past:

Be prepared. Have your agenda prepared ahead of time. Be very specific about the purpose of your meeting and what your intended results are. Many groups rehearse their meeting beforehand so that partners can give feedback to each other and calm some of the "jitters." Do your homework. What are the issues that your member of Congress cares deeply about? How can you tie your issues into ones that he or she is already committed to?

Be courteous. Even if you disagree on an issue, being courteous may help make the member more willing to reconsider his or her position or react favorably to future requests. While it is important that you be firm and resolute in your advocacy work, nothing is ever gained by being discourteous or provocative. Remember to dress appropriately, be on time, and keep your agenda to the time allotted.

Acknowledge previous actions. It is important that you begin meetings by thanking your member of Congress for previous requests that have been accepted. Supplement "thank you's" expressed in private meetings with public ones; for example, thank your member of Congress at a town hall meeting, in a letter to the editor, or in a special ceremony.

Be inspiring. Perhaps the two most successful ways to inspire a member of Congress are (1) your own passion and commitment and (2) showing a powerful video. Taking the time and trouble to select and bring a moving video and needed equipment is more valuable than you might imagine. It's been said that "a picture is worth a thousand words." A powerful video is worth many more.

Make specific requests. Often the main reason groups have unsatisfactory meetings is that their requests are not clear and specific enough. Your member of Congress needs to understand exactly what you want. At the end of your meeting, review each request and make arrangements to follow-up. Many groups prepare packets ahead of time to leave with their member of Congress—including a sheet that summarizes the requests that have been made at the meeting.

Demonstrate your strength in the community. Describe to your member of Congress your activities in the community aimed at creating a base of support for the taking of action on hunger legislation. Show clippings of letters and editorials your group has generated, or play radio or television clips. You may also want to invite representatives from other community groups to the meeting.

- **Working with Legislative Assistants:** Every member of Congress has legislative assistants or aides. These people are very important in the policymaking process. While your member of Congress makes all final decisions, the aides make recommendations and are charged with implementing most decisions.
- **Using the Media:** A very effective way to influence members of Congress is to get the media on your side.
- Be sure to send all media you generate to your member of Congress and the staff. In addition to mailing it or faxing it when it appears, bring it along to your next meeting. That way you can make sure that they see it and know that you were behind it.
- If you are trying to shift the position of your member of Congress on an issue, the media is a place to get your message across. By using "free" media, such as editorial pages or radio interview programs, you are involving more people and building awareness of the issue. If the coverage you generate is sympathetic to your view, an elected official is likely to reconsider opposition.
- If you and your member of Congress agree on an issue, you can use the media to publicly express your thanks. The member of Congress will then want to be more publicly associated with the legislation and more open to spending time lobbying peers on its behalf.
- **Networking:** For increased success, many RESULTS groups have formed alliances with other community groups. These alliances have greatly improved their capacity to influence Congress. Remember that if your member of Congress knows that the local chapter of RESULTS

supports a bill, it elicits one response. But if he or she knows that the local chapter of the American Academy of Pediatrics, the local Council of Churches, and professors from the local school of public health support it as well, it elicits an even stronger response.

For more than a decade, RESULTS has focused on having our members of Congress support our issues by cosponsoring a bill or signing a letter to the chair of a key committee or subcommittee. We are beginning to look for ways our members of Congress can demonstrate their support by speaking out on our issues (e.g., joining us for a radio interview on the release of the *State of the World's Children* report, speaking for one minute on C-Span at the beginning of a Congressional day, speaking at a community meeting on our issues, etc.).

For some time we have encouraged other groups to join us at meetings with our members of Congress. We have begun to look for ways to encourage and train other groups to have their own meetings with their member of Congress on issues we all care about.

CHAPTER 27

Working with the Media

Speaking to the Entire Community

If you're not legislative or you're not political, you are purposely or accidentally avoiding the arena in which decisions affecting the earth are made. And that's irresponsible to the earth.

David Brower, Earth Island Institute

Rationale: Working with the media is perhaps the most leveraged way of getting an issue on your member of Congress's priority list.

Needs: A clear and compelling angle. Materials such as a news advisory, a news release, or an editorial writer packet.[31]

What makes it work: Good timing (usually when a bill is about to be introduced, a report is about to be released, or some other action is about to be taken). Well-written materials that include a compelling vision along with accurate information. Powerful speaking by committed, courageous volunteers. Persistence and support.

Pitfalls: Inability to speak, lack of support, weak materials, timidity.

The following is excerpted from the RESULTS Group Manual:

In late 20th-century society, the role of the media has gone well beyond "reporting" on current events. The media plays a central role in selecting, shaping, and prioritizing the public discussion. Elected officials use the media

[31]An editorial writer packet includes: (1) a one-page summary with names, titles, and phone numbers for further information and (2) a background paper of four pages or more.

as a barometer of public opinion as well as a vehicle for promoting their political objectives.

Hunger will end only when the media adopts the issue wholeheartedly and begins to monitor all progress or lack thereof. Your work with the media contributes to giving hunger and poverty the attention and priority they deserve. After all, more people have died from hunger and related illness in the last six years than in all the wars and violence in the previous 150 years.

Here are the major types of projects to work on with your local media:

Writing Letters to the Editor: Letters to the editor are a newspaper's way of getting feedback from its readers. While they may only be able to publish a few of the letters they receive, editors are influenced by the volume. An article or editorial which readers respond to is more likely to be followed up with future pieces.

Tips on writing a letter to the editor:

1. Respond to a recent news story or editorial. A good letter might begin, "Your article on the new poverty statistics ("Poverty Rate is Increasing," Dec. 4) was excellent. Readers might also want to know that...."
2. Make your letter short and legible. It should contain a few striking facts that might surprise an editor or a reader. ("Studies show that millions of destitute families worldwide could lift themselves out of poverty with loans of $50 to $100, less than many American families spend on a pair of sneakers for their children!")
3. Use descriptive words which communicate how passionately you feel about the issue. Don't be dry. ("The discovery of oral rehydration therapy has given humanity the potential to save more lives, at a lower cost, than perhaps at any time in history.")
4. Include your address and home and work phone numbers.

Getting an Op-ed Piece Published: "Op-ed" stands for "opposite the editorial page." In larger papers like the *New York Times,* the op-ed page is the page after the newspaper's editorials and letters to the editor. Smaller papers may combine all three on one page: editorials, op-eds, and letters to the editor.

Generally, there are two types of op-ed pieces. One is a column from syndicated writers such as George Will or A.M. Rosenthal. Newspapers "subscribe" to wire services which send out these columns. Another type of op-ed, sometimes indistinguishable from a letter to the editor, is from a local writer.

You should ask the op-ed editor, or in the case of smaller newspapers, the editorial page editor, if you can write an op-ed, sometimes called a "guest editorial." Sometimes RESULTS volunteers have been given this opportunity in lieu of the newspaper running its own editorial. While it varies from paper to paper, an op-ed is usually about 750 words.

Initiating an Editorial: Successfully urging a newspaper to publish an editorial on legislation RESULTS is supporting is one of the biggest "wins" our groups can have. Not only does an editorial get the word out to the public and elected officials, but it says that the newspaper itself endorses the legislation. An article or op-ed, on the other hand, publicizes the information, but is not an endorsement by the newspaper.

You need to know which editorial writer covers the topic you are interested in. Call your newspaper and find out who the editorial writers are. Depending on the size of the paper, there may be as few as one or two, or as many as eight or more. Find out who covers the kinds of issues the current legislation addresses and then ask for that person.

After introducing yourself, engage the editorial writer by asking a question. When we worked on microenterprise loans for the poor, we might have begun with a question such as, "Have you heard of the bank in Bangladesh which makes tiny loans to destitute women to start businesses? No? Well, do you have a few minutes for me to tell you about it and legislation which builds on this amazing success story?"

At some point, ask the writer if you can drop off or mail information. Then follow up on the phone within a week to see that they got the information and if they have any questions. It is always good to provide them with a piece of new information, so it won't seem like you're only calling to nag them. As with all work with the media, be brief, energetic, and appreciative for their time. Keep trying even if the first editorial takes some time to initiate, and be sure to respond to editorials with letters to the editor complimenting the paper for running the piece.

Getting on a Radio Talk Show: The same principles apply here as above. Once you have gained some experience with RESULTS' issues, you are ready to approach a radio talk show. In a small community with limited radio coverage, it is easy to pick and choose the shows you would like to be on. Call the hosts with your idea for the show. Much the same as with calls to editorial writers, you need to be prepared with a concise and enticing "hook" to pique their interest. This is where all your work preparing Laser Talks and practicing speaking will pay off. If you get them interested, they will trust that their listeners will be interested, too.

The release of a major report, such as the *State of the World's Children*, will carry more weight with talk show hosts than a general conversation about ending hunger and poverty. Be as specific with them as possible.

The two most important things you can do to prepare yourself for a radio talk show are (1) to practice by having someone interview you over and over and (2) to write up four or five main points you'd like to see covered during the interview. If the interviewer isn't bringing up these issues, you can weave them in by saying something like, "Let me digress for a minute and tell you about a piece of legislation before Congress right now...."

Hosting a News Conference or News Event: Since 1985, RESULTS groups have organized news conferences each December on the release of UNICEF's *State of the World's Children* report. Whenever RESULTS invites volunteers to organize news conferences, enormous amounts of support materials are provided, including time-lines, sample news advisories and news releases, talking points, and press kits.

Choosing to put on a news conference provides your group with an unprecedented opportunity for networking and coalition-building within your community.

Tips on holding a news conference:

1. Be sure you have a compelling answer to the question: What's the news?
2. Choose a site the news media is used to going to or one that is visually compelling and easy to get to. Your news conference should usually be in the morning so the television stations have time to get back to the studio, prepare their segment, and get it on the evening news.
3. Find speakers who will attract the media: members of Congress, local celebrities and sports figures, experts who can speak with authority, etc.
4. Create powerful visuals that help get your message across and attract television cameras and newspaper photographers.
5. Compile a media list which includes the assignment editors of the local television and radio stations and the city editors of the local newspapers.
6. Mail a news advisory 10 days before the event which tells the basics: who, what, where, why, and when. Have your speakers and visuals lined up and feature them in your news advisory. Phone the people on the media list to see if they got the news advisory, and engage them in a conversation about the event.
7. Prepare a news kit for the members of the media who attend.
8. Write a news release for the day of the news conference. Write it as if it were an article in the newspaper that day.
9. Rehearse with the participants or have breakfast together and talk it through.
10. Call the media again the day before and continue to impress upon them the importance of the event. Your job isn't to get a crowd there—it's to get the media there.

Hosting a news conference is the quintessential act of a community leader. Basically you are gathering the media together because you have a message to deliver to the community. One of the best things you can do as a first-time news conference host is to attend someone else's news conference weeks before your own.

CHAPTER 28

1991–2004

From Civic Cynics to Empowered Citizens

When *Reclaiming Our Democracy* was published ten years ago, it outlined the birth of RESULTS in 1980 in a Van Nuys, California, living room and its growth over the next decade from a fledgling organization with no full-time staff to its emergence as a major force in the fight to end world hunger and poverty.

Over that first decade, RESULTS played a lead advocacy role in a campaign that produced a dramatic increase in U.S. government funding, which fueled a boost in global immunization rates, saving the lives of some three million children a year. RESULTS was also the lead advocate for increased U.S. government assistance to support a revolution in banking that was providing microloans to several million of the world's poorest families. At the end of that period, RESULTS Educational Fund organized Candlelight Vigils where more than one million people gathered in 75 countries to shine a light on the 1990 World Summit for Children.

Perhaps RESULTS' greatest achievements, however, and the ones most difficult to maintain, were the innovations and breakthroughs in citizen transformation—transformation from "I don't make a difference" to "I do make a difference"—a tremendous journey for most of us. RESULTS had difficulty maintaining that citizen transformation, starting during my last few years as Executive Director, from 1991 to 1995.[1] Very little in our educational system or culture roots for powerful citizen education and action. To become an empowered citizen, one must ford a very deep river of civic hopelessness and cynicism. This challenge and opportunity crystallized for me in a 2004 coaching

---

[1]In August 1995, I left my position as Executive Director of RESULTS to begin work on the 1997 Microcredit Summit, a project of RESULTS Educational Fund, aimed at reaching 100 million of the world's poorest families with microcredit by the end of 2005.

call with Ian Sansom, a RESULTS leader who lives in Tasmania, Australia. The call was focused on expanding RESULTS groups.

"We had 15 people at our meeting last night," Ian told me with great enthusiasm, "and 10 of them agreed to become monthly letter writers."

"Congratulations!" I replied. "What was your goal for the evening?"

"We wanted two new partners,"[2] he answered. "We already have two and wanted two more to bring us up to the four that most groups have."

"Well, did you get the two new partners?" I asked.

"No," Ian replied, "we got 10 new letter writers."

"Did you invite people to be partners?" I queried.

"No," Ian responded, "we told them that being a partner was an option, but we didn't actually ask if they wanted to be one."

For many, it's tough to stand in front of a group and make bold requests—to ask for money or for significant volunteer commitments. To do so can tap into a deep fear of rejection and feelings of unworthiness. One RESULTS leader, Marshall Saunders, described it this way. "It's like being the first boy to walk across the gym floor at a junior high school dance to ask a girl to dance," he said, "and being rejected—*in front of everyone*."

When they begin, most volunteers and staff don't have the ability to articulate the vision of ordinary citizens making a difference in the world. This ability has to be developed. That is the challenge of RESULTS and of all other organizations committed to civic transformation and breakthrough action.

Understanding that Ian hadn't reached his goal that evening, I asked him what his purpose was.

"Our purpose was to inform people about RESULTS," he told me.

"That's interesting," I responded. "When I used to lead presentations, my purpose was to inspire people about the difference they could make, working with others, to generate the political will to end hunger. Most people walk into their first RESULTS meeting believing they *don't* make a difference. If, by the end of the evening, they are inspired about the difference they can make, a transformation will have taken place, or at least have begun. Your purpose was to inform, my purpose was to transform."

We talked about the continuum from inform, to entertain, to transform and how a meeting could aspire to any of these goals.

"In the United States," I continued, "people don't have to leave their homes to be entertained. They can stay home and watch *American Idol*, *The Bachelor*, or other television shows aimed at entertaining people. In this country it would be difficult to get people out of their homes consistently just to be informed, when they can stay home and be entertained.

"People *will* leave their homes to get transformed," I continued. "That's

---

[2]Partners are the more active volunteers who take on day-to-day operations of the local RESULTS chapter.

what we need to offer. That's what we have to stand for. That's what we have to plan for, prepare for, and deliver. But that's the hard part."

Techniques for achieving this transformation are described in Chapter 24. Essentially, transformation is what I mean when I speak about "healing the break between people and government."

Dan Zukergood, a former junior and senior high school social studies teacher, recalled his own transformation from "civic cynic" to "empowered citizen."

"As a new social studies teacher living in upstate New York in the mid-1980s," Dan recalled, "I remember telling my students, 'kids, as members of a democracy, you must communicate with your representatives and tell them how you want to be represented.' Yet, even while I was saying this, the little voice in my head was saying, 'my representatives would never listen to me. So why would they *ever* listen to a bunch of junior and senior high kids?'

"I also remember telling my students, 'kids, you know that each one of you can make a big difference in the world.' Yet, even while I was saying this, the little voice in my head was saying, '*I* can't even make a difference, so why should a bunch of teenagers be able to?' *And I was their social studies teacher!*"

It was after Dan and his wife, Laurie Herrick, started a RESULTS group in Oneonta, New York, in the mid-1980s that Dan's eyes were opened to the power of citizens educating themselves and taking action.

"Even when I taught at the junior and senior high school level," Dan recalled, "I learned that kids can make a difference—even if they are not old enough to vote. The first RESULTS-like action my students ever took was a letter they wrote to Rep. Sherwood Boehlert (R-NY). They asked him to co-sponsor a bill. I can't remember what the actual bill was, but I can recite his response to the students pretty much by heart. The letter looked like this:

> Dear Students,
>
> Not only was I NOT going to co-sponsor the bill you described, but I had intended to vote against it. But, due to your excellent argument, I have decided to co-sponsor the bill.
>
> Thank you for making me more aware of this issue.
>
> Sincerely,
>
> Rep. Sherwood Boehlert
>
> P.S.—Never let anyone ever tell you that five seventh graders can't change the vote of a Congressman!

"And so began my journey as a teacher of active citizenship!" Dan declared.

Dan and Laurie's work with Representative Boehlert, along with others in the Oneonta RESULTS group, and their work to build a new chapter when they moved to Syracuse, New York, would come together at a pivotal moment for the Child Survival Fund.

The Child Survival Fund was created in a 1984 lobbying effort led by Bread for the World. It focused on funding key elements of the "child survival revolution" promoted by the late Jim Grant, former Executive Director of UNICEF. These elements included immunization of children against six childhood diseases, like measles and tetanus, that were taking the lives of nearly 9,600 children each day and the promotion of oral rehydration therapy to prevent the deaths of some 13,700 children each day due to dehydration. RESULTS' persistent lobbying and leadership over the ensuing 19 years would cause the Child Survival Fund to grow from $25 million in 1985 to $370 million in 2004. This helped reduce child mortality from 41,000 child deaths a day in 1986 to some 29,000 child deaths a day in 2004.

The Child Survival Fund had grown from $0 in 1984 to $200 million in 1990 with dramatic help from RESULTS-generated actions, like the 90 editorials published in 1986 in support of universal childhood immunization by 1990 (see Chapter 8). In 1990, RESULTS groups shifted their focus from intense lobbying to drawing large crowds to the Candlelight Vigils, which were organized to attract media attention to the World Summit for Children that year (see Chapter 22).

Therefore, it was a shock to RESULTS' system, and to my own, when President Clinton's first budget in 1993 called for and succeeded in achieving a $40 million cut in the Child Survival Fund from $275 million to $235 million, the first cut ever.

"It's not so much that they were targeting the Child Survival Fund for cuts," recalled RESULTS legislative director Joanne Carter, "It's just that they weren't prioritizing it, or saw it as a larger pot of money that they could take from for other priorities."

I had distracted myself from lobbying work by our focus on the Candlelight Vigils in 1990 and the Keeping the Promise Campaign in 1991 and 1992. We wanted to go beyond lobbying, to building a larger movement committed to forwarding the child survival revolution. The Campaign included lesson plans for school children, materials for places of worship, and general media outreach.

But with the Clinton cuts in 1993, we dropped the more educationally focused Campaign and I returned my full attention to lobbying. The Child Survival Fund increased the year following the Clinton cuts, but then came the next big shock.

In the Congressional elections of 1994, Republicans took control of the House of Representatives for the first time in 40 years. The new chair of the Foreign Operations Subcommittee of the Appropriations Committee, the subcommittee that appropriated funds for foreign aid (which included programs like the Child Survival Fund) would be Sonny Callahan (R-AL), who had *never* voted in favor of a foreign aid bill before taking over as chair of the subcommittee. Big changes were afoot and we had to make sure the Child Survival Fund remained a priority.

Three days after the 1994 election, with much of the development community still in shock, Joanne Carter and I sat down to breakfast with Sherry Boehlert, the Congressman whom Dan and Laurie had worked with in upstate New York 10 years earlier. By then, Rep. Boehlert had joined the RESULTS board. We turned to him for advice and leadership. At the end of the breakfast we asked Boehlert to be the lead Republican sponsor of the World Summit for Children Implementation Act. Boehlert agreed to be lead sponsor, but said Rep. Jim Walsh (R-NY) was likely to become chair of one of the 13 House Appropriations Subcommittees, and as a subcommittee chair, he would be a better lead sponsor. "Ask Walsh," Boehlert told us, "and if he says no, then I'll do it."

With Representative Boehlert's request, we knew just whom to turn to: Dan and Laurie. They had started a RESULTS group in Oneonta, New York, and then another in Los Angeles, when they moved there.

"After L.A.," Dan recalled, "We knew we would start RESULTS groups wherever we went."

In 1991, they moved to Syracuse, New York, so Dan could complete a Ph.D. in education at Syracuse University. Syracuse was the Congressional district of Rep. Jim Walsh, the very Representative to whom Boehlert had pointed us.

After getting settled in Syracuse, Dan and Laurie began to form a RESULTS group and work on what RESULTS would call the two top "trim tabs," relationships that could make the biggest difference in creating the political will to end hunger: the local Congressman, Rep. Jim Walsh, and the local editorial writer, Fred Fiske.

"We tried to get a meeting with Fiske," Laurie recalled, "but he was too busy. I invited him three or four times to do something, but with no success. After a while, he agreed to participate on a RESULTS-organized conference call for editorial writers. Being active in the association of editorial writers, he was impressed by the number of colleagues from large newspapers who were also on the call. Afterward, I called him up and he said, 'We should talk. Let's have coffee sometime.'

"We went out for breakfast," Laurie continued. "He was really intrigued by what we were talking about and impressed by our connections internationally. Through RESULTS, he could be on a call with Grameen Bank founder Muhammad Yunus or UNICEF Executive Director Jim Grant. But early on he made it clear that he wasn't supportive of Representative Walsh. In fact, it took a few years before he finally gave good press to Walsh, and that was based on Walsh's work on RESULTS' issues."

Support for the Congressman would come frequently, however, in letters to the editor written by Dan, Laurie, and their RESULTS partners in Syracuse.

"Once Representative Walsh saw the support we would give him in the press," Laurie continued, "his attentiveness shifted."

It was after several years of establishing the Congressman's trust, giving him excellent support in the newspaper, and honoring him at press conferences, that Dan and Laurie got the call from Joanne Carter and me.

We asked Dan and Laurie to meet with Walsh in Syracuse to discuss the possibility of his leading on the bill and arranged to have them connect Joanne and me by phone. A few weeks later, Dan and Laurie went with Walsh to the office of Sen. Alfonse D'Amato (R-NY), where they used the Senator's video machine to show Walsh *341*, the video that was shown at the World Summit for Children four years earlier. Afterward, they went downstairs to Walsh's office.

"When we arrived at his office," Dan recalled, "we noticed a picture on the wall of Walsh as a young man, during his stint as a Peace Corps volunteer. We spent some time talking with him about his time in Nepal those many years before. He shared how much he wanted to make a difference with people in developing countries."

Then the three of them called Joanne and me in Washington. Walsh wanted us to walk him through the bill.

"When we finally asked for his decision," Dan remembered, "he was excited about the opportunity we were offering him, but had some reluctance. A portion of the bill included family planning and Walsh was a conservative Republican with a large conservative constituency. He discussed the issue with us candidly and decided that, despite the fact that some constituents may lump family planning with abortion services, there were too many great opportunities in this bill to let it go."

We were elated. It was just weeks after the election and we had a Republican lead sponsor who was to become chair of one of the Appropriations Subcommittees. Republican Walsh, a returned Peace Corps volunteer and son of the former mayor of Syracuse, joined Ohio Democrat Tony Hall, also a returned Peace Corps volunteer and son of the former mayor of Dayton, Ohio, to lead on the bill. With the death of UNICEF's Jim Grant in January of 1995 after a bout with cancer, the bill was renamed the James P. Grant World Summit for Children Implementation Act.

Over the next several months, RESULTS generated dozens of co-sponsors in support of the legislation. There were RESULTS groups in many districts and members of Congress were jumping on to help the bill move along. Walsh and Hall testified before Chairman Callahan and spoke with him privately.

That first year, Callahan created a Children and Disease Programs earmark for 1996 at $484 million, which included $275 million for Child Survival Fund and $100 million for UNICEF. Over the years, Callahan was heard to say that he would not go to conference with the Senate unless this earmark was 'off the table,' which meant it was not negotiable.

When introducing the overall foreign aid bill on the House floor, Callahan said, "We receive more requests, more indications, more letters of support about Child Survival . . . than any other single issue in this bill."

Dan and Laurie were certainly no longer "civic cynics." Now, twenty years later, Dan is an Associate Professor of Education at Springfield College in Massachusetts. With the training he received in RESULTS, he is clear about his ability to make a difference and to prepare his students, part of the next generation of classroom teachers, to be active citizens.

By 1993, my own focus in RESULTS shifted from the movement-building activities of the Candlelight Vigils and the Keeping the Promise Campaign back to lobbying. But a year later, John Hatch, a speaker at the 1994 RESULTS International Conference, planted an idea that began to move me away from lobbying once again.

Hatch was the founder of FINCA, a leading U.S.-based microcredit institution, and father of the village banking methodology used by FINCA and many other groups around the world. He was also a member of the RESULTS board. A six-page paper he wrote for the RESULTS conference called for a Microcredit Summit and campaign to reach 200 million of the world's poorest families within a decade. We showed the paper to Grameen Bank's Muhammad Yunus, another member of the RESULTS board and a leading figure in the field of microcredit. Yunus suggested that a goal of 100 million would be more achievable.

I had been elated by the clear and dramatic impact of RESULTS' citizen lobbying, but was driven by a constant desire for even greater impact. We were able to create small miracles, largely unseen by the general public, which meant that the scandal of global poverty remained unknown to most.

Even in 2004, I could quiz groups of bright high school students on current-events trivia (questions about the celebrity trials of Martha Stewart and Michael Jackson, for example) and they would pass with flying colors. But give them multiple-choice questions about the number of children who die each *day* from largely preventable malnutrition and disease (more than 29,000), the number of primary school–aged children *not* in school (more than 120 million), or the number of people living on less than $1 a day (1.2 billion), and they would flunk miserably.

What is it about our culture that makes the marital status of Jennifer Lopez a bigger priority than the largest solvable problems of our planet: world hunger and poverty and our fragile environment? It's often bizarre to observe the gap between what our culture says matters and what my heart tells me is most important. More often than I'd like to admit, I find myself in my kitchen in the morning, with a spoonful of Cheerios in my hand, talking to Katie Couric on television. "Come on Katie," I tell her. "Aren't you embarrassed to be talking about this nonsense [*crap* is the actual word I use]?" I don't think she hears me. In any event, the popular culture is not where I turn for my inspiration.

Where I do turn for inspiration is to people like UNICEF's Jim Grant,

Grameen's Muhammad Yunus, and FINCA's John Hatch—visionaries with a track record of achievement who point to *a world that could be*—rather than the world that is. They don't want incremental change; they want breakthroughs—and so do we!

A campaign to reach 100 million of the world's poorest families with microcredit was stunning. It was clear that none of the important United Nations Summits of the 1990s[3] emerged with a singularly compelling goal on this.

I've often asked myself why microcredit was given so little attention. Was it because it was a relatively new intervention? The first loans in the developing world were not made until the early 1970s. Certainly basic education and health were available in Asia, Africa, and Latin America long before that. Was it that there was no UN agency with microcredit as its central mandate in 1995? UNICEF made sure that children's well-being was on the world's agenda. The UN Population Fund saw to it that reproductive health issues were raised. The UN Environment Program spoke up for the planet's ecology. But which UN agency spoke for microcredit with equal authority? None!

At first we lobbied to insert the 100-million-poorest target into the 1995 Social Summit to be held in Copenhagen, but we were told that they weren't accepting any new goals. It became clear that if there was to be a compelling, measurable goal for microcredit, we'd have to establish it.

Hatch, Yunus, and I were the first to be galvanized by the vision of a Microcredit Summit, an effort to reach 100 million of the world's poorest families by the end of 2005. With back-of-the-envelope calculations, we estimated that no more than 8 million clients were reached in 1995. This meant we were calling for a dramatic increase from 8 million to 100 million poorest families over a 10-year period. Those 100 million families would include some 500 million family members.

I realized that if I were to take this on, however, I would have to step down as RESULTS' Executive Director so neither the lobbying work of RESULTS nor this non-lobbying project, the Microcredit Summit, would suffer from insufficient attention as had happened with the Candlelight Vigils and the Keeping the Promise Campaign. I discussed this decision at length with Dave Ellis, my life coach. Dave and I spoke weekly about all aspects of my life and our conversations played a crucial role in having my plans and insights expand to match this new vision.

I must admit that my first image of the Summit was of a hotel meeting room with 300 delegates. What we created instead was a civil society–organized summit to rival the UN summits, not in the number of participants, but in vision and especially in follow-up.

I took one staff member with me to launch the Summit, my executive

[3]The UN organized the Children's Summit in 1990, the Earth Summit in 1992, the Social Summit in 1995, the Housing Summit in 1996, the Food Summit in 1996, and all the other conferences including the Women's Conference in Beijing in 1995.

assistant, Ayala Sherbow. In August 1995 I became the volunteer President of RESULTS and full time President of RESULTS Educational Fund—with my entire focus on what would become the Educational Fund's largest project, the Microcredit Summit. Lynn McMullen was promoted from Director of Organizing and Development to Executive Director of RESULTS.

Just as with the Candlelight Vigils and the creation of RESULTS itself, the 1997 Microcredit Summit was another profound example of the W.H. Murray statement from *The Scottish Himalayan Expedition*:

> Until one is committed, there is hesitancy, the chance to draw back, always ineffectiveness. Concerning all acts of initiative (and creation), there is one elementary truth, the ignorance of which kills countless ideas and splendid plans: that the moment one commits oneself then Providence moves too . . . I have learned a deep respect for one of Goethe's couplets:
>
> Whatever you can do or dream you can, begin it.
> Boldness has genius, power, and magic in it.

The magic would come in large doses, and we would need it, as "summit fatigue" could have been one of many impediments. The Microcredit Summit came three months after the UN Food Summit, the last of six UN summits. The attitude could have been, "What, another summit? Forget it!" But people saw that microcredit was a powerful intervention that had been given short shrift at the UN summits.

A Microcredit Summit Organizing Committee was created with 12 members. The committee included practitioners like Ela Bhatt of SEWA in India, Nancy Barry of Women's World Banking, Michael Chu of ACCION, Connie Evans of Women's Self-Employment Project in Chicago, and, of course, Muhammad Yunus and John Hatch. Other members were from the World Bank, the Carter Center, and Citicorp.

We started with a mailing list of 200. We sent them John Hatch's six-page paper and asked for feedback. The Organizing Committee weighed in on all rounds of the feedback. By the fifth round we were mailing a 50-page document to 5,000 people (the Internet was still in its infancy in 1996) in order to fine-tune the Microcredit Summit's Declaration and Plan of Action.

"Preparation of a draft declaration proved to be a real hornets' nest," wrote Muhammad Yunus in his book *Banker to the Poor*. "I was shocked to see how the Summit preparations began opening up conflicts. Sam became extremely disappointed. I tried to cheer him up by saying that we had to confront all our academic, institutional and philosophical differences. It was easy for me to say this and disappear into safety in Dhaka," Yunus continued, "but Sam was the one who had to be in the eye of the storm. He had no place to run."

I felt it was essential to work through the issues—and there were many. Some believed the goal was too bold or the poorest couldn't be reached. I was committed to having a final document *before* the Summit so the event could focus on celebration and next steps, not wordsmithing. I wanted the Summit to be more than a photo-op. I wanted to make sure it launched a campaign that made good on the Summit's promise.

We agreed on a structure to help ensure action. We created 15 different Councils including Councils of Practitioners, Advocates, and UN Agencies, among others. To attend the Microcredit Summit an institution had to join one of the 15 councils, commit to the Summit's goal, and promise to report annually by submitting an Institutional Action Plan.

We reaffirmed our goal: to reach 100 million of the world's poorest families, especially the women of those families, with credit for self-employment and other financial and business services by the end of 2005, and outlined three core themes: *reaching the poorest, reaching and empowering women,* and *building financially self-sufficient institutions.*

I spoke everywhere I could about the Summit, including a public meeting in the U.K. that was particularly painful.

"What difference does it make if you reach the very poor sustainably," they challenged in a rough and tumble discussion, "if there's no impact on their lives?"

We had *assumed* impact. They were right, so we added a fourth core theme: *ensuring a positive measurable impact on the lives of clients and their families.*

We had 2,000 delegates registered the week before the 1997 Summit and extra materials in case 500 more registered on site. But more than 900 registered on site. In the end there were more than 2,900 delegates from 137 countries.

"Life leads us in mysterious ways and calls us to achieve our greatest potential in a manner we can never predict or know in advance," wrote Yunus, reflecting on the Summit. "Microborrowers, who grow up accepting that they are nobody, they are worth nothing, were placed by this Summit in the global spotlight and held up as the great heroes in the fight for world development. Speaker after speaker lauded them for their endless patience and skill in micro-managing tiny pieces of resources to craft a life with dignity.

"In teaching economics I learned about money," Yunus continued, "and now as the head of a bank I lend money, and the success of our venture lies in how many crumpled bank bills our once starving members now have in their hands. But the microcredit movement, which is built around, and for, and with money, ironically, is at its heart, at its deepest root, not about money at all. It is about helping each person achieve his or her fullest potential. It is not about cash capital, it is about human capital. Money is merely a tool that helps unlock human dreams and helps even the poorest and most unfortunate people on this planet achieve dignity, respect, and meaning in their lives."

The Summit attracted Presidents and Prime Ministers from five countries, and First Ladies from another five, along with Queen Sofia of Spain and Queen Fabiola of Belgium.

"I am thrilled to see such a turnout for this Summit which is one of the most important gatherings that we could have anywhere in our world," declared U.S. First Lady Hillary Rodham Clinton in her remarks to the Summit.

UN Development Program Administrator Gus Speth read a statement from Secretary General Kofi Annan who said, ". . . I therefore fully endorse the goal of this Summit to reach 100 million of the world's poorest households by the year 2005. . . . You can count on the UN to be there with you throughout this effort between now and the year 2005."

"We commit ourselves to be your partner," announced World Bank President Jim Wolfensohn. "We will help in whatever way we can."

After the Summit came a flurry of kudos. ACCION Senior Vice President Bill Burrus wrote, "The Summit was truly an historic occasion and there is no doubt in my mind that we will all look back to this moment as a watershed for the microenterprise movement worldwide."

". . . I am awed by the experience I just had," said Freedom from Hunger President Chris Dunford, "aware of having been witness to a moment in history."

"Many, many congratulations on what you accomplished last week!" Bill Drayton, President of Ashoka wrote. "You had a very smart, if audacious, strategy—and, true to form for you, you made it happen. Very, very few other people could conceivably have pulled this off."

Four years after the Summit, a practitioner came up to me at the 2001 Asia/Pacific Microcredit Summit in New Delhi, India, and said, "I was at the Summit in Washington. It was a wonderful fanfare."

And so it was, but we had not set out to perform a fanfare. We were committed to reaching 100 million of the world's poorest families with microcredit and we immediately faced opposition to a number of our core themes. A group of specialists in the field challenged core theme number one: *reaching the poorest*, arguing that it is too costly to identify and motivate the poorest people.

They continued by arguing that if you do reach the very poor, you can't build a financially self-sufficient institution, challenging core theme number three: *building financially self-sufficient institutions.* They also challenged core theme number four: *ensuring a positive measurable impact on the lives of clients and their families*, arguing that small loans only add a debt burden to the very poor.

Immediately after the Summit, our staff spoke by phone with practitioners to urge them to send in their Action Plans.

"We want to serve our clients, don't we?" my staff would say to me after calls to a number of practitioners.

"Yes," I replied, "of course we want to serve our clients."

"Well, some of them are telling us we should drop our focus on reaching the poorest," they continued.

These were pivotal moments for me and for the Campaign. Others would call these debates academic. But it's not academic if you are among the very poor, those living on less than $1 a day, the group that is most often excluded from development.

"It's true that we want to serve our clients," I responded, "but not at the expense of our mission. Our first commitment is to serving our mission, reaching 100 million of the world's poorest families. Our second commitment is to serving our clients. We want to bring our clients up to our mission, not weaken our mission to please our clients."

For nearly two decades I had seen this particular failure in development, the failure to reach the very poor. A number of times RESULTS succeeded in helping to pass a new law. On occasion, RESULTS Educational Fund would take time to study the law's implementation. A 1990 review of USAID's work in basic education, for example, found that $64,000 was spent on *each* foreign national who received an advanced degree in the U.S. How many African children could have been sent to primary school for $64,000?

A review by the General Accounting Office of USAID's implementation of the Child Survival Fund found that USAID was counting more than $2 million spent on a bridge in Mozambique toward the Child Survival Fund, money that was intended for vaccinating children and promoting breast-feeding.

And in Jordan, loans of $15,000 to $20,000 were counted toward USAID's mandate to reach the very poor with loans under $300. These were gross examples of the law's being broken, but beneath these examples was a persistent assumption that the very poor could not be reached.

This was not Muhammad Yunus' analysis or that of BRAC founder Fazle Abed. Freedom from Hunger's Chris Dunford and Didier Thys, the head of the Microfinance Information Exchange (MIX) didn't concur either. But many other people in positions of influence, especially within donor agencies, did write off the very poor.

The Microcredit Summit would not buckle. On the goal of reaching the poorest, the Summit became an inspiration to some and an irritant to others, depending on where one stood on the issue.

Until 2003, loan size was used to determine whether the very poor were being reached, a very crude, if not useless, indicator of poverty. As Freedom from Hunger's Chris Dunford would say, "Loan size tells you more about the institution making the loan than it does about the poverty of the person receiving the loan."

Over the first seven years of the campaign, the Microcredit Summit led the fight to make sure that the very poor were included and that something more reliable than loan size was used to measure the poverty of clients. The Summit identified and disseminated cost-effective poverty measurement tools, tools that would identify the very poor without significant additional cost. One such tool found that a home with a leaking roof and walls that were no more than four feet high were strong predictors of poverty. Another tool showed that, with proper facilitation, three separate groups of community members could reliably identify the very poor within their community. By 2002, our Asia and Africa organizers had used Microcredit Summit–commissioned training videos based on these tools to lead two-hour classroom sessions in 35 countries for more than 3,000 practitioners.

Unfortunately, the donor agencies and the U.S.-based groups working around the world largely ignored this work. Ignored it, that is, until RESULTS stepped back into the fray with new legislation. For the first four years after the Microcredit Summit (1997–2000), RESULTS played a very subdued role in lobbying on microcredit.

"We hadn't taken on microcredit as a major campaign," recalled RESULTS legislative director Joanne Carter, "but we continued to work with allies from both parties during those years. In 2001, Rep. Tim Roemer (D-IN) came to us asking what needed to happen next." Carter continued. "'Is it more money that's needed,' he wanted to know, 'or is it more focus on the very poor?' The latter had been our struggle for so long."

Fourteen years earlier Roemer was an aide to Sen. Dennis DeConcini (D-AZ). In 1987, DeConcini was the lead sponsor of microcredit legislation in the Senate. Now Roemer was a member of Congress himself, with a strong passion for microcredit.[4]

Congress had a decade-long commitment to ensuring that half of microenterprise funds reached the very poor. Now, at Roemer's request, legislation was drafted that would bring accountability to this commitment. The legislation would require the head of USAID to work with others to develop two or more cost-effective poverty measurement tools and specified that institutions seeking funds for the very poor must use one of these yet-to-be-certified tools.

In the fall of 2001, Roemer hosted a briefing for Congressional staff with Chris Dunford and me and mentioned that he was going to introduce legislation. An aide to Rep. Chris Smith (R-NJ) was at the briefing. Smith was vice chair of the International Relations Committee and a child survival and microcredit powerhouse. Within a couple of weeks, Smith introduced his own version of the legislation, and then Roemer introduced his bill.

Only RESULTS, Freedom from Hunger, and Grameen Foundation USA supported the initial bill. Everyone else opposed it—CARE, Save the Children, Catholic Relief Services, FINCA, ACCION, Opportunity International, and, of course, USAID. The opponents were concerned about the potential for burdensome new requirements for their programs, the use of these yet-to-be-developed poverty measurement tools. I assume a few were also worried they might find that their clients weren't that poor to begin with.

The microfinance field had been focused on strong financial performance, a key goal that could also push programs away from the very poor. A $500 loan is more efficient than a $50 loan and a $1,000 loan even more efficient. The field was increasingly focused on commercialization, transforming microcredit groups from non-governmental organizations to regulated banks. This,

[4]Roemer retired from Congress in 2002 and currently serves as President of the Center for National Policy and as a member of the 9/11 Commission (The National Commission on Terrorist Attacks upon the United States).

too, could push institutions away from the very poor because of high capital requirements and mandates for more rigorous reporting.

Representative Smith wanted the House International Relations Committee to take up the bill. The Committee's chair and ranking Democrat, along with Smith and Roemer, worked to combine and further develop the legislation.

"There was a lot of debate around the legislation," remembered Joanne Carter, "and what impressed me was how the committee staff really listened and delved into the substance of the issue. They saw that if you were committed to reaching the very poor, then you had to measure it better."

A series of meetings took place with Congressional staff and members of the Microenterprise Coalition, the group of U.S.-based microenterprise networks working overseas.

"Even though the majority of practitioners were arguing against it," Carter recalled, "the members of Congress were persuaded on the importance of the bill."

A week after one particularly crucial meeting, the bill passed in committee by unanimous consent. Three weeks later, it passed by unanimous consent in the House.

"There were some key offices in the Senate that wanted to move forward on the legislation," Carter continued.

A new version was drafted in the Senate. It gave more time for development of the poverty measurement tools and specified that it was USAID that had to have 50 percent of its funds reaching the very poor, not the individual microcredit programs such as FINCA and Opportunity International.

"The practitioners and USAID felt it gave them more flexibility," Carter concluded. "I think people were persuaded once they got into the process of developing the tools. You had to pry open that political space with a law, however, in order to get to the point where people were working on developing the tools."

Just as I was astounded by the passage of the bill and its signing into law in June 2003, I was similarly impressed by the work done on its implementation by groups like FINCA, Opportunity International, ACCION, and Freedom from Hunger. Jim Grant's call for a World Summit for Children and John Hatch's call for a Microcredit Summit moved me away from lobbying to movement-building activities. Now RESULTS' work on this microcredit legislation made me wish I were back in the game of citizen lobbying.

By 2003, the Microcredit Summit had spent eight years offering brilliant carrots to encourage practitioners to reach the very poor: papers, plenary discussions, training videos, two-hour classroom sessions, four-day trainings. But this legislation—a stick, not a carrot—changed everything. When the bill was finally signed into law in June 2003, the word I kept using to describe what had just happened was "astounding."

Astounding, but not easy. The stories RESULTS volunteers tell usually begin with their own hopelessness, which covers a deeper desire to make a difference. Their hopelessness then collides with the inspiration of a RESULTS volunteer or staff member, a seemingly ordinary person doing extraordinary things. The volunteers tell of their initial involvement, usually consisting of repeated and often unsuccessful calls for an appointment with a member of Congress and invitations initially ignored by members of the media. And, of course, if it's really a RESULTS volunteer's story, there are huge doses of persistence, because without persistence, one is left with appointments denied, requests rejected, and no success, no interaction with decision makers, and ultimately, no transformation.

Kerry Langan, a RESULTS volunteer in Cleveland, remembered that her initial inspiration came from Jennifer Robey, a young RESULTS staff member who visited the Oberlin College campus in what would be a failed attempt to start a RESULTS chapter there.

"My family is Irish and about one-third of my father's family starved to death in the Irish Famine," Kerry recalled. "Hunger is something I always wanted to work on, but didn't know where to start. Jennifer was fun. I was energized by the evening. She seemed to be an ordinary person like myself, but was out there changing things. She really gave me a sense of the possibilities."

The Oberlin group never got off the ground, so Kerry called the RESULTS office and learned of an upcoming presentation in Cleveland by RESULTS staff member Nick Arena.

"In July of 1993, I joined the Cleveland chapter of RESULTS," Kerry continued. "I enthusiastically learned the material on the basics tape[5] and was determined to make contact with editors at the Cleveland *Plain Dealer* and to schedule a meeting with then freshman Congressman Sherrod Brown (D-OH). My first few months as a partner were filled with frustration. Although I convinced a writer at the *Plain Dealer* to participate in a RESULTS conference call on the World Summit for Children anniversary, the newspaper didn't publish anything. Still, I called every two weeks and soon staff members became familiar with my name.

"Meeting with Sherrod Brown proved even more difficult," Kerry remembered. "I wrote letter after letter discussing the foreign aid budget, microcredit, child labor, and other poverty-related issues. On our monthly conference calls, I listened enviously as partners across the country described meetings with their representatives and thought, 'what am I doing wrong?'

"On a Sunday evening in late March 1994, while eating dinner with my husband, the phone rang. I reluctantly left the table, still savoring a mouthful of mashed potatoes. As soon as I picked up the telephone, I heard a deep voice say, 'Kerry Langan?' 'Yes,' I answered, swallowing hard to speak more clearly. 'Sherrod Brown,' the voice responded. 'Talk to me about these issues.'

[5]New partners must pass an oral test on materials contained in a cassette tape, which includes the basics on RESULTS, the problems and solutions to hunger and poverty, and how a bill becomes law.

"I blinked. The phone call I had waited for for months was taking place, *now*. Details of microcredit flashed through my mind. Should I start with statistics on the number of children who died each day from preventable malnutrition and disease? There was a Congressman on the other end of the telephone—*say something!* I told myself. I blurted, 'I need to meet with you. These issues are very complicated.' I sensed reluctance on his part, but he told me to call his scheduler."

After getting the appointment Kerry called Nick Arena, who coached the group on the upcoming meeting. They gathered information and rehearsed over and over.

"At our first meeting with Sherrod," Kerry recalled, "we all spoke well. Only one of us had ever met face-to-face with a Member of Congress before. Sherrod listened, asked questions, thanked us for coming, and committed to nothing. My first impression of him was this guy is really, really smart. Although he held his cards close to his chest, I sensed he was a deeply compassionate person. We presented him with an autographed copy of Sam's book, *Reclaiming Our Democracy*.

"Three days later," Kerry continued, "there was a message on my answering machine: 'Hello. This is Sherrod Brown. I read the book! I'm a convert. Stay in touch.' I replayed the message at least a dozen times. I called the other members of our group. I called Nick and played the message for him. 'Stay in touch,' he said. We sure did."

The more they worked with Brown, the more they knew he had major leadership potential. In RESULTS, we track "leader spokesperson actions" and "audacious leader spokesperson actions." The latter refers to Members of Congress leading on an issue even in the face of opposition from the Administration or the chairman of a committee. Eventually, the Cleveland partners asked Joanne Carter what it would take to have Brown go to the next level of leadership, to go beyond just co-sponsoring legislation.

"I was looking for someone to lead on the TB issue," Carter remembered, "because of its great link with poverty and because it was the biggest curable infectious disease on the planet. Some two million people died each year of TB, and, by 1993, the World Health Organization [WHO] had declared TB a global health emergency."

"It was 1997 when we met with Sherrod on tuberculosis," recalled Allison Gallaher, another Cleveland Partner and part-time RESULTS staff member. "As a ranking member of the Health Subcommittee of Energy and Commerce, he saw health as his purview."

Out of these beginnings, Sherrod Brown became one of the leading spokespersons in Congress for U.S. funding to combat TB. He introduced legislation authorizing funds and requiring that the money be spent in effective, life-saving programs. When he started, less than $1 million a year was spent on TB control. By 2004, it had grown to $85 million.

"In the summer of 2001," Allison remembered, "Sherrod introduced an amendment to the foreign aid spending bill to increase funding to $80 million. As the debate on the amendment unfolded on C-SPAN, I heard RESULTS laser talks, the presentations we made on TB, coming out of the mouths of members of Congress. I remember watching the vote count appear on the television screen, and the moment that it became clear that the amendment had enough *yes* votes to pass. I was jumping up and down in my living room and screaming as though the Cleveland Indians had just won the World Series."

An important victory it was, truly deserving of celebration. However, RESULTS' World Series victory, its Super Bowl, World Cup, and Olympics will come when the 29,000 child deaths each day from preventable malnutrition and disease are reduced to zero; when *all* primary school–aged children are in school—good schools; and when all people can live in dignity.

In the years since *Reclaiming Our Democracy* was published, we have faced a number of challenges and opportunities. One opportunity was to create a new option within RESULTS for people whose primary concern was hunger and poverty in the United States. We had worked on some domestic issues all along, but our international work had always taken precedence. Before 1994 a small effort was put into support for domestic programs such as the Head Start Program and the Supplemental Food Program for Women, Infants and Children (WIC).

In 1994, we decided to create a separate track, RESULTS Domestic, on which we would apply proven RESULTS methods to domestic issues. Karen McQuillan came on staff as the first domestic coordinator. The domestic side of RESULTS quickly became the fastest-growing part of the organization. By the end of 1995, there were 15 local volunteer groups working primarily on U.S. issues; now there are 34.

RESULTS worked with other child advocates in 1994 to educate the public and Congress about WIC and Head Start. In a year of very tight budget constraints, fiscal year 1995 funding for WIC was increased $260 million, to $3.47 billion. The Head Start Program got an increase of $210 million, to $3.53 billion. In 2001, Head Start funding jumped by nearly $1 billion, to $6.2 billion.

As the millennium approached, we focused our domestic lobbying on early childhood education and childcare. More and more studies were showing that quality preschool programs had lifelong benefits for children who participated. Early intervention was a key to ending the cycle of poverty. The most effective programs were those like Head Start that dealt with all of the needs of the child and involved the entire family. A research brief from Fight Crime: Invest in Kids, an organization of more than 2,000 police chiefs, sheriffs, prosecutors, and crime survivors dedicated to preventing crime and violence, notes, "Investing in quality services now will help millions of vulnerable children become productive, responsible adults, and will prevent millions of Americans from becoming victims of crime."

In 2003, our early education work faced a new challenge. The Bush Administration announced a plan that would dismantle Head Start by turning over control to the 50 states. RESULTS and allies dove into action, organizing a media and public education campaign to defend Head Start. RESULTS organized our largest media conference call ever with 53 journalists. The call launched a campaign that generated over 150 media pieces, including 27 editorials. A watered-down version of the Administration plan, which would allow up to eight states to administer Head Start, passed the House of Representatives by one vote. The corresponding Senate bill had no such provision, effectively killing the scheme, for now.

For most of the last dozen years, the number of RESULTS groups with a global focus has declined, although it has stabilized in recent years. Just because the work of RESULTS is important, even urgent, that doesn't make it easy.

A decade has passed since *Reclaiming Our Democracy* was first published. The world has changed and RESULTS must change too. As is true for other organizations, RESULTS must learn to use new technologies to their fullest potential. But we must not become too enamored of technology because the ultimate difference in creating the political will to end hunger will come through face-to-face interactions by articulate, passionate citizens—citizens who ask for and receive loving, rigorous support. That is why the people and stories in this book are so vital to creating the world we want.

Essentially, this book is filled with miracles: *The miracle of people realizing their true purpose in life*—serving others, making a difference, or, as one friend put it, "leaving the campsite cleaner than we found it."

The miracle of acting on one's purpose with true commitment—as if one's life depended on it.

The miracle of leadership—especially in unlikely leaders—you and me. Leadership ultimately requires going beyond one's comfort zone, agreeing, for example, to host a news conference without ever having *been* to a news conference. The *Fear Factor* that matters most for this planet concerns not how many insects one can swallow in 60 seconds, but, rather, how much discomfort and discouragement one is willing to endure while acting to serve others and make a difference in the world.

Lastly, this book is filled with *the miracle of holding on to a vision of what the world could be*, when others are filled with doubt. Susan B. Anthony and Elizabeth Cady Stanton; Mahatma Gandhi, Martin Luther King, and Nelson Mandela—all demonstrated this kind of fierce, single-minded determination. It is what each one of us must emulate if we are to have a purpose-filled life. As Goethe said, "Whatever you can do or dream you can, begin it. / Boldness has genius, power, and magic in it."

Yes, begin it!

CHAPTER 29

The RESULTS Model Takes Aim at Climate Change

Climate change can be paralyzing. Because it is so big it can produce fear and inertia, and because its causes and solutions are so diffuse it can frustrate and discourage action. Perhaps the biggest challenge for climate activists to overcome is to remain truly hopeful—something Citizens Climate Lobby (CCL) has mastered better than any other organization.

That hope was in clear view as I listened to CCL's monthly conference call that first Saturday in August, 2012. The United States was headed to what would be the hottest year on record. CCL was also going through the hottest year in its five-year history with volunteers hurtling to the following year-end achievements: 537 letters to the editor published (up from 36 in 2010), 534 meetings with members of Congress or their staff (up from 105 in 2010), and 87 op-eds published (up from 20 in 2010).

"If you want to join the fight to save the planet, to save creation for your grandchildren," wrote leading climate scientist James Hansen, "there is no more effective step you could take than becoming an active member of this group."

The group Hansen was talking about was Citizens Climate Lobby.

So what is going on here? One thing is clear. CCL is the first organization to deeply empower grassroots citizens with a stunningly effective replication of RESULTS' methodology—so effective that some in RESULTS are asking CCL leaders how they are doing it.

The guest speaker on the CCL conference call had just finished and the moderator moved to a discussion of the workshops from CCL's International Conference the month before. Elli Sparks, a volunteer from the Richmond, Virginia area, was introduced. Sparks had joined CCL 18 months earlier and often said that when she joined, she was suffering from "climate trauma." I asked what she meant by that.

> My second child has a terrible heart defect and had to have five open heart surgeries. After the surgeries were over and my children got settled at school, I won-

> dered what was going on with the environment. I went to my local library and got Bill McKibben's book *Eaarth*. It was the summer of 2010. I read it and wept. My friends had been involved with the Al Gore documentary a few years earlier but I had a kid that I was taking to the Cleveland Clinic twice a year. My daughter wasn't getting what she needed from me and my marriage had suffered. I had been dealing with survival issues. Now I was weeping at work and at home, constantly crying and I thought, "I take 10 years off to start a family and the world falls apart. . . ."

When Sparks joined CCL she had never met with an editorial writer and hadn't been on a Congressional lobbying visit for 12 years. But now, 18 months after joining CCL, she would describe the workshop she co-led on creating relationships with members of Congress and the media.

I had heard her speak before and was inspired by the work that she and her team were doing in Richmond, but I wasn't expecting to hear what she was about to say. Her remarks were the purest expression of the transformation that my new Center for Citizen Empowerment and Transformation sought to create.

> . . . Our director Mark Reynolds likes to say, "We're betting the farm on relationships." Then he tells us that we need to build relationships with members of Congress and editorial writers. Most of us CCL volunteers have never done that before!! What in the world does a relationship with a member of Congress look like? How do we connect with an editorial page editor? Some of us have found models for those relationships in other parts of our lives. Gary in Boston uses the model of a work relationship. . . .

This was a good start, honest and probing, but nothing mind-blowing. That would come next.

> My relationship model is different. I adore romantic relationships, so I use romance as my model. That first meeting with the editorial writer . . . it's like a blind date, only you've decided beforehand you are going to marry this fellow. You are going to be sweet and interesting, but not too intense . . . if it doesn't work out with the editor, you are going to marry one of his friends at the newspaper—the business editor, environmental writer, or city editor. Someone at this paper will find you interesting and compelling—it's just a matter of being persistent until you find the right connection.

Who talks like this? Certainly not someone still suffering from climate trauma. And you probably wouldn't hear it from typical climate activists or activists of any kind. It was music to my ears.

> . . . I see the relationship with a member of Congress as an arranged marriage. If you live in her district, the member's aide has to meet with you. That's what our Congressman's legislative director (LD) told us in January. Since then, we've met

> five times with the LD in 2012. We schedule 45-minute meetings with him. He keeps us for well over an hour. He doesn't want us to leave! Why? Because a good arranged marriage starts out cold and heats up over time. That's different than a love match, which starts out hot and slowly cools down.

From "climate trauma" to this, and she was just getting going.

> . . . I see the editorial page writer as a painter. His canvas is the editorial pages. His pallet is filled with letters to the editor, op-eds, and editorials. I am his muse, model, and assistant. . . . I want him to fill his canvas with colors that I like, so I'll have my group send 3–5 letters to the editor whenever the opportunity arises. The more colors I put on his pallet, the better chance of having him pick one or two of my favorite colors.
>
> . . . Last summer, he printed three climate denier letters from international denier groups. At first, the denier letters felt like a blow to the gut. Then, I dug deep for the love language. . . . My editor was proud of his work in standing up for the climate. Those denier letters were in response to his own articles encouraging conservatives to help conserve the climate. He had been courageous in writing those editorials. He was getting national attention because of them. He was not backing down. I thought he might enjoy a pat on the back from across the nation. I called Gary in Boston, a scientist in NY, and our CCL director [in California]. All three sent letters. All three letters were printed! I guess I was right . . . my editorial page editor likes national attention!!

And then she got to the essence of citizen empowerment and transformation, the breakthrough that eludes almost every national advocacy effort.

> . . . During our conference I met with 20 congressional offices. I met with many folks whose view of the world was very different than mine. Going into their offices was hard. I had to let go of a lot of emotional baggage. I could no longer judge them or hold hostility in my heart towards them. I had to let go of my fear of climate change and my fear that they wouldn't listen to me. I had to center myself in love. Releasing fear and centering in love . . . this is sacred and profound work. . . .

And so it is. But how do you start an organization that sets out to create the political will to ensure a stable climate and delivers "sacred and profound work" in the process? It is definitely not a matter of luck but the result of some serious planning and commitment. That was the journey that CCL's founder Marshall Saunders began when he kept returning to see "An Inconvenient Truth" in 2006—three times over a 10-day period.

Actually Saunders' journey began long before his repeated viewings of the climate change documentary. It's hard to put a finger on one event in a person's life that leads to the founding of an organization like CCL, but when I look for clues, I search for existential moments in which the preciousness of life is so profoundly experienced that it launches a continued quest to live a life that truly matters. So what were those moments in Saunders' life? As you will see, at first, his life was as ordinary as any.

"I was a guy who played everything safe," Saunders recalled. "I wanted a peaceful life with my wife and two kids and wanted to be left alone."

But in 1980, Saunders took a human development course and made a contract with himself that said, "I trust myself as I seek out new risks and commit to new responsibilities."

"At first I softened it so I didn't have to take risks," he remembered, "but then I realized that risks are at the heart of it."

Maybe that's the beginning, shifting from a life of safety to a life that incorporates some risk. But for most people that might lead to taking up sky diving, skiing black diamond trails, or running a marathon or two, all of which require courage and bring some risk but don't exactly result in starting a life-altering organization that addresses one of the greatest challenges of our time.

But Saunders didn't hit the slopes or jump out of airplanes. Instead he joined Rotary and started visiting community service projects like the Pan American Institute, a private junior high school for the poor in Tijuana, Mexico.

"I visited the school in 1987," he recalled, "and Rotary gave about $600 for their library. It is in a really run-down neighborhood, but if you went inside the school you would see that everything was spotless and the kids were well groomed. When the kids arrived each morning they got a broom or a mop and they would clean the school every day. But if you went out the back door the neighborhood was a trash heap."

At about this time Saunders began receiving dividends from Big Red, his family's soda company founded decades earlier in his hometown of Waco, Texas. The experience with the school and the new income led Saunders and his wife Pam to eventually provide about 15,000 meals a year to the students. But now life had a new lesson to deliver.

> Right after I joined Rotary I had a physical and learned I had prostate cancer. . . . Unfortunately the surgery didn't get all of the cancer and it is incurable. At the time I was beginning to get family money off the Big Red, I had the desire to make a difference, and now I learn I'm going to die. It became a race to see how much I can get done before I get too sick to do it and die.

But to the great good fortune of Saunders and an untold number of others, he would not die any time soon, but would instead live his life as if he were.

Maybe trusting oneself to seek out new risks and committing to new responsibilities coupled with the specter of death looking over your shoulder are part of what fuels the founding of an institution like CCL.

Saunders' work in Rotary led him to start the first Rotary chapter in Leningrad, one of the first in what would soon be the former Soviet Union. Soon after, he was given a Rotary newsletter with a piece by John Hatch, founder of the microfinance group FINCA. In it Hatch said, "Let historians record that Rotary led in ending the scourge of polio followed by ending poverty."

Saunders found a Rotarian in Orange County, California, who was making Rotary matching grants to FINCA in Mexico. It was clear that Saunders didn't do things half way, so he jumped right in. This would be his new calling. Talking to Rotary groups across the country, Saunders completed 72 grants totaling $9,000 each which provided nearly $700,000 for FINCA's work in Latin America. "We had about $2 million more in the pipeline," Saunders recalled, "but the Rotary Foundation Trustees said, 'No more grants to FINCA.'"

Saunders was on FINCA's board at the time and an invitation after one of their board meetings led him to RESULTS and his next calling—citizen empowerment.

> I was going to take a nap after one of the FINCA board meetings but Lawrence Yanovitch, one of their senior staff, said, "Let's go to the RESULTS conference which is meeting in Washington, DC this weekend. You'd like this group."
>
> I walked into the back of the meeting room where about 300 RESULTS Partners were seated. On a raised platform were four men in dark suits, three managers from the World Bank and the Director of RESULTS, Sam Daley-Harris. It was Question and Answer time and the RESULTS Partners who came to the microphone to ask a question had done their homework. They asked good questions, and seemed to be in disagreement with the policies of the Bank on a range of issues, especially on school fees for children in very poor countries.
>
> I was not surprised by that, but what did surprise me was that in the face of their disagreement the RESULTS Partners were very polite. More than polite, they were generous in their appreciation of these men. That continued with every questioner: disagreement with the Bank's policies, politeness, and appreciation. When the session was complete the RESULTS Partners gave them a standing ovation. I hadn't seen anything like that ever before. . . .
>
> It reminded me of the title to that movie, *The Unbearable Lightness of Being.* I felt like I was floating six inches above the floor. I went to the back table and picked up a tee shirt that had a quote by Senator Mark Hatfield (R-OR) on it, "We stand by as children starve by the millions because we lack the will to eliminate hunger. Yet we have found the will to develop missiles capable of flying over the polar cap and landing within a few hundred feet of their target. This is not innovation. It is a profound distortion of humanity's purpose on Earth." I was blown away by it.

Years later, at the launch of Citizens Climate Lobby, when there weren't any CCL chapters yet, Saunders said this to the group:

> So the manner in which we will work with Congress is non-partisan, of course, but much, much more than that. It is respectful and generous in our appreciation of those who oppose us. It is patient and kind. This extends to how we think about people who disagree with us. And yet through all of the patience and kindness there is an indomitable will, never being defeated, never giving up.

This idea of being respectful and generous in our appreciation of those who oppose us is quite foreign to most advocacy efforts. When I started the Center for Citizen Empowerment and Transformation in 2012, I met with dozens of non-governmental organization (NGO) leaders. I would tell them about CCL volunteers meeting with the legislative director for one of the top House Republicans—a Tea Party ally. The volunteers spent four hours planning for the meeting and when the meeting ended the legislative director said they were the most prepared group with whom he had ever met.

"If I asked an ordinary climate activist to meet with a top House Tea Party leader," I would say to the NGO heads, "I think the climate activists would say, 'Now which wall do you want me to bang my head against, this wall here or that wall over there?'" Almost to prove my point, at a meeting with the head of an environmental group with millions of stakeholders the leader jumped in at the end of my story and said, "We wouldn't meet with Tea Party leaders in Congress. We'd meet with those who are with us or those whom we feel we could convince, but we wouldn't meet with Tea Party leaders."

This was not the lesson that Saunders would bring to CCL, however.

While he had been invited to RESULTS meetings in San Diego before, he had never gone. This time he would go.

> I came back to San Diego and Rotary had said "no more loans" so I wondered if RESULTS would let me be one of them. I called Bruce Underhill, the local RESULTS leader, and I was welcomed. . . . One of the first things I remember doing was going to meet with Rep. Brian Bilbray (R-CA) along with about six others. We went to a Denny's restaurant across from his office to do a little planning. I had experience in microcredit so I was going to speak about that during the meeting.
>
> We went into his office and he came out from behind his desk and sat in a mahogany, leather-covered chair. I sat across from him and felt a little nervous. Before RESULTS, I didn't know who my member of Congress was. I really didn't follow politics at all. Now I had all these thoughts running through my head. "Should I cross my legs? Should I fold my hands in my lap? How would I look?" Then it was my turn to talk and Bruce said, "Marshall is going to talk about microcredit." After I spoke the Congressman said he would look into the microcredit legislation. I called back a day later and the aide said . . . the Congressman would cosponsor the bill. . . .
>
> The main thing RESULTS gave me was the realization that I could participate and that my voice mattered. The feeling of family was also very important to me.

Saunders met with members of Congress and invited people to RESULTS' conference calls but left the work with the local newspaper to others. That was until one of the RESULTS partners, out of sheer frustration, proposed a protest in front of the newspaper to say that they were killing babies by refusing to cover life-saving interventions like vaccinations in the Third World. That's when Saunders stepped in and began calling the editor of the editorial pages.

I called for almost two years and he never called me back. One time I called somebody else at the paper and he said, "I can't help you on Tuberculosis or microcredit but why don't you call Bill Osborne." That broke the thing wide open. Osborne, who was also on the editorial board, must have just cared about global diseases. I was so excited after the first call that I put the editorial packet in a manila envelope, took it to the paper and asked the lady at the front desk if she would give it to him. I called him later and he said what he would come to say so very often, "I can't promise anything but maybe." About a week later I opened the paper and there it was. I took the editorial to my wife Pam and said, "look here, sweetheart" and I just had a moment of being really proud. . . . Osborne tended to write several editorials on our issues each year.

Saunders' view of the world was also shaped by an earlier encounter with RESULTS. He was in Costa Rica for a FINCA Board meeting and was invited to join me by phone on a radio interview I was doing at the San Diego NPR station. During the interview I mentioned that RESULTS had successfully lobbied Congress for $200 million for microcredit.

At first I thought, "that's not right." I had busted my butt for three years to raise nearly $700,000 through Rotary, and RESULTS had raised $200 million in their lobbying . . . it didn't seem to be realistic, the $200 million. I did make a mental note of it, however.

The mental note would be an early lesson on the road to his climate work showing the difference between important changes that individuals can make and the critical work that governments must do. Saunders continued his work with RESULTS and made a serious commitment to Grameen de la Frontera, the microfinance institution he founded in the state of Sonora, Mexico. He had read about climate change and realized that sea level rise would affect some of his clients.

It occurred to me that I was trying to get 5,000 more borrowers in Mexico and that Bangladesh might lose millions due to sea level rise. I felt I had to get to the bottom of this. I went to see *An Inconvenient Truth* and went back about a week later. . . . Then I read that Al Gore was going to train 1,000 people. I said, "holy socks, of course that's what I want to do."

Saunders sent in his application and didn't hear back at first. But in January 2007, he joined about 250 others in Nashville for one of the trainings. Vice President Gore went through the slide show and gave the group permission to lead the presentation.

I was excited to get home and start practicing. There were 300–400 slides which I reduced to 60 or so. I polished my presentation for each slide and tried to get it down to 20 minutes. My first presentation was to the United Methodist Women at my church.

Saunders led the slide show dozens of more times but early on he realized that 98 percent of the information focused on the problem of climate change and that barely 2 percent focused on what people could do about it. Many of the actions seemed to center on using more energy-efficient light bulbs and buying hybrid cars but didn't really get at the big picture, public policy. There was something else he saw as missing that most advocacy initiatives omit.

> I was expecting Vice President Gore's Climate Reality Project to operate somewhat like RESULTS, providing lots of support. I was expecting that we would have monthly conference calls and that there would be a Group Leader nearby that I could talk to who would occasionally call me to ask me how I was doing. I expected that I could call headquarters in Nashville and ask for clarifications occasionally. And I expected a format in which I could talk to other participants on a regular basis. None of that existed. When I suggested some of these things to headquarters they didn't understand what I was talking about and when they did, they didn't think it was necessary.

Saunders certainly saw this extra support as necessary and would make sure that it was part of any initiative he would launch.

This hunger activist and newly minted climate educator was now reading the newspaper every morning. On one of those mornings, cup of coffee in hand, he read in the *San Diego Union Tribune* that Congress had just approved $18 billion in subsidies to the fossil fuel industry.

"I'd gotten people to change 18 light bulbs yesterday," he thought, "and that same day Congress approved $18 billion in subsidies to the fossil fuel industry. This is never going to work."

Perhaps that is why, during a Q&A session at one of his talks, he told participants that the climate issue needed the methodology of RESULTS. When a participant asked, "Why don't you do that?" he replied that he didn't know if he could get a room full of people who would be open to being politically active on climate. Clearly this was only one of several insecurities around starting a new organization, but the questioner said she would help, and even after her help fell through, Saunders decided to forge ahead anyway.

Saunders' realization was similar to the experience that led me to start RESULTS 30 years earlier. I had read the experts' calls for the "political will to end hunger" and asked 7,000 high school students the name of their member of Congress. When fewer than three percent knew the answer, I realized that something more had to be done. And now, with Congress approving $18 billion in fossil fuel subsidies and Saunders encouraging people to change their light bulbs and trade-in their gas guzzlers, he also knew something more had to be done.

Saunders asked several large environmental groups if they would train a small number of their members to become deep advocates on climate. When they all said no, he asked me to coach him on starting Citizens Climate Lobby because he knew he wanted to model it after RESULTS.

I had founded RESULTS in 1980 and left in 1995 to found the Microcredit Summit Campaign. But in 2007, six months before Saunders' call, I had gone back to RESULTS half time with a focus on starting chapters around the U.S. So there we were, both immersed in this question: "What will it take to deeply empower citizens at a time of great cynicism and despair?" We spoke once or twice a week by phone as Saunders prepared for his very first presentation.

With assistance from a new friend, Jean Seager, 29 people gathered on October 6, 2007, in Rancho Bernardo, California, for the first group start workshop of Citizens Climate Lobby. Saunders had picked that name because he wanted it to be as explicit as possible.

"That morning before the group start meeting I called Sam on the cell phone and we talked for a while," Saunders recalled, "and then we talked again afterward."

I took those calls on a baseball field in Princeton, New Jersey, before and after one of my son's Little League games. Saunders hoped that at least some of the people in the room would understand what he was proposing and agree to join him. To his great surprise everyone said yes.

> I was elated and exhausted. I am often tired after a presentation like that. Of the 29 people all of them wanted to be in the group so we divided up by area and started three groups in San Diego. They had finally found something to do about the climate. They knew they were getting into something brand new and wanted it to be as successful as I did. I wanted to be alone after being so open and vulnerable but I went with 5 or 6 others to the Mongolian restaurant in the shopping center. I went back a week or two later and gave them a test on the basics of CCL and climate. They loved it. The next step was to have a conference call. There would be three groups on the call and they were all in San Diego County.
>
> The first conference call was November 3, 2007. I woke up at 4:30 that morning and worked on the script. Brent Blackwelder, the head of Friends of the Earth, was our first guest speaker. I told everyone that they could tell their grandchildren they were on the very first CCL call. Before introducing Brent, I read an excerpt from a Thomas Friedman column. I was on fire. I didn't see any impediments. I was alone in my office on the telephone and the three groups were in their own three living rooms.
>
> But after the call I was thinking, "How was it?" I felt kind of empty and I couldn't see anyone's response. "Holy socks, I'm not good enough to be doing this," I thought. "I just don't think people liked it." It felt like I was speaking into a vacuum.
>
> Thankfully, soon afterward somebody reassured me that it was good.

Saunders' insecurity should be a reality check for any grassroots effort to create change on a grand scale. If insecurities are not present then volunteers and staff are probably not being encouraged to move out of their comfort zones and take new territory. But it can't be discomfort for the sake of discomfort, but must be in pursuit of a compelling vision.

Madeleine Para, a teacher in Madison, Wisconsin, who joined CCL in 2011, experienced those insecurities. The difference with Para and her CCL colleagues is that they have a deep structure of support and an ethos of joyful aspiration that keeps pulling them toward the vision and prevents their fears from stopping them.

"I made a decision that fundamentally changed my life," Para recalled looking back on some of her climate activism. "I decided the survival of life on planet earth mattered more to me than any discouragement, fear, or self-invalidation I might carry."

This is a powerful declaration that is critical to CCL's breakthroughs. I refer to it when I delineate 13 commitments[1] necessary for real citizen empowerment and transformation to occur. Under the section titled "Empowering breakthroughs" I write: "For a citizen to go from not knowing the name of their member of Congress to having a deep, trusted relationship with them requires a series of breakthroughs—it requires moving out of their comfort zone. That is essentially the definition of a breakthrough, seeing something that seems difficult or impossible, having some discomfort in taking it on, and then, with coaching and support, going through that comfort zone to experience the joy and accomplishment on the other side. . . . Empowering others in this way and providing opportunities for them to express their greatness is one of the gifts of deep advocacy."

I am reminded of the drawing that has a small circle on the left side of the page with an arrow pointing to it saying, "Your comfort zone." To the right is a much larger circle with these words written in the center: "Where the magic happens." It's so very clear.

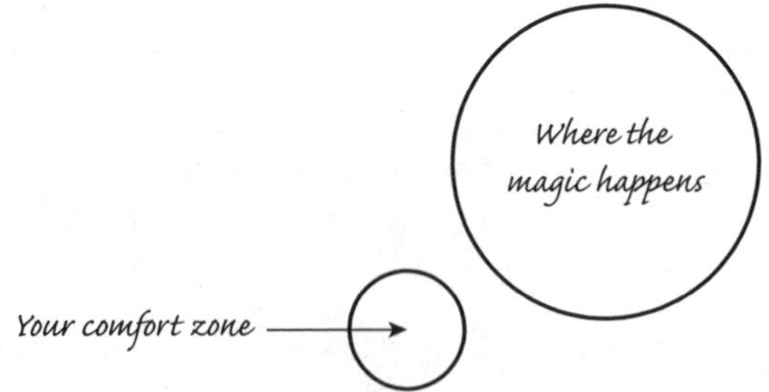

Para discussed another level of breakthrough.

> It's not that hard for me to connect with "regular" people. It's been a stretch, but not so far that I couldn't figure it out mostly on my own, using the powerful motivator that I care more about the planet than my old feelings of shyness or inadequacy. I used to hate to be in any situation where someone might say no to

[1]All 13 commitments are discussed in Chapter 30.

> me, and I would avoid asking for anything in order to avoid how bad it might feel if they said no. Now I regularly ask different people to help me with things. I'm too busy having fun to worry about whether they will say yes or no.

I discuss dropping the fear of "no" in another of the commitments required for success. Under "enrolling others" I write: "Engaging other community members in being empowered volunteers is part of the structure of support. If one invites a friend to a meeting there is always the fear that they will say no or that they will come and see this as a useless activity. When volunteers become senior to that fear, when the commitment to the purpose and vision is greater than the fear of rejection, then big things can happen."

Para then spoke about her greater fear.

> The bigger challenge for me has been the idea that a member of Congress or a newspaper editor or some other important person is going to want to talk with me or care what I think. I'm not really over this yet. I believe it intellectually but not emotionally so far. So it's a breakthrough every time I have contact with any "person of importance."

And she said this about her very first meetings on Capitol Hill—five in one day.

> . . . I did not grow up with privilege, as a working class child living in a middle class neighborhood, and I really was not used to the idea that important people would want to be bothered with me. The phrase "who do you think you are?" kept going through my head. But my commitment to the planet and the confidence of the people around me required that I at least pretend to know what I was doing, and maybe it would turn out to be true.

Para's route into climate change was through reading James Hansen's book *Storms of My Grandchildren*. After reading it she joined the Sierra Club's Beyond Coal Team, and organized a fairly large event for 350.org's global day of action on 10/10/10. When she received a call from Citizens Climate Lobby she was too busy to join, but was intrigued by the fact that they were the only group she'd found that was actively working on Hansen's carbon fee and dividend idea. The proposal would put a rising fee on carbon with the collected fee going back to the public.

Para would look back on the action she had taken and see that she had stretched herself and had fun doing it, but like Saunders' reaction to the $18 billion Congress approved in fossil fuel subsidies, she said, "I was dissatisfied with my activities because I did not think they were going to get us where we needed to go. . . ."

That was the feeling that Cheryl McNamara had with her work in Toronto, Canada. McNamara's route into action was also prompted by a book, in her case Ronald Wright's *A Short History of Progress*.

Wright shows how civilizations like the Mayans and the Polynesian society on Easter Island rose and fell because they gobbled up the environment that sustained them. McNamara had been alarmed years earlier by the toll climate change was taking but she quickly put it to the back of her mind—but not this time.

> When I lay down Ronald Wright's book I envisioned myself as an elderly woman on her death bed, ashamed that I could have done something about this problem but did nothing and now that I lay dying, I was powerless to do anything.
>
> But it was not too late. I was in my prime, perfectly capable of helping to solve this gargantuan and dangerous problem.

McNamara was experiencing one of those existential moments that launches a continued quest to live a life that truly matters. She decided that she would start with herself and began chronicling her and her spouse's attempts to reduce their carbon footprint in a weekly blog called Carbon Slim. They stopped eating meat, bought local and organic produce, travelled by bicycle and public transit, reduced their air travel, changed all their light bulbs, reduced their garbage, bought a small home, learned to grow vegetables in their backyard, and brought their home's efficiency up from 43 to 76 percent.

> After all the effort and money to reduce our household's carbon footprint, I realized that while it was much lower than the North American average, it wasn't enough. We needed help. We needed others to drastically reduce their personal footprints too, and only government policy could make that happen.
>
> Around that time, I was part of the communications team for a rally on Parliament Hill in Ottawa called C-Day: Fill the Hill. Two things struck me about that experience. One—that journalists are, for the most part, clearly uneducated on the issue, and two, we spent a lot of time and effort on an event that was largely ignored outside of the few thousand people who made a lot of noise outside Parliament that day. I asked myself, what was preventing us from going inside and actually talking to policy and law makers about this pressing problem? Why weren't we doing that?

Her question, "What was preventing us from going inside and actually talking to policy and law makers about this pressing problem?" reverberates through our mostly hollow lives as citizens. That is the question for all mouse-click advocates who are serious about systemic change and who want to do more than just lift a finger for the next mouse-click. The sad answer as to why we aren't going inside and actually talking to the law makers is that most people who want big change cannot find an organization capable of empowering them at a level equal to their desire for change. Most organizations ask us for nothing more than a click and a check. They see us as little children who are too busy with play, too distracted, too naïve, and too incapable of doing the homework necessary to go really deep with our democracy.

But when citizens find an organization that treats them as capable adults miracles can happen. This adult treatment includes providing monthly conversations with leading climate scientists on a nationwide conference call, using the monthly call to teach short talks that can be used in letters to the editor or in conversations with editorial writers, and providing constant opportunities to take new territory with your member of Congress or other community leaders. Listen to Para describe the 2012 achievements in Wisconsin on CCL's January 2013 conference call:

> We had six editorials including two on our local CBS television affiliate, six guest columns, and 49 letters to the editor (I think I missed a few outside of Madison). Also in 2012 we added four new chapters, we got 20 people to the national conference in Washington, DC . . . and we had five face-to-face meetings with Wisconsin Members of Congress.

CCL's success wasn't limited to Wisconsin. In the United States and Canada the totals included: 711 pieces published in 2012 (letters to the editor, op-eds, editorials, and articles), 534 meetings with Congressional offices that same year, and 26 new chapters.

When you talk with CCL volunteers and look for the secret to this five-year-old organization's success—one thing that emerges over and over is the brilliance of CCL's Executive Director Mark Reynolds. Each CCL volunteer has their own way to describe it and Peter Joseph, an emergency room physician in California, certainly had his way. Joseph co-founded the San Francisco chapter of Physicians for Social Responsibility in the late 1970s. Haunted by the holocaust which his family escaped, Joseph has dedicated his own life to preventing the global destruction that nuclear war, and now climate change, could bring.

> After jumping in, the first thing I noticed was that their executive director, Mark Reynolds, seemed insanely positive, almost manic. I wondered what he was on, but I then realized that it was his commitment to a goal that seemed achievable. . . . There is no trace of gloom or doom in him. His organizing calls are fast-paced and packed with actions to take, all of which are intended to empower each individual. This is not a group of followers or side-line observers. Every action by participants is made public and supported by the group. We inspire each other. Participants can gorge themselves on positive reinforcement, and the results are impressive.

When Madeleine Para finally decided to check out CCL's introductory call, she found the same thing.

> What I heard in that phone call made so much sense to me that I knew immediately I was going to throw in my lot with CCL. It made sense to me that Congress was key and that we should work with them based on respect. I appreciated someone who could laugh while talking about climate change.

That person was Mark Reynolds.

"I did make a conscious decision early on that if we didn't bring joy and celebration to what we were doing we would never have success," Reynolds recalled. "It's not that I don't take climate change seriously, but we needed a different way to deal with the issue."

Reynolds went on to outline another distinction.

> Early on someone said, "Wow, these phone calls are really good."
>
> I thought, "We can't afford a good phone call, we have to have great phone calls each time. Good will never be a big enough answer for what we are dealing with. We have to ask for something more from ourselves every day. We can't afford to just go through the motions for even one day."

Reynolds knew that you can't ask more from volunteers every day by being a scold, but you can by modeling inspiration and hope. Twenty-five years ago RESULTS was probably the only advocacy organization connecting hundreds of volunteers on a monthly conference call. Now more and more organizations are hosting conference calls and events with both audio and visual components called webinars. But often these sessions are wonk fests with little in the way of inspiration or aliveness. CCL calls have their share of wonkiness with climate scientists and other experts speaking on most of the monthly calls, but Reynolds constantly brings in the human dimension. In December 2012, he introduced CCL's conference call guest, Dr. Kevin E. Trenberth, Distinguished Senior Scientist in the Climate Analysis Section at the National Center for Atmospheric Research and a lead author of the 1995, 2001 and 2007 Scientific Assessment of Climate Change reports from the Intergovernmental Panel on Climate Change (IPCC). Listen to how Reynolds described the CCL volunteers to Trenberth before the scientist addressed the group.

> I want to tell you just a little bit about the people who you're speaking with before you begin making your comments. I think most people on this call have been on airplanes where just before you take off they make the announcement: "Here's where the exits are, if we lose pressure the oxygen masks will fall down from the ceiling." As that announcement is being made people are usually reading their book or introducing themselves to the person next to them, doing their last couple of e-mails or, in my case, I'm such a nut about maps, I open the magazine every time and I look at the map and I think "that's a great map." But nobody is paying attention to the announcement.
>
> The way the people listen on this call is as if that announcement is being made but the person making the announcement said, "The left wing is on fire, we're going to attempt a landing and if you pay careful attention there's a chance you'll survive." So I just want you to know there are no casual listeners on this call. The people are very intent in pulling what they need to pull from your comments to help solve the issue of global warming for our country and for the world.

> The other side though is that they're not grim and they don't run around like crazy frightened people. These are the happiest warriors I've ever met.
>
> This week one of our volunteers said that she had a call with a former candidate for President of the United States. They were having a discussion about what we're trying to do, put an effective pricing mechanism on carbon based fuels and do it on an economy-wide basis.
>
> And he said, "That's impossible."
>
> She said that before she started volunteering with CCL she would have thought, "Well, he's an expert—I'm not an expert, so if he says it's impossible it must be. And he's an insider and I'm not an insider and so I must throw in the towel." But she said, "since I've taken on the view that I'm not going to be a cynical, detached observer of my government, but rather someone who says this is my democracy, this is my government, I have something to do about it, I was able to just include his comments with a lot of other people I talk to." And she said that while she was respectful and took good notes, and set up their next meeting, the thought that went through her mind when he said you could never get something that big done was, "Well thank you for sharing, I'm glad you have opinions, a lot of people have opinions."

This introduction to Trenberth is not unusual. Reynolds is always sharing a story that returns people to their commitment and vision. The CCL volunteers I spoke with told me about months or even years of hopelessness until they found the structure of support and empowerment CCL provided. If you have a big policy idea or a big concern but you know it's only rolling around in your head and nowhere else, that can be debilitating. But if you begin reading about it in the newspaper and you know that hundreds of members of Congress or their staff are discussing it and you are one of the people making that happen and you are connected to hundreds of others who are doing the same, then your hopelessness turns into hope. That's just the way it works.

Reynolds told me that he didn't want it to seem like his personality or anyone else's was the thing that makes the difference. I could see his point but it was also critical to acknowledge CCL's unique ethos and the difference that ethos makes. Another of the commitments I outline in Chapter 30 as a key to success speaks to this issue in a section titled, "Humor, joy and celebration," in which I write: "The issues of global poverty and climate change often involve addressing great personal or global pain or sounding an alarm for action on a dire and critical issue. We must not let the heaviness inherent in the task overwhelm us. Instead we must find the joy in the work so it does not become drudgery. That joy can be found in the act of making a difference, having personal breakthroughs, assisting others in making a difference, finding partners who share your commitment, and being inspired by living a committed life. Approaching the work with lightness and cheerfulness and celebrating the victories along the way, both large and small, will help bring joy and sustain the volunteers and staff for the long run."

Reynolds described his approach to visiting new cities and starting new groups as similar to Elli Sparks' model for relationships with members of Congress and editorial writers—romance.

> Remember how Elli saw that first meeting with the editorial writer as a blind date and how she decided beforehand that she was "going to marry that fellow"? Before I go to a city to start a group I decide that I am going to fall in love with them before I get there. So I try to find evidence in them and in the environment about why I will never be the same from having spent time with them. . . .

Maybe that is part of the ethos that nurtures volunteers and spurs people like Sparks to move from climate trauma to this:

> . . . During our conference I met with 20 congressional offices. I met with many folks whose view of the world was very different than mine. Going into their offices was hard. I had to let go of a lot of emotional baggage. I could no longer judge them or hold hostility in my heart towards them. I had to let go of my fear of climate change and my fear that they wouldn't listen to me. I had to center myself in love. Releasing fear and centering in love . . . this is sacred and profound work. . . .

When cap-and-trade legislation finally died in Congress in 2010, the environmental community in the United States was in deep despair. CCL was barely three years old and had 26 chapters at the end of that year, hardly the recipe for dragon slaying. But they did grow, with triple the number of chapters just two years later and hundreds of deep advocates awakening across the U.S. and Canada.

On a call with CCL group leaders at the beginning of 2013, Charles Komanoff, co-founder of the Carbon Tax Center, said, "It amazes me that you had the fortitude, vision, and commitment to pursue this issue during the 'dark times' and to continue forward in a brighter time."

The difficult journey toward ensuring a stable climate will surely require fortitude, vision, and commitment in the dark times and the brighter times. It will also require releasing fear and centering in love and will turn out to be sacred and profound work—the work of the soul.

In my mind, one more thing is certain: for this aspect of the work, Citizens Climate Lobby will lead the way.

CHAPTER 30

Center for Citizen Empowerment and Transformation

In 2012, I launched the Center for Citizen Empowerment and Transformation to help large, non-governmental organizations find and train that small portion of their members who want to go far beyond mouse-click advocacy and create champions in Congress and the media for their cause. Five years earlier, I had gone back to RESULTS half time and was traveling around the country starting and empowering grassroots groups in a quest to better understand what made citizen empowerment and transformation work.

That quest helped me identify 13 commitments needed for success which are discussed in this chapter. As I was developing the concepts, my wife wondered if circulating the list was tantamount to giving away the store. I saw her point but also knew that so little is understood about true citizen empowerment and transformation that even if I nailed the list to every tree in the nation and circulated it online as widely as possible, people still wouldn't get it. There are so many misconceptions on this topic that even if we think we understand a concept, our instincts lead us astray.

For example, one principle that almost every organization gets wrong is the fact that campaigns must be focused if volunteers are to go deep enough on an issue to have real breakthroughs with their members of Congress and the media. But the conventional wisdom mistakenly assumes that if you focus on one issue over the course of a year the volunteers will get bored, which is only true if the curriculum is shallow and the issue lacks vision. What the conventional wisdom doesn't understand is that gaining mastery on a topic over time—deeply understanding the legislation, players, arguments, and politics—is thrilling for a volunteer and gives them a confidence that is exciting, not boring. Rejecting the conventional wisdom, Citizens Climate Lobby (CCL) has focused on a carbon tax and dividend for two years and yet, as I write this chapter, their volunteers had 108 letters to the editor published in one month alone, January 2013—142 total pieces published that month. Is that what boredom looks like? I don't think so.

While my aim with the Center for Citizen Empowerment and Transformation (CCET) is to spread these 13 commitments that are so critical to deep empowerment, what I mostly encounter are organizations fascinated by the latest technological innovations: Facebook, Twitter, e-mails, on-line petitions, and text messages. Most are uneasy with a focus on personal empowerment and transformation, uncomfortable with the deeper social innovations. While advances like Twitter and on-line petitions are useful tools, I find it misleading to call these tools "social media" when these so-called social media tools often help people avoid the deepest social interactions on which true change so often depends. For example, feeling nervous beyond measure before calling an editorial writer to initiate a conversation on an issue you care about, but picking up the phone and calling anyway, is the first step toward one of those deep personal interactions that are so often avoided.

Why don't our major non-governmental organizations (NGOs) provide real empowerment and transformation for even a small portion of their members? I believe it comes down to not knowing what to do, not knowing what works, the fear of failure, and that same fear of being told "no" that keeps volunteers from picking up the phone as described above. It also comes from NGOs taking comfort in the clout they already have, even if that clout is insufficient to reach their ultimate goals.

Another way of looking at our nation's failure at citizen empowerment and transformation is to consider what journalist and Tarrytown Conference Center founder Robert L. Schwartz called the much-needed social innovations. When he introduced Muhammad Yunus before a lecture some 15 years ago, Schwartz outlined seven inventions that allowed for the development of the modern city. He cited steel frame construction and the elevator which enabled the building of skyscrapers and discussed other innovations like the subway.

Then, he said, what the world needs now, more than ever, are not so much the technological innovations, but social innovations like Muhammad Yunus has created with the Grameen Bank in Bangladesh.

This distinction between technological and social innovation is at the heart of this book and of the Center for Citizen Empowerment and Transformation (CCET).

I may be alone when I say this, but I agree with Schwartz that social innovations, innovations that deeply empower and transform, are the innovations that are most needed today. Let me explain what I mean.

An inventor can develop a breakthrough in solar technology, but if our governments continue to deny or downplay the role greenhouse gasses play in climate change, we are doomed. A researcher can discover a vaccine that will prevent an intractable disease, but if our governments can't find the political will to make its dissemination a priority and if nations and communities can't build the social structure and outreach necessary to ensure its use, then the innovation will lie dormant. If the ten nations of the world that spend the most on defense can allocate over $1 trillion a year combined and there is little or no outcry for a change in priorities then how will we ever be good stewards of the planet?

But as with any innovation, there are the early adopters and those waiting to see if it works. Up until now, my experience with citizen empowerment and transformation has been with RESULTS some 30 years ago and with Citizens Climate Lobby (CCL) over the last five years. In both cases the work was with start-ups. Now I am working to bring these innovations to established organizations.

During 2012, I met with dozens of NGO leaders, some with millions of stakeholders and some with thousands. At a meeting with the head of one of the smaller organizations, a group with an annual budget of about $1.5 million and no more than seven on its staff, the CEO explained that the organization did not have the budget or staff to take on a new program to empower their grassroots base. I found myself agreeing with the CEO during the meeting only to realize on the train ride home that the group's budget was 100 times greater than that of RESULTS in its early years and that RESULTS had no full-time paid staff during its first four and a half years. What RESULTS did have was an ethos of and commitment to empowering ordinary citizens to take extraordinary action.

Even though RESULTS was able to do it as a start-up 30 years ago, I can understand a large organization's caution about going down this path. All too often, however, leaders mistakenly believe they must open 10 or 15 offices around the country and hire 10–15 staff to fill those offices. But that is not the case. Citizens Climate Lobby, for example, has grown and empowered its volunteers with only five staff. So if it is not major funding or a significant number of staff, what is needed for an organization to succeed at citizen empowerment and transformation?

I began identifying the commitments necessary for success, essentially distilling the heart and experience explained more fully in this book. There are 13 commitments listed below. The first six focus a bit more on the organizational infrastructure needed for success and the final seven offer a way for volunteers and staff to embrace a series of personal breakthroughs. As you study the commitments beware of the tendency to dismiss them as too difficult or to see your organization as already fulfilling them. While you may be achieving them, it is more likely there are deeper levels yet to be reached.

A powerful structure of support. This is the first commitment—the foundation. A powerful structure of support is where this model differs from that of most other organizations. If greatness is expected from volunteers, then a great structure of coaching and empowerment will be required from the organization and its staff, something beyond e-blasts and the occasional webinar.

Among the failures of grassroots empowerment is the myth that all volunteers need is a training session on meeting a member of Congress, a packet of materials, and a sense that their cause is just. But this analysis ignores the heavy layer of cynicism and despair found in each of us and throughout society. Each of the items mentioned in this list comes to life in a powerful structure of support which includes inspiring 1) monthly conference calls for groups, 2) weekly coaching calls for group leaders, 3) monthly action sheets, and 4) packets for editorial writers. Without that, all of the commitments listed below become interesting ideas that are seldom implemented.

It must be emphasized that a structure of support can either fall in the "going through the motions" category or, instead, consistently strive to be groundbreaking. For example, one component of the monthly conference call is the guest speaker. Even if the guest speaker is dazzling each month, if they are given 25 minutes but leave no time for questions, the volunteers will become the proverbial "bumps on a log" and not as profoundly engaged as they would with a 10-minute talk followed by 15 minutes of discussion. Another section of the monthly conference call is when a few volunteers share their successes. But if all the volunteer says is, "We had a great meeting with our member of Congress and can't wait to do it again," and they leave out the fact that it took 11 phone calls to get the appointment, they had to meet with the district director first, and their knees were knocking as they walked into the meeting, it won't be as useful for the others on the call. Another section of the monthly conference call, something most organizations omit entirely, is practicing to be more articulate through a role play or some other form of training. If a volunteer tries the role play and does a terrible job, but the staff can say no more than "Thank you for volunteering," then we have missed an opportunity for real growth and are left with a moribund structure of support. But with a profound structure of support, people are empowered to live their lives aligned with these words from George Bernard Shaw's *Man and Superman*:

> This is the true joy in life, the being used for a purpose recognized by yourself as a mighty one, the being a force of nature, instead of a selfish, feverish little clod of ailments and grievances complaining that the world will not devote itself to making you happy. I am of the opinion that my life belongs to the whole community, and it is my privilege to do for it whatever I can. I want to be thoroughly used up when I die, for the harder I work, the more I live. I rejoice in life for its own sake. Life is no brief candle to me, it is a sort of splendid torch which I've got a hold of for the moment, and I want to make it burn as brightly as possible before handing it on to future generations.

Inspiration and idealism. Being at peace with and confident in one's idealism and vision and one's commitment to inspiring others is critical. This idealism includes holding ourselves to our fullest potential and our governments to their greatest ideals. If government is broken, we are part of that brokenness and must engage in healing ourselves too. In working with grassroots advocates one can often hear a staff member say, "People are too busy to get involved." People *are* too busy for gestures, for going through the motions, but there are some who are not too busy to make a real difference. One's idealism and inspiration should not be surrendered to reason or to the petty pace of everyday life. The dictionary defines "inspire" as to fill with an animating, quickening, or exalting influence; to influence or impel. The purpose of deep advocacy is to influence or impel, to change hearts and minds. That cannot be done with facts and figures alone. The urgency of the need for change must also be conveyed with inspiration. When a monthly conference call or weekly group leader call agenda is being created, it must be filled not only with accurate information but also with moments that truly inspire and move the volunteers and staff.

Selecting the right staff. Building a unit that truly delivers citizen empowerment and transformation requires the commitment of a successful startup. Therefore, another critical ingredient is selecting the right staff. One must select a staff that is entrepreneurial, unstoppable, and inspiring or committed to learning to be more inspiring. No matter how good the outside coaching, if the staff is not entrepreneurial and unstoppable and is not committed to being inspiring, the effort will not succeed. There must be a perceived pain that this program will relieve and a true sense of calling that goes far beyond the effort put into a typical 9–5 job. There must be an attitude of "we will get this done, no matter what." The staff must own the vision completely as any great entrepreneur would do and be persistent in the face of opposition.

Focused, inspiring agenda. Another piece of the organizational DNA and a clear failure of most deep grassroots empowerment efforts is the lack of legislative focus and the mistaken belief that if there is one major issue that is returned to throughout the year, the volunteers will become bored. That is only true if the grassroots are given a simple request to make over and over on the same issue. But if the groups are not just trying to get a co-sponsor on a bill but are instead working to really create champions in Congress, the media, and among community leaders to take a little-known issue and make it a political imperative, then boredom will not be a problem. Developing a legislative agenda that is *inspiring* and *focused* allows volunteers and staff to drill down deep on an issue rather than flit from issue to issue and, as a result, allows volunteers to be moved by their own growth as community leaders.

Practice and coaching. One of the great challenges to the future of our planet is our short attention span. But when one has a 20–30 minute meeting with a member of Congress, editorial writer or other community leader, what had been a superficial understanding can now go much deeper. But this is only possible if the volunteer has practiced and prepared and has something profound to offer. Practice builds confidence and develops one's leadership. We shy away from arranging a meeting with a member of Congress, writing a letter to the editor or calling into a talk show because we think we don't know what to say. Only real practice can change that. The organization must be committed to ensuring the volunteers have ongoing opportunities for real practice in order to become spokespersons themselves. This call for practice includes an organizational commitment to improvement, coaching, and being coached.

Integrity. Volunteers give a very precious commodity: their time. There must be a deep commitment as an organization and as individual staff members to keeping one's word. If there is a conference call, be on time and deliver a quality agenda. If there is an action sheet, have it arrive on time and be both accurate and inspiring. One could say that global poverty and a deteriorating environment are the result of a lack of integrity on a global scale. They cannot be solved by individuals and organizations that have questionable integrity themselves.

While the previous six commitments would also live in the volunteer body, these next seven are a particular promise to the volunteers, a stand for a program that delivers excellence. While they must be encouraged by the staff, their achievement is more in the hands of the volunteers themselves.

Empowering breakthroughs. For a citizen to go from not knowing the name of their member of Congress to having a deep, trusted relationship with them requires a series of breakthroughs—it requires moving out of their comfort zone. That is essentially the definition of a breakthrough, seeing something that seems difficult or impossible, having some discomfort in taking it on, and then, with coaching and support, going through that comfort zone to experience the joy and accomplishment on the other side. These breakthroughs can happen with a member of Congress, with an editorial writer, with other leaders in the community, and with oneself. Empowering others in this way and providing opportunities for them to express their greatness is one of the gifts of deep advocacy.

Enrolling others. Engaging other community members in being empowered volunteers is part of the structure of support. If one invites a friend to a meeting there is always the fear that they will say no or that they will come and see this as a useless activity. When volunteers become senior to that fear, when the commitment to the purpose and vision is greater than the fear of rejection, then big things can happen. This commitment to enrolling others, be they friends or guest speakers or movement leaders, is also applicable to the staff.

Building deep relationships. When an op-ed is selected for publication it has less to do with the quality of the op-ed and more to do with the relationship one has developed with the op-ed editor. Of course timing and quality are important, but it is more valuable to have 10 people who have great, trusted relationships with op-ed editors pitch a *good* op-ed than to send a *great* op-ed to 10 editors with whom there is no relationship. So the commitment is not so much to having an editorial writer or member of Congress say yes to every request, but to building a deep, trusting relationship. Hearing "no" from a member of Congress early on should be seen as just one step along the path to building a great relationship over time.

Being vulnerable. Showing an emotional video or reading convincingly an excerpt from an evocative article to a member of Congress is more important than just sharing information. The goal is to tap into their humanity and create a deeply memorable moment. If your issue is poverty, for example, the goal is to have the meeting be as close to an actual field visit as possible. But people shy away from being vulnerable, especially with those in positions of power. Bringing an emotionally moving video or reading to a member of Congress can make a volunteer feel especially vulnerable. Instead we are more likely to hide behind a presentation of facts and figures. However, a willingness to be vulnerable is essential to having breakthroughs, engaging others, building powerful relationships, and, ultimately, success.

Partnership, not partisanship. The most profound breakthroughs and transformations come when those whom we perceive as against us or our cause begin to see the truth and importance of our issue and embrace it as their own. But that can only happen through partnership, not partisanship. We must see the humanity and essential goodness in each person, especially those who are seen to oppose us. In 1987, the RESULTS group in Atlanta, Georgia adapted the following prayer for their own member of Congress, a prayer that had originally been written by Newton Hightower of Houston for his member of Congress. They would read this prayer at the beginning of each of their meetings and think, a touch cynically, "Yeah, right" when they first read it. But they continued to read it as a way of opening their own hearts to the humanity of their member of Congress who had voted *against* famine relief for Ethiopia in 1985.

> Thank you God for Pat Swindall. We know that he is a good man who wants to do right in the world. We know that he struggles with the same problems we do: closing our hearts to those who don't agree with us. There are no thoughts or feelings that he has had that we haven't had and vice versa. We pray for all of us to have compassion for people in our country and far away, for rich and poor. We pray that Pat and we will be less frightened of each other. We pray our focus will be more to love and appreciate him and less to change him. Help us to remember that sharing love with the world is the highest contribution we can make and will lead to children being fed and the planet surviving. Forgive our righteousness and anger. Open our hearts and minds to find the next expression of love for Pat that he can receive.

When we are faced with someone who appears to oppose us the normal tendency is to give up. If we don't give up we are likely to be defensive, retaliatory, or argumentative, but this seldom works. The commitment being discussed here has nothing to do with being weak or without resolve. Rather it is a clear understanding that change is not likely to occur without communication. No matter how backward one's member of Congress's views might seem, one must decide whether one wishes to be right about their backwardness or, instead, engage him or her in a deep conversation for change.

Being unreasonable. *Time* magazine once stated: "Visionaries are possessed creatures, men and women in the thrall of belief so powerful that that they ignore all else—even reason—to ensure that reality catches up with their dreams. But always behind the action is an idea, a passionate sense of what is eternal in human nature and also what is coming but as yet unseen, over the horizon." Taking a stand for a stable climate, the end of poverty, or for achieving world peace is seen by most people as naïve and futile. It is the visionaries whose actions get us closer to those goals and whose actions are buttressed by "an idea and a passionate sense of what is eternal in human nature and also what is coming but as yet unseen, over the horizon." A program for citizen empowerment and transformation is an incubator and nurturing place for visionaries.

Humor, joy and celebration. The issues of global poverty and climate change often involve addressing great personal or global pain or sounding an alarm for action on a dire and critical issue. We must not let the heaviness inherent in the task overwhelm us. Instead we must find the joy in the work so it does not become drudgery. That joy can be found in the act of making a difference, having personal breakthroughs, assisting others in making a difference, finding partners who share your commitment, and being inspired by living a committed life. Approaching the work with lightness and cheerfulness and celebrating the victories along the way, both large and small, will help bring joy and sustain the volunteers and staff for the long run.

What Are People Capable Of?

This list of commitments is a tall order, but what is at stake is the quality of life on this planet and perhaps life itself. There are two competing visions of people and their ability to change the world for the better. One sees individuals as weak, inadequate, inconsequential, and just not up to the job. The other sees people as being strong, committed, brave, visionary, audacious, and heroic. Honestly, when it comes to ending global poverty or ensuring a stable climate or an enduring peace, how do *you* see people? How do you see yourself?

If you see yourself in the bold and audacious category, that boldness can easily die without a profound structure of support.

I agree with Apollo Astronaut Rusty Schweickart who said, "We aren't passengers on Spaceship Earth, we're the crew. We aren't residents on this planet, we're citizens. The difference in both cases is responsibility."

If our species is to have any hope of living up to our responsibility, of succeeding and thriving, we must see people as strong, brave, visionary, audacious, and heroic. And if we embrace that vision we must return to Robert Schwartz's assertion that now, more than ever, we need *social* innovations that empower individuals to have breakthroughs in expressing their personal and political power for the good of humanity. But we know that these breakthroughs do not occur spontaneously or without being nurtured. If we are to help people achieve them, we must create the profound structures of inspiration, challenge and support that enable individuals to do the work of protecting the planet and all of creation.

Twentieth Anniversary Edition

Acknowledgments

When I left the Microcredit Summit Campaign and launched the Center for Citizen Empowerment and Transformation (CCET) in 2012, I was essentially returning to the work I started 33 years earlier with RESULTS, the work of citizen empowerment and transformation. So it made perfect sense to return to this book and share the new lessons I have been learning.

I am grateful to the Citizens Climate Lobby volunteers and staff who shared their stories with me: David Folland, Peter Joseph, Cheryl McNamara, Cathy Orlando, Madeleine Para, Mark Reynolds, Joseph Robertson, Gary Rucinski, Marshall Saunders, and Elli Sparks.

A number of people have read the new material at various stages and I thank them for their valuable feedback: Anna Awimbo, Amy Bennett, Sharron Botwinick, Eliot Daley, Jad Daley, Shannon Daley-Harris, Lisa Marie Laegreid Gatti, Peter Joseph, Cheryl McNamara, Madeleine Para, Ken Patterson, Mark Reynolds, Marshall Saunders, Linda Schatz, Elli Sparks, Jean-Francois Tardif, and Steve Valk.

It is a very special honor to have the Foreword for this edition written by Nobel Peace Prize Laureate Muhammad Yunus, a friend and colleague for more than 25 years.

In this new chapter of my life I have been blessed by partnerships with colleagues new and old: Dave Ellis, life coach extraordinaire, Joanne Carter and all of the volunteers and staff at RESULTS and the Microcredit Summit Campaign, Mark Reynolds who shows what citizen empowerment training should look like, Pachamama Alliance, and the support of David Douglas and Fred Mulder.

A special thank you is extended to Edward Jutkowitz and Camino Books for their work on all three editions of this book.

More than anyone, I must thank Marshall Saunders. His inspired launch of Citizens Climate Lobby based on the RESULTS model, his openness to my coaching, and Marshall and Pam Saunders' support of the Center for Citizen Empowerment and Transformation have been pivotal to this next phase of my life and to this new edition of *Reclaiming Our Democracy.*

Shannon, Micah, and Sophie light up my life and make it so very clear why citizens everywhere must awaken to their power and solve the challenges that face our planet and its people.

Tenth Anniversary Edition

Acknowledgments

This tenth anniversary edition of *Reclaiming Our Democracy* would not have existed were it not for Scott Swearingen. He lobbied early for this edition and I am grateful that he did.

Many have taken the time to read versions of the new chapter, and I am indebted to each and every one of them. Anna Awimbo, Anjum Khalidi, David Dresner, Lisa Laegreid, Sherine Mahmoud, and Brian McConnell of the Microcredit Summit staff. Joanne Carter, Joyce Lee, Alan Gold, Meredith Dodson, Stacey Carkonen, Leila Nimatallah, Peggy Long, Kolleen Bouchane, Barbara Wallace, and Sue Perez of the RESULTS staff.

I am grateful to Dan Zukergood and Laurie Herrick, Kerry Langan and Allison Gallaher, Fred Fiske and Joanne Carter for taking the time to contribute their reflections.

I am honored to have forewords to the new edition by colleagues and heroes of mine, Marian Wright Edelman and Marianne Williamson.

Karen McGuinness, Dan Zukergood, and my wife, Shannon Daley-Harris, offered comments that were invaluable.

Barbara Gibbons, my editor, has been a joy to work with. Edward Jutkowitz, my publisher, has been a true partner every step of the way.

Among the changes in my life over these many years have been the births of Micah in 1998 and his sister Sophie in 2001. Micah, Sophie, and Shannon have blessed me beyond measure.

As with the original, the true spirit behind this book comes from the volunteers of RESULTS. Their inspiration, their struggles, their willingness to move beyond their comfort zones, and their breakthroughs are what move me to this day and it is to them that I dedicate this book.

First Edition

Acknowledgments

This book began ten years ago as a handful of sheets in a file folder. Its champion at the time was K.A. Parker who offered an encouraging word every now and then—words that I wouldn't heed until years later. Only in a conversation with Ken Schatz in early 1991 did I see that I was ready to take on this project. I am grateful to both.

Linda Schatz came forward first and helped me with the proposal and the initial drafts. I appreciate her ever-ready support and encouragement. James Morris's publishing experience, honest feedback, and friendship helped me find my voice. I thank Andy Rice for introducing me to James.

This project would have been impossible without the support of the RESULTS Board of Directors, and especially the RESULTS Educational Fund staff, past and present. I am especially grateful to staff members who supported me by taking on much of the day-to-day responsibility of running RESULTS when the writing began in earnest: Peter Rickett and Kim Posich, Lynn Walker-McMullen and Nick Arena, Ann Reedy and Sharon Mason, Alex Counts and Joanne Carter, David Schnetzer and Alan Gold, Keith Johnson and Barbara Charbonnet, Jennifer Robey and Paula Jennings, Michael Jones and Steve Lake, Roohi Husain and many wonderful interns.

For me, the heart of the book is the stories of the RESULTS volunteers. I am ever grateful to those who took the time to look at their trials and triumphs with RESULTS—and to share those stories with me: Anna Amarandos, Nick Arena, Steve Arnold, Barbara Charbonnet, Karen Cloud, Alex Counts, Heide Craig, Bruce Davidson, Martin Delker, Stephen Dewhurst, John DiMura, Dan Doerfer, Jo Marcia Feinberg, Ron Fischman, Holly Garrard, Alan Gold, Jeff Golden, Peter Graves, Dixine Hardesty, Eileen Hasday, Newton Hightower, Debbie Hirsh, John Hotson, Terry Imhoff-Gannett, Jim James, Keith Johnson, Glenna Keefe, Sara Keeney, Gerry Klamon, Marilyn Kodish, Larry Ladell, Kylie Langdon, Dorsey Lawson, Scott Leckman, Eric Lindblom, Mary Coleman Martin, Sharon Mason, Karen McQuillan, Karen Mitura, Barbara and Woody Moore, Don Munroe, Toshihisa Nagase, Gail Neumann, Deborah Norton, Kip Phelps, Carol Pierce, Dave Ransome, Peter Rickett, Michael Rigby, Jennifer Robey,

Joel Rubinstein, Michael Rubinstein, Bob Sample, Frank Sanitate, Suzy Shure, Margo Stahl, Chuck Sutherland, Scott Swearingen, Shirley Tainton, Jean François Tardif, Nancy Taylor, Terry Thirion Fitzpatrick, Mark Toogood, Marjorie Trifon, Bruce Underhill, Steve Valk, Bob Van Olst, Jessica and Matthias von Boeventer, Lynn Walker-McMullen, Bev Wason, Jack and Lori Waters, Amanda Watson, Keith Wilhelmi, Shirley Williams, Nancy Wimmer, and Chuck Woolery.

I owe a special debt of gratitude to Michael Rubinstein. His insights and the depth of his story showed me what I was looking for and served as a model for the others.

I interviewed a number of people not in the RESULTS organization, and I appreciate the time they took to share their perspectives: Peter Davies, Rep. Edward Feighan, Rep. Ben Gilman, Brad Gordon, James P. Grant, Rep. Tony Hall, John Hatch, Idriss Jazairy, Rep. Mel Levine, Rep. John Miller, John Mitchell, Doug Siglin and Tom Getman.

Thanks go to Andy Krieger for introducing me to his agent, Jane Dystel. Her advice was particularly helpful during the short time we worked together.

I'm grateful for the help I received from Mary Jane Turner and Lynn Whittaker of the Close-up Foundation, and Trish Reynolds and Krishna Sondhi from Kumarian Press.

Many people took the time to read the manuscript at various stages and offer their feedback. I am grateful to David Cohen, Stephen Commins, John Coonrod, Eliot Daley, Dennis Farrier, John Haskell, Samuel Koo, James Morris, Ellen Pearl, Linda Schatz, Arthur Simon and Paul Thompson.

I offer a special thank you to Alex Counts, Steve Dewhurst, Alan Gold, Keith Johnson, Ernest Loevinsohn, Sharon Mason, K.A. Parker, Ann Reedy, Peter Rickett, Michael Rigby, Jennifer Robey, Michael Rubinstein and David Schnetzer, who offered pages of notes and gave useful feedback on several drafts.

My publisher, Edward Jutkowitz of Camino Books, has been a pleasure to work with, and I am also grateful for the work of my editor, Joan Bingham.

I owe a debt of gratitude to Valerie Harper who encouraged me beyond my first rejection letters and agreed to write the foreword to the book.

Over the years, many people have given generously of their time and commitment to the experiment in citizen activism that is RESULTS. Many are mentioned in the pages of this book and in these acknowledgments, but many are not. Their contribution has been no less vital than those named. My deepest love and appreciation to all those who have given of themselves to this endeavor.

I'm grateful to my family for their support and understanding, especially my mother and father and my brother and sister.

No one read as many drafts as Shannon Daley, nor read them at their earliest and roughest stages. Her thoughtfulness and love are throughout this book and throughout my life. Thank you.

To find out more about RESULTS, the Microcredit Summit Campaign, Citizens Climate Lobby, the Center for Citizen Empowerment and Transformation and how you can get involved, contact:

RESULTS
1101 15th Street NW
Suite 1200
Washington, DC 20005
Tel. 202-783-4800
http://www.results.org

Microcredit Summit Campaign
1101 15th Street NW
Suite 1200
Washington, DC 20005
Tel. 202-637-9600
http://www.microcreditsummit.org

Citizens Climate Lobby
1330 Orange Ave. #300
Coronado, CA 92118
Tel. 619-437-7142
http://www.citizensclimatelobby.org

Center for Citizen Empowerment and Transformation
1101 15th Street NW
Suite 1200
Washington, DC 20005
Tel. 202-390-0012
http://www.citizenempowermentandtransformation.org